I0762905

HOLLYWOOD VS NAZIS

Books by
MICHAEL BENSON

Betrayal in Blood

Lethal Embrace (with Robert Mladinich)

Mommy Deadliest

A Killer's Touch

A Knife in the Heart

Gangsters vs. Nazis: How Jewish Mobsters Battled Nazis in Wartime America

Moguls: The Lives and Times of Film Pioneers

Nicholas and Joseph Schenck (with Craig Singer)

Mafia Secrets: Untold Tales from the Hollywood Godfather (with Gianni Russo)

Hollywood vs. Nazis: How the Movie Studios Took On Nazis Infiltrating Los Angeles

Books by
FRANK DIMATTEO and MICHAEL BENSON

Carmine the Snake: Carmine Persico and His Murderous Mafia Family

Lord High Executioner: The Legendary Mafia Boss Albert Anastasia

Mafia Hit Man: Carmine DiBiase, the Wiseguy Who Really Killed Joey Gallo

The Cigar: Carmine Galante, Mafia Terror

Red Hook: Brooklyn Mafia, Ground Zero

Carlo Gambino: Boss of Bosses

HOW THE MOVIE STUDIOS TOOK ON NAZIS INFILTRATING LOS ANGELES

MICHAEL BENSON

CITADEL PRESS
Kensington Publishing Corp.
www.kensingtonbooks.com

CITADEL PRESS BOOKS are published by

Kensington Publishing Corp.
900 Third Avenue
New York, NY 10022

All Kensington titles, imprints, and distributed lines are available at special quantity discounts for bulk purchases for sales promotions, premiums, fund-raising, educational, or institutional use. Special book excerpts or customized printings can also be created to fit specific needs. For details, write or phone the office of the Kensington sales manager: Kensington Publishing Corp., 900 Third Avenue, New York, NY 10022, attn: Sales Department; phone 1-800-221-2647.

CITADEL PRESS and the Citadel logo are Reg. U.S. Pat. & TM Off.

Library of Congress Control Number is available

First hardcover printing: April 2026
ISBN: 978-0-8065-4478-6

ISBN: 978-0-8065-4480-9 (e-book)

10 9 8 7 6 5 4 3 2 1

Printed in the United States of America

The authorized representative in the EU for product safety and compliance
is eucomply OU, Parnu mnt 139b-14, Apt 123
Tallinn, Berlin 11317, hello@eucompliancepartner.com

To Gary Goldstein,
who's had my back since Day One.

CONTENTS

AUTHOR'S NOTE

This book is a work of nonfiction. It depicts actual events. However, dialogue and actions consistent with these historical figures have been supplemented. Chronology has been adjusted in some instances to smooth narrative flow. Some persons portrayed may be composites.

SPY CODE KEY

Agent #	Name
1	Leon Lawrence Lewis
7	C. Bert Allen
8	Captain Carl F. Sunderland
11, 74	Captain John H. Schmidt
17	Alyce Schmidt
33	Walter Clairville
C19	Charles Slocombe
F	Mrs. Anna Friedman
G2	Mrs. Grace Comfort
J2	John Barr
M	LAPD Detective William "Red" Hynes
N2	Neil Howard Ness
P8	Harwood E. Park
R3	Roy Arnold
S3	Sylvia Comfort
S4	Julius Sicius
WC	William C. Conley
W2	William A. Bockhacker
Y2	Charles Young

It will be to Hollywood's credit that its anti-Fascist activities pre-dated the swing in American public opinion and diplomacy. It will be to Hollywood's credit that it fought the Silver Shirts, the German-American Bund, and the revived Ku Klux Klan at a time when few realized their ultimate menace.

—Leo Rosten, sociologist, 1941

INTRODUCTION

"Judenfilm!"

The first Hollywood film to tick off the Nazis was *All Quiet on the Western Front*, from Universal Pictures in 1930. The studios were still transitioning to talkies, exploring the possibilities of synchronized picture and sound, and scenes of soldiers advancing in rhythm played like a macabre dance. The movie was antiwar and a tremendous artistic achievement, winning Academy Awards for Best Picture and Best Director, Lewis Milestone.

Like many Hollywood pictures, this one played in Germany, dubbed into German. Opening night in Berlin went smoothly. Audiences appreciated the film in solemn silence.

But on the second night, a screening was attended by Dr. Paul Joseph Goebbels, a small, weak-chinned, and clubfooted man of the burgeoning Nazi party, antisemites extraordinaire, hell-bent on genocide. He came prepared, accompanied by a school of brown-shirted Nazis.

During the film the Nazis rose and shouted, "*Judenfilm!*" (Jew film). Stink bombs exploded, a cage full of mice were released. Women screamed. A man hopped for the exit, shaking one pant leg. The screen went dark. When the lights came up, only brown shirts remained, their trousers tucked into their boots. They laughed, oblivious to the stink.

In response to the incident, which made the papers, riots erupted over the next week at screenings across Germany and Austria. Nazis took to the streets in protest. Within days, the German motion picture theater owners banned the picture.

Hollywood was confused. Why would this work of art bring

such anger? It took Billy Wilkerson, publisher of the *Hollywood Reporter*, to correctly diagnose the situation. *All Quiet on the Western Front* was not offensive to Germany. That was just the excuse. Problem was, it was an anti-war picture, and in Germany single-minded Nazis were busy kindling pro-war fervor, expansionism, based on Adolf Hitler's uniquely charismatic anger. There was no anti-war in Nazism. Also, the head of Universal Pictures was a Jewish man, and Jews to a Nazi were the root of all evil. The *Judenfilm* must be burned, purged from immaculate Nazi society.

Veterans of the Great War (now known as World War I) got a sinking feeling at the new German rhetoric: "The military spirit of the German people," Wilkerson wrote, "is only dormant. Not dead."

All Quiet on the Western Front was the first but certainly not the last Hollywood film to anger the Nazis. As the Nazi Party gained influence and then absolute power in Germany, it allowed fewer and fewer Hollywood movies to bump up against the Nazis' cool and pristine spell. German regulations on Hollywood content started out along then typical racist lines. Stop sending pictures that "depict Negro culture." Nazis liked Shirley Temple as much as the next guy—but not when she's dancing with Bill "Bojangles" Robinson. Nazis called it "racial defilement." Eventually, the Nazis only wanted movies that glorified their own image, as crisp as a winter morning and orderly as an ant hill.

Carl Laemmle

The man responsible for *All Quiet on the Western Front* was a German himself, Carl Laemmle, head of Universal Pictures. He grew up on the Blue Danube and came to America at seventeen, ran a store in Chicago until he was thirty-nine and, after seeing a line outside a nickelodeon in 1906, invested in the flickers. Eventually, he made, distributed, and exhibited his own films.

The first Universal Studios, built around 1912, were housed in an abandoned brewery at Sunset and Gower, the first time there was filmmaking in Hollywood. In 1915, Laemmle purchased a 230-acre lot on the Valley side of the hills and called it Universal City.

For years, a homesick Laemmle vacationed in Germany, a land that still panged his heart. But the Great War ended that. When peace came, Germany was a shadow, poor and torn. Visiting became depressing. What Laemmle did do was try to raise money in America to help the desperate civilian need in Germany, but it was too soon. Americans still thought of Germans as "the enemy."

Thus, Laemmle came to hate the war in a special way. Not just for its amorality, but for what it did to his fatherland. When Laemmle read the book *All Quiet on the Western Front* by Erich Maria Remarque, he saw *film art.*

"If there is anything in my life that I'm proud of, it is this picture. It's a picture that will live forever," Laemmle said.

Laemmle was befuddled but not terribly bothered by the Nazis' hostile reaction to his masterpiece. He was still blissfully unaware of what madmen they were.

Hitler Takes Charge

Push ahead two and a half years . . . January 30, 1933. Adolf Hitler rose to Reich Chancellorship of Germany. One day after that profane ascension, William Dudley Pelley held his first Silver Lodge meeting in Asheville, North Carolina. It was a big week for fascism on both sides of the Atlantic.

The great puzzle pieces of global conflict fell into place. A few weeks after Hitler assumed German command, Franklin Delano Roosevelt (FDR) was inaugurated as president. They would become adversaries to the death, neither surviving the war they'd wage.

Hitler's rise to power signaled an episodic internal campaign of violence, the stuttering start of a purge against those non-Aryans that Hitler thought best removed from the earth, unwanted people, Jews, communists, homosexuals, the mentally and physically infirm, and pretty much anyone who wasn't pro-Nazi. Hitler called it the Ultimate Solution. Anyone who disagreed was the enemy.

Aryanization would grow into the Holocaust. It wasn't until the liberation of the death camps in 1945 by American soldiers that reports of starvation, ovens, and gas pellets ceased to be criticized as "Jewish/Communist propaganda."

Newsreels

Throughout 1933, Americans' limited knowledge of Hitler and his policies came from newspapers and newsreels, the short films that preceded the feature in cinemas. Most of the major Hollywood studios (Paramount, Fox, Universal, RKO, and MGM) produced their own newsreels, each edition running about six minutes, or the length of a Bugs Bunny cartoon.

From the beginning of his reign, Hitler's image on screen drew tremendous audience reaction—although in most theaters those who booed and hissed were playfully combatted by those cheering and shouting "*Heil!*" Americans learned the word *swastika* and in those naive days of 1933 sometimes referred to Hitler as "Swastika Man." RKO's newsreel shorts, known as *The March of Time*, were most successful when it came to a behind-the-scenes look at Adolf Hitler's Third Reich. (See chapter 16, "On the Rhine with *The March of Time*.")

Somnambulant Obedience

There was still optimism in the New World that Germany, its population seemingly in a trance, would come to their senses and stop following this maniac who blamed all the world's ills on Jews. Germany's Jewish Central Association (JCA), in a haze of hope, issued a statement: "We do not believe our German fellow citizens will let themselves be carried away into committing excesses against the Jews."

The JCA's optimism was short-lived. The "excesses" began immediately. Stink bombs were hurled into Jewish-owned businesses. Pickets chanted hatefully outside Jewish stores. Those who tried to shop were harassed: "Buy Gentile," the Nazis commanded, "if you know what's good for you."

In Hollywood, there were high hopes that the studios would continue to make tons of money in Germany exhibiting American pictures dubbed into German, despite the new chancellor's "anti-Jew thing," as it was called in *Variety*.

In those early days of Hitler's reign, the Ultimate Solution was only hinted at. Goebbels, asked if there was a moral issue with "ridding the world of Jews," conceded, "Here and there it might lead to a human tragedy."

The Inner Sanctum

Hitler's inner sanctum, where plots of global domination were conjured . . .

Hitler and Goebbels are alone. It is Goebbels, now minister of propaganda and popular enlightenment, speaking: "Eventually we will have to deal with the Japanese, whose grand vision is second only to yours, *mein Führer*."

"I have decided to make them all honorary Aryans," Hitler said, with a laugh. His sense of humor. This was beside the point to the new leader, whose first order of business was dismantling Germany's democracy so that he wouldn't have to worry about reelection.

But the minister of propaganda relentlessly distracted Hitler, a steady flow of grandiose rhetoric to keep the egomaniac from imploding. Goebbels also sought to distract Hitler from truly looking at him. He wore a special shoe for his clubfoot, but there remained a shameful hitch in his giddy-up. He was aware of Hitler's opinion of gimps and distracted him from his bad foot with *ideas*. After all, it was Goebbels who instigated the German protest of *All Quiet on the Western Front*. Hitler's rapid rise to superstardom was due in large part to Goebbels's genius manipulation of the German media.

Their faces were close. Goebbels leaned in and whispered.

"The most important city to conquer in America is Los Angeles."

"Yes, strategically, it is a major western port," Hitler replied, impatient.

"Yes, true, and many German ships dock there—"

"It is halfway between Berlin and Tokyo, no?"

"Yes, but that is not what I mean. What you want *under your thumb* is Hollywood. The motion picture studios are the world's greatest propaganda machine. Hollywood movies are not only shown across the U.S. but everywhere in Europe as well. To control that message is to win the hearts and minds of millions without firing a shot."

"Hollywood *Judenfilm!*"

"It can be yours. *Hitlerfilm!*"

"We will purge Hollywood of the Jews," an invigorated Hitler said, almost spitting the last word. "With the movies, we will undermine the morale of the American people. We will undermine their faith in their own government. A new group will take over. This will be the German group, and we will help them assume power."

It was a nice burst of enthusiasm, but brief. Goebbels kept at it, regularly trying to get Hitler to think about the U.S., to try to understand its complexities—so many different sorts of people all living under a "united" banner. But Hitler never found America interesting enough to learn what it was really like. He was a student of European history. The New World was a footnote. Hitler thought America's attempt to mix races was its fatal flaw and tended to underestimate what America could do. He was hopeful he could conquer America with a minimum of sweat.

But Goebbels's point was a good one. First, he would conquer Hollywood and convert the big studios into pro-Nazi propaganda machines.

"What about counterespionage?" Hitler asked.

Goebbels said there was nothing to worry about. The United States in 1933 was a sleeping giant. "The U.S. is by far the largest country in the world without an espionage or counterespionage system in place," Goebbels said. "Our plot against America can be executed without opposition."

"None? They are more foolish than I believed."

"There is a Federal Bureau of Investigation, but only

three-hundred agents to cover forty-eight states. None of them have been trained in espionage."

"We will be able to do as we please. We will make them think it is their idea. There is no one to stop us," Hitler said. His eyes narrowed. "And another thing: Americans have the stomach for ultimate solutions. They call it 'Manifest Destiny.' Just look at the American Indians. What became of them?"

Goebbels laid out the plan. The Hollywood Studios were run by Jews, a fact that had been kept quiet. To start, there would be a paper propaganda campaign in America: Jews were the enemy, Jews ran Hollywood, they shouldn't be making motion pictures. Leaflets, Goebbels added, would call for a purge and crudely ridicule U.S. democracy.

Later, Goebbels said in public, "We are convinced that film is one of the most modern and far-reaching means for influencing the masses. A government therefore cannot leave film to the world itself."

Though America was embroiled in the Great Depression, in Hollywood that spring, the party raged on. Everyone was talking about *King Kong*, and no one was paying attention to Swastika Man. Well, almost no one.

Give the Moguls Their Due

Today, eight and a half decades after America's entrance into World War II, sour-faced historians criticize the prewar Hollywood moguls of the 1930s for not doing enough (in their films and business practices) to combat the growing Nazi menace.

The men who owned and ran the studios have been accused of greed, hesitating to pull their movies from Germany despite Nazism because there was so much money to be made. Truth is, the men who ran Hollywood kept their own anti-Nazi heroics secret.

This is the story of those heroics.

The Hollywood studios did much to combat Nazism in southern California. They financed the undercover investigations and incredible adventures of an organization called the Los Angeles

Jewish Community Council, the LAJCC. (As this doesn't exactly easily slip off the tongue, for the purposes of this book, the LAJCC will be called the "Nazibusters"; their job: to infiltrate, expose, and disrupt the growing number of organized Nazis in Los Angeles.)

The Nazibusters would operate for years, deep undercover, men and women, from the secretarial pool to the upper echelon, their officers meeting weekly, but never once did a member of the press learn that they existed.

The head Nazibuster was a man who would come to be known in Nazi circles as "The Most Dangerous Jew in L.A." He had an alliterative name . . .

Leon Lawrence Lewis

Lewis was a forty-five-year-old, six-foot-one Jewish lawyer. In 1933, he was almost always the tallest person in the room, and he knew how to use that advantage to get his way.

Lewis was first in L.A. to react to the Nazi insurgence, and he would stick with the battle the longest. He learned of Nazis spouting hate speech near downtown L.A., and within weeks was ready to table his lucrative private practice and prosecute his own war against the L.A. Nazis.

He correctly assumed that infiltration by the correct agent would be easily accomplished. The Nazi's primary trait was their smugness. Overconfidence. They were aglow with their own theories of superiority—and often a large amount of alcohol. A side-effect of this psychology was that Nazis were neither exceptionally suspicious nor inquisitive. Lewis's operation would have gone a different route if he'd thought newcomers to the Nazi fold would be thoroughly vetted. But he knew they were bound to be in recruiting mode, and by pushing the right buttons, telling them what they wanted to hear, getting in would be easy.

As our story begins, Lewis was working in an inconspicuous office, end of the hall, sixth floor of the Roosevelt Building at Seventh and Flower in downtown L.A., a twelve-story building shaped like an E, built in an Italian Renaissance Revival style.

(Though the neighborhood has deteriorated, the Roosevelt Building still stands and in 2007 was added to the National Register of Historic Places.)

The door read: LEON L. LEWIS, ATTORNEY AT LAW. In the waiting room, he had one secretary behind a desk and three chairs, then his private office with his desk, upon which sat a leather-bound inkblot and photos of his wife and two daughters. Facing the desk were another three wooden chairs.

It couldn't have looked less like the future nerve center of a complex intelligence and counterintelligence operation.

True Patriot

Lewis was born in Wisconsin to German Jewish immigrants, attended public school there, got his BA at George Washington University and his JD at the University of Chicago Law School. His private practice in Chicago leaned toward helping Jews in trouble long before he decided to go after Nazis.

Lewis wasn't just interested in fighting Jewish battles. Lewis had served his country, eighteen months of service with the National Guard, fought in the Somme, battlefield promotions taking him from private to captain. He was a patriotic American and saw the Nazis as a threat to all Americans, not just the Jews.

As it was for many veterans of the Great War, Lewis felt it was bad news that Germans were getting aggressive again. After the war, Lewis returned to Chicago and, along with resuming his practice, he became the Anti-Defamation League's national executive secretary. He wrote about antisemitism for twenty years in the periodicals of the ADL and B'nai B'rith, where he served as first executive secretary from 1913 to 1925. (In 1933, B'nai B'rith was still the only major Jewish organization in Los Angeles.)

Lewis was a newcomer to L.A., arriving with wife, Ruth, and daughters, Clair and Rosemarie, from Chicago in 1930. If you had to be a neophyte, L.A. was the place. Sometimes it seemed like everyone was new in town. Too many were actors, but luckily for Lewis, not enough were lawyers. He hung out his shingle and went to work.

Strategic Political Support

By financing Lewis's Nazibusters, the movie-studio moguls gave more than just money. They gave "strategic political support." The heads of all the major studios were represented. Each studio appointed representatives to form a subcommittee to monitor anti-Nazi spy activities—in essence, to keep track of how the studio money was being spent.

That subcommittee was known to the Nazibusters as the "Hollywood Branch." In time, the Hollywood Branch did more than just monitor. They held weekly meetings in the neo-Gothic, eight-story Hollywood Professional Building—home of the Academy of Motion Picture Arts and Sciences—where they mounted a "National counterpropaganda campaign."

Would that "propaganda machine" that Goebbels wanted so badly roll over for the Nazi invasion, or would weaponized Hollywood one day have him and his mustachioed buddy in its formidable celluloid crosshairs? To learn the answer, we must return to the beginning . . .

CHAPTER 1

L.A. in 1933

Agitators for communism and agitators for fascism play each into the hands of the other; the avowed purpose and intention of both being equally dangerous to the perpetuation of democratic principles of liberty.

—Captain Carl F. Sunderland (a.k.a. Agent 8)

In much of 1933, Los Angeles views of the sky were crisscrossed with electrical wire. The major streets of L.A. were cut down the middle by rail tracks for streetcars but already overwhelmed by automobiles, particularly downtown. The freeways had yet to be built, and you didn't have to get far from Downtown to find desert. Wherever you looked, there were oil wells. Paradise remained unpaved.

Looking up, some asked what that thing was they were building atop Griffith Park. The Observa-*what?* Seemed like bad timing. People were hungry, dammit, and they were spending a mint on stargazing.

Depression-era Los Angeles was a gloomy place. The economic malaise left a gray cloud over the basin that competed with the smog. With the entire nation feeling destitute, a mass migration had taken place: dust bowl migrants, Hollywood wannabes, with eyes like a blank slate, in desperation heading where you could sleep outdoors, if need be, live like a coyote.

Why was everyone poor? Who was to blame? The despair and ignorance rendered the public vulnerable to disinformation.

Brainwashers could make quick work of that steady supply of tabula rasa and anger. The Nazis were hawks, the incoming newcomers quarry, helpless prey to be taught and trained by fascist predators.

Folks were deeply frustrated, disappointed by life, ready to believe that Jews were responsible for all their ills. There was no logic to those antisemitic Nazi lessons, no evidence offered, none demanded. Repetition made it true: Jews had all the money. That's why the good people, the *Christian* people, were poor. Plus, Jews were all Communists.

Before the Nazis arrived in 1933, there were already many antisemitic groups ready to pitch that theory, none of them terribly large, usually working out of a small office space in downtown L.A. The KKK was around, gathering in the hills above Hollywood where, hooded-up and mounted, they galloped around whooping and carrying torches.

These groups, though not everyone's cup of tea, didn't cause the automatic outrage that they would today. The loud and angry hate speech was less offensive in a world in which all prejudices were mainstream.

L.A. Jews received letters from Europe that spring. The Nazis were formally boycotting Jewish businesses.

Boyle Heights

In 1933, Los Angeles had 1.4 million people, about 30,000 of whom were Jewish, or just over 2 percent. With more coming. The number was up to 70,000 ten years later. There were three distinct groups of Jews in L.A. at the time Hitler took Germany: Downtown Jews, many of them second-generation Angelinos and well-monied; Hollywood Jews, who had money but, as they were in show business, were considered a bit unsavory. These two groups would join once they found a common enemy but accounted for less than half of the total number of Jews in L.A.

The third and largest group lived in the east side neighborhood of Boyle Heights, tucked in between downtown Los Angeles and East L.A. The neighborhood was not exclusively Jewish by any means, but a melting pot, proud of its inclusivity, of citizens unwanted in the "nice" areas. Boyle Heights' main drag back then was called Brooklyn Avenue. That was where the original Canters Brothers Deli was, before it moved to Fairfax and became a tourist attraction. (Still great, though.)

As the first Nazis silently arrived in L.A. by boat and rail, the men of Boyle Heights were talking about Abie Miller, the lightweight prizefighter who was taking on all comers at the Pasadena Arena. Miller was a veteran of the smokers, and the men of Boyle Heights schlepped to the Pasadena to watch him fight. Boyle Heights men loved the very concept: fighting Jews. It remained a relatively new notion in America but one that would grow increasingly familiar as the decade and its terrors wore on.

The Jews of Boyle Heights lived in a system of xenophobia typical of any Depression-era American city. All Jews knew the limits: where they could live, what they could do for a living, where they shouldn't walk at night. Banks redlined the district on maps. *No loans.*

The Boyle Heights Jews, working class, pro-labor, were considered by their richer counterparts to be too liberal and unhelpful when trying to get gentiles to distinguish between Jews and Communists, something antisemites found difficult to do.

Political Climate

The rise of Nazi activity in L.A. during the bleakest years of the Great Depression coincided with other political city battles, sometimes verbal, sometimes physical. The Los Angeles Police Department ran a "Red Squad," which absolutely equated the (not necessarily Jewish) labor movement and the attempted formation of unions with Communism. The city was polarized between the ultraconservative business community and the radicalized labor movement. This was a rift that the incoming Nazis felt they could exploit.

Not all the antilabor forces in L.A. were affiliated with the police. The self-styled Better America Federation paid members of the Ku Klux Klan to bust up Communist get-togethers.

Point is, when spies were sent to take on the Nazis, it was a *very* L.A. thing to do. From San Fernando to Long Beach, political espionage was everywhere.

First Concentration Camps

The Nazis worked quickly. By March 1933, the Nazis in Europe were opening the first concentration camps. Jews were being rounded up. Those left behind managed to write to relatives in America. Bad things were happening. Non-Jews didn't get the message. America was slow on the uptake.

Someone asked Hermann Goering, the top Nazi who would run Hitler's Luftwaffe after war came, if he would do anything to protect the Jews of Germany.

His reply was tepid: "I shall employ the police and without mercy whenever German people are hurt, but I refuse to turn the police into a guard for Jewish stores."

Not all Jewish groups were as naive as the JCA in Germany. A joint committee was set up by the American Jewish Committee, the American Jewish Congress, and B'nai B'rith. The committee decided not to stage protests in America out of fear that they would result in reprisals against Jews in Germany.

"We'll only make it worse," was the initial opinion. What they didn't know was it couldn't get worse.

Call to Action

"Let's do nothing" didn't last long. In March 1933, an emergency conference of Jewish organizations was held and fifteen hundred people showed up. At that meeting, the commander-in-chief of the Jewish War Veterans called for a boycott of German imports.

A call to action was voiced by Rabbi Stephen S. Wise: "The time for prudence and caution is past. We must speak up like men. How can we ask our Christian friends to lift their voices in protest against the wrongs suffered by Jews if we keep silent? What is happening today in Germany may happen tomorrow in any other land on earth unless it is challenged and rebuked. It is not the German Jews who are being attacked. It is the Jews."

On March 27, 1933, there were simultaneous protests in Chicago, Boston, Philadelphia, Baltimore, Cleveland, and New York. A Madison Square Garden anti-Nazi rally was broadcast by radio throughout the world, and an estimated 55,000 showed up, most of whom never got inside the building, but packed the streets around the arena. Politicians came. AFL union president William Green, Senator Robert F. Wagner, and New York Governor Al Smith were all on hand, calling for an "immediate cessation of the brutal treatment being inflicted on German Jewry."

As anticipated, the Nazis back in Germany used news of the American protests as an excuse to step up their anti-Jewish campaign. Goebbels announced that because of the activity in America being organized by "Jews of German origin," he planned a campaign of "sharp countermeasures." He also announced that on Saturday, April 1, 1933, all "good Aryan Germans" would boycott Jewish-owned businesses. If the protests in the U.S. stopped, so would the boycott, he promised. If not, "the boycott will be continued until German Jewry has been annihilated."

The "boycott" was misnamed. The campaign to keep Germans from buying from Jews had been in place for weeks. What Goebbels was calling for was terror and violence. Jewish-owned stores were not just shunned, they were smashed and befouled.

In response to the "boycott," U.S. Secretary of State Cordell Hull issued a lukewarm protest, referring to the "unfortunate incidents" in Germany, commenting that "the whole world joins in regretting them." Hull added his own opinion that the reports of violence against Jews in Germany were "probably exaggerated."

While violence in Germany escalated, the Jewish-led boycott in the U.S. against German products continued. Rabbi Wise said that while the effect of the boycott in Germany was minor, it remained the American Jew's "moral imperative" to boycott.

"At least we have spoken," Wise said.

What German Section?

The first Nazis in L.A. belonged to an organization called the Friends of New Germany. The Friends, as they were called, also had representatives meeting and recruiting in other cities, but as we know, Hitler had special designs on southern California.

However, when Hitler and Goebbels eyed Los Angeles hungrily, they couldn't conceive of just how new and *without tradition* the city was.

"Where's the German section?' the first Nazis asked.

"What German section?" was the response. In New York City, the Friends merely had to set up shop in the Yorkville section of Manhattan and everyone for blocks around spoke German. It wasn't that easy in L.A.

The Friends didn't panic, though. They merely cast a wider net—distributed pamphlets, set up a recruiting center. They still hadn't quite come to grips with L.A.'s rootlessness and vastness. As our story takes place, fully half of L.A.'s residents had been in the city for less than five years, and ninety percent had been in town for less than fifteen. Second-generation Angelinos were few and far between.

Whereas N.Y.C. was a place where the space between things had been removed, L.A. was the opposite. Space seemed infinite and the growing city sprawled in the baking heat, gobbling up the valleys, canyons, and smoggy basins.

First Olive out of the Jar

The first film to deal with Hitler did not come from Hollywood but rather was produced by the New York–based Film Forum (not to be confused with the Houston Street cinema of the same name). It was a two-reeler (one reel equals about ten minutes), entitled *Hitler and Germany.* Released in April 1933, it featured filmed interviews with "notable anti-Nazis" discussing what Hitler might mean for the future of the country and Europe. One of the experts was Norman Thomas, a perennial presidential candidate, after whom a Manhattan high school is named. The movie played for a week here and there, then vanished.

Friends Get Together

The L.A. chapter of the Friends of New Germany held their first public meeting in April 1933. Speakers told the men in the room about the greatness of Adolf Hitler, and how Nazis would rise up to save America.

Afterward, one man who attended the meeting spoke to Leon Lewis. Speakers urged their followers to wrest Jewish people from the fabric of America—just as Hitler was doing in Germany.

Lewis already knew he needed to do something to stop the Nazis, but what? Using what framework? Relying on which allies? It was hard to tell the white hats from the black in this Wild West called L.A.

CHAPTER 2

Corruption, Oil, and Burning Books

The most difficult attack to combat and repulse is the attack that comes from within.
—Captain Carl F. Sunderland

Corruption was assumed at the Los Angeles Police Department (LAPD). The worlds of crooks and cops hopelessly overlapped, two sides of the same street. Politicians were bought and sold. Police officers paid for appointments. Madams and bookies greased the palms of the vice squads. Squawkers had their cars blown up.

There was a big overlap between the ranks of the LAPD and the Ku Klux Klan (KKK). The Los Angeles County Sheriff's department was just as bad. One sheriff's deputy once opined, "Jews should have their nuts cut out."

To further complicate matters, there'd been a seamless blend of L.A. law enforcement and organized crime since the 1920s. Some guys were all-of-the-above corrupt, L.A. citizens who had busy schedules, being gangsters, cops, and KKK riders.

Goebbels figured that, once the Friends of New Germany determined the palms that needed greasing, weaving Nazi ways into the corrupt L.A. fabric would be a snap. He had no clue what he was up against.

Oil Money

The handful of rich Jews in Hollywood represented only the region's *new* money. There were riches in L.A. several decades before the movie studios came west. *Oil money.* The boom came in 1892. Echo Park first. Edward L. Doheny whittled a eucalyptus log to a point and drove it into the ground at the corner of Patton and Colton. Boom!—gusher.

Within a year there was drilling everywhere, more than a thousand genuflecting derricks. The two most popular neighborhoods eventually became just south of Downtown and around La Brea Avenue and Wilshire Boulevard. People with modest homes drilled in their backyards. If you lived in L.A. during the 1930s, there were constant reminders that the oil fields were busy, pumping new money to put on top of the old for the lucky landowners. It was that purely gentile oil money that Berlin wanted on its side. With the oil millionaires' help, Jews could be extracted from Hollywood.

Hollywood During the Depression

Movie moguls of the 1930s were of a type: Jewish dreamers who came over on the boat—restless, ambitious, restricted in their pursuits in America due to their religion—and so invented their own industry.

It is possible to trace the birth of the motion picture industry to one meeting in New York, 1904. The men at the table would go on to run Twentieth Century-Fox, United Artists, MGM, and Paramount. They were Joseph and Nicholas Schenck, Marcus Loew, and Adolph Zukor. At that time motion pictures were brand new and considered a novelty. The men, who were all involved in the vaudeville industry, had assembled in the dimly lit back room of Shanley's Grill Room, a Times Square tablecloth joint. It was Zukor who saw the future, that this novelty was an embryonic body of artistry. The men agreed that they should be *making* motion pictures. Even if Zukor's vision was mere fantasy, he was right about one thing: good pictures would outsell hastily slapped together pictures.

"One day, photoplays will be as long as stage plays," Zukor said.

The others argued, saying no one would have the patience to sit still staring at a screen for that long.

"It is not a novelty," Zukor insisted. "It is only a novelty because we treat it that way. Pictures can be used to *move* an audience."

What Zukor was suggesting was that the new technology, moving images, be injected with a strong dose of show business. The others got the idea. Film could be used to tell stories, tell jokes, explore the psyche, the imagination, create a product every bit as addictive as an opiate. Zukor predicted pictures would sell out houses for a time side by side with vaudeville, but eventually flickers would kill vaudeville, *become* the show, and dominate the entertainment industry.

And it all came true—and when it did, the men at that table owned a huge piece of the motion picture pie. At first, they made their pictures in the East, but unpredictable weather made shooting difficult. Carl Laemmle of Universal had the right idea. They schlepped west to the land of sunshine.

Those moguls kept their heads above water during the Depression. Movies had sound now. They sang and danced. Hundreds of show girls tapped as one. Busby Berkeley fantasies soothingly titillated, a sparkly ball of fluff and thigh to get the world through its doldrums.

And among those moguls, there was a hesitance to overreact to Nazism. Germans loved their movies. Who wanted to turn off that cash faucet until it was absolutely necessary?

Only Harry Warner—born Hirsz Mojzesz Wonskolaser, surname shortened on Ellis Island to Wonsal, and de-ethnicized to Warner for business purposes—the eldest of the Warner brothers, wanted to discontinue business with Germany from the start. The other moguls hung back. Jack Warner called his brother Harry "the conscience of the company" and Warner Bros. halted business with Germany years before the other studios.

Sparks of Oppression

On May 10, 1933, Hitler ordered all banned books to be piled in the street and burned. Across Germany mass bonfires were held. Film crews memorialized the conflagration. Intellectuals cried, watching sparks soar into the sky, then die like dissipating freedom. The pyre process was carried out by student groups, tasked with seizing all books deemed to be un-German, most pulled from public and university libraries.

As the flames grew higher, Goebbels delivered a speech in which he proclaimed, "No to decadence and moral corruption!"

The mistreatment of Jews in Europe hadn't raised much of a fuss in the U.S., but book-burning touched a nerve. More than a hundred thousand people, many non-Jews, marched in New York City in protest of the literary bonfires. Smaller protests were held in Chicago, Philadelphia, and Cleveland. Almost every daily newspaper in the U.S. condemned the fires.

The Good Father

America's most popular antisemite was a Catholic priest named Father Charles Coughlin, who had a coast-to-coast syndicated radio show on Sunday afternoons. In those days before TV, families gathered around the living room console radio and listened to the good father, who wrapped his anti-Jewish rhetoric in a warm and fuzzy voice. During his show Coughlin explained that all the world's ills were brought upon good, God-fearing men and women by dirty Jews—Communists, all of them—and they wouldn't be content until they ruled the world.

German Film Under Hitler

Goebbels took control of the German film industry and purged it of "undesirables." Films existed only to fulfill the National Socialist ideal. No one said boo.

He believed there was no such thing as "public taste." Use a command voice and the public could be dictated to. He could shape the taste of his people at will. He'd nailed down political taste; artistic taste was next.

Germans no longer had points of view. Now instead of film criticism, only "film observation" was allowed. Journalists were allowed to describe pictures and, even then, only in terms reflecting the glory that was All Things Hitler.

Goebbels founded a Nazi film school so that filmmakers would learn to make films that best created public support for their agenda, and set up a board of "master censors" to review all films prerelease for hints of subversion.

It amounted to a ban on creativity. One result was a mass flight of German filmmakers (such as Fritz Lang, Robert Siodmak, Douglas Sirk, and Billy Wilder) and performers (Peter Lorre and Marlene Dietrich) to the U.S.

Germany's loss. Hollywood's gain.

An estimated fifteen hundred members of the German film industry fled before they could be purged. Goebbels offered Fritz Lang—director of *Metropolis* and *M*— the job as head of propaganda films, but Lang instead got out of Dodge, came to Hollywood, and put his talents toward the slanted light of film noir.

All Things Offensive Will Be Burned

On June 28, 1933, Hitler severely restricted the distribution of Hollywood movies in Germany. "Films considered detrimental to Germany will be confiscated and burned," Goebbels said.

And what constituted "detrimental to Germany"? That was strictly Goebbels's call. If a Jew was in the picture, banned. If a Jew composed the music, banned. "Any film in which Jewish characters appear or that presents a cheerful aspect of Jewish life," banned. One movie, MGM's *The Prizefighter and the Lady*, starred Max Baer, a real-life boxing champion who, though Christian, had worn a Star of David on his trunks into the ring to fight the German champ Max Schmeling in Yankee Stadium—banned! Banned with the greatest enthusiasm was anything featuring or mentioning Charlie Chaplin, who was also mistakenly thought to be Jewish. Chaplin irritated Nazis with his mustache and physical resemblance to Hitler.

On July 1, the Aryanization of the German film industry was made law. It was illegal to allow any Jew to participate in German filmmaking. The law included Jews working for Hollywood film studios in Germany.

Hollywood had to scramble to get their Jewish employees out of Germany as fast as possible. For those that remained, bad things happened. The owner of a theater in Rochester, New York, Nathaniel Wolff, was kidnapped from his hotel room in Berlin and beaten. In Austria, theatrical impresario Alfred Rotter and his wife were killed by Nazis. In Berlin, a German film exhibitor, David Oliver, and his wife narrowly escaped death when their taxi was firebombed. Warner Bros. sales rep Philip Kauffman had his car stolen, his house broken into and ransacked, and he was beaten.

Now, all film industry employees in Germany were forced to show their passport, birth certificate, and proof of their grandparents' religion, anytime anyone in a brown shirt wanted to see them.

The Hollywood moguls were confused by this. Aryanization was bad for business. They could understand bigotry, but to purposefully lose money to reorder society? This was madness.

Hitler's a Dirty Word

The first time the name Hitler was to be spoken in the dialogue of a Hollywood picture, censors freaked out and the line was rewritten.

(For the record, the word was to be spoken as the punchline to a joke by Jerome "Curly" Howard in the pre–Three Stooges MGM film *Dancing Lady*, 1933.)

"Hitler was ignored by the Hollywood screen even as he redrew the map of Europe," says historian Thomas Doherty.

In the meantime, Nazis in L.A. were putting it around that Hitler just wanted to be friends with the United States. Nothing to worry about. Embrace the new age. And the U.S. was vulnerable. For Hitler, it might have been a happy coincidence, but an America battered by economic gloom was ripe for playing ball—if the pitch was right.

CHAPTER 3

Let's Be Friends

The youth of Germany will be conscripted for government work just as in the past they were conscripted for military service. This is part of Hitler's program to give every person a job. The young men will be assigned to labor camps for work on highways, forest, and government projects.

—Heinz Spanknöbel

As 1933 got under way, dusty Angelinos had things on their minds. The Depression was getting old. Panic crept up from a baser instinct. Scofflaws ran wild, rolling through the hills and valleys like tumbleweeds of corruption. Black markets flourished. Mattresses were stuffed. Financial institutions, demonized in the stock market crash of 1929 and the subsequent runs on the banks, were going out of their way to seem trustworthy. It was a wasted effort. It would be years before Americans trusted banks again.

FDR's Ticking Package

For the U.S. president, the world was a dangerous place. Seventeen days before Franklin Delano Roosevelt's inauguration, a thirty-two-year-old Italian immigrant named Giuseppe Zangara fired five shots at him as he gave a speech in Miami Beach, Florida. Chicago Mayor Anton Cermak was killed, four wounded, but FDR was unharmed. Zangara was tried, convicted, sentenced to death, and executed in a swift eight weeks. Less than a month into FDR's first term, there was a second attempt, this one a bomb sent through the mail.

The world was growing faster, too. The Englishman Malcolm Campbell set a new land-speed record for automobiles, bulleting down the flat sands of Daytona Beach at more than 270 mph (and was knighted for his efforts). Roscoe Turner flew in a prop plane from Burbank to New York in just over ten hours, setting a record.

Of specific interest to L.A. that spring, the Reconstruction Finance Corporation gave the Metropolitan Water District of Southern California more than two million dollars for construction work on the Colorado River aqueduct. Fresh water and lots of it was coming. Imagine having an outdoor hose and a lawn. L.A. had visions of a desert turned green. With water, greater L.A. could grow unchecked.

Glitz and Dirt

In Hollywood, there was the usual combo of glitz and dirt. A starlet named Peg Entwhistle leaped to her death off the H in the HOLLYWOODLAND sign. (The damn sign used to light up at night, flashing HOLLY, then WOOD, then LAND. But money was tight in 1933, and the sign, dark.) The most talked-about picture of the year would be RKO's *King Kong*, whose title character climbed the Empire State Building with a blond shiksa in his fist. The Marx Brothers made *Duck Soup*, which many think was their best movie. Charles Laughton and Katharine Hepburn won the year's acting Oscars. Darryl F. Zanuck and Joseph M. Schenck joined forced to form a new studio that would be known as Twentieth Century Pictures, Inc. The Fox wouldn't be added till a few years later. All the studios were shut down for a time that year by a soundman strike.

And Jewish Angelinos were thinking for the first time about Nazis. Relatives in Europe were frightened. Terrifying leaflets littered downtown L.A., distributed by the Friends of New Germany. The leaflets contained provocative disinformation, statements purposefully designed to deceive, such as the nonsense that "Jews had all the money" and "Jews were responsible for the Depression." The propaganda rapidly evolved until there were calls for violence and thinly veiled references to genocide. "Jews are a cancer that must be removed from society." The leaflets had that Nazi ha-ha sense of humor, calling FDR's New Deal the "Jew Deal" and referring to the president as *Rosenfeld.*

The new Nazis in town were busy spreading Hitler's word, trying to recruit L.A.'s German American men, and antisemitic men in general, to join their fold.

Who were these Friends of New Germany? Nobody knew. The justified fear was that the group was acting on direct orders from Adolf Hitler, that they were *foreign agents.*

The Friends of New Germany was led by Heinz Spanknöbel, who presented himself as a man of the cloth and a German diplomat. He was neither. He was, as feared, an agent of Hitler working in the U.S.

Looking to build an army, Nazis in the beginning took any gig they could get. They stood on street corners. They promised free beer. They addressed women's groups in L.A.'s suburbs.

"Tell your husbands about the Commie threat," the women were instructed.

On September 18, 1933, a big Hollywood studio first parodied Adolf Hitler in a picture. It was Warner Bros.—and the film was a six-minute Looney Tunes cartoon called *Bosko's Picture Show.* The cartoon pretended to be a newsreel and included a segment on the town of Pretzel, Germany, where the leader was a buffoon, with toothbrush mustache and lederhosen. (For more on *Bosko's Picture Show*, see the Appendix.)

The Tough Jews of Newark

In October 1933, Germany pulled out of the League of Nations. Stateside, the Nazi movement was drawing violent resistance, in particular a brawl in Newark, New Jersey, where the Jewish gangster Abner "Longie" Zwillman was financing a violent group known as the Minutemen—Jewish boxers and other tough guys—who could respond to and bust up a Nazi rally in sixty seconds, busting a few Nazi noses while they were at it.

According to one eyewitness account, the Nazi event was "stormed" by the anti-Nazis: "Volleys of stones and stench bombs crashed through the windows before a police cordon, thrown about the building, restored order. After the meeting sporadic street fighting broke out."

The Nazis were learning that winning the hearts and minds of America with their hate talk was not going to be accomplished without suffering a few bumps and bruises from Jewish tough guys. (For more on these battles, see this author's book *Gangsters vs. Nazis*.)

For the Nazis, there was more bad news later that month from back east, this time from New York, where a warrant was put out for the arrest of Friends leader Heinz Spanknöbel. News broke that he was to be charged with espionage, but the arrest was never made because Spanknöbel disappeared. Nobody was sure where he went. One story goes that Spanknöbel was at the home of a man named Ignaz Griebl (more about him later) when he was abducted, forced into a car and then onto a ship, and sailed back to Germany. The reason: insubordination. Which command had he failed to obey? We don't know. What we do know is that Griebl entered the Friends of New Germany at a high level and was reporting back to German intelligence what was going on.

Because Spanknöbel was the Friends' founder, an attorney for the Jewish War Veterans, Julius Hochfelder, asked the New York State attorney general's office to call witnesses, with a view to canceling incorporation papers of the Friends of New Germany.

The Brown House

Robert Pape was the first *Obergauführer* (regional leader) of Nazi Germany's L.A. operation, a Great War veteran and charter member of the Nazi party. He set up Friends HQ in a mansion at 902 South Alvarado Street, corner of Ninth Street, west of Downtown. The former home was converted into a Nazi complex, formally called Alt Heidelberg, but known by the Nazis as the Brown House because that was the name of Hitler's HQ in Munich. Alt Heidelberg was also the name of a popular German beer, and the title of an MGM picture from 1928 with Ramon Navarro and Norma Shearer.

The center on Alvarado was a German American "community center," featuring the Aryan Bookstore, *the* place to go for all your antisemitic, pro-Hitler propaganda. Magazine titles included *Beacon Light*, published in L.A., Father Coughlin's *Social Justice*, published in Michigan, the Silver Lodge's periodical *Liberation*, printed in North Carolina, and *The American Gentile*, published in Chicago. There were many others.

The Alt Heidelberg was a place to go in general, as Pape built a little entertainment and business complex around the store. There was a *biergarten* and a restaurant that resembled an old German beer hall. It had a comfortable "Old Country" ambiance. The food was excellent and cheap. Beer cost a nickel. Full meals, sixty cents. Very Depression-era-friendly. During the day, older Germans filled the restaurant, but after nightfall the crowd changed, becoming younger—and louder in their praise for Hitler. Sometimes an oom-pah band played, tubas blowing a resonant wind, while ruddy-faced men performed sudsy dances. Upstairs, there was space for administrative offices.

To sell more copies of *Silver Ranger*, the newspaper of the Silver Lodge fascists, the Friends hired a newsie to stand outside the Aryan Bookstore with copies in a burlap sack.

"Extry! Extry! Free speech halted by Jew riot!" the kid would shout. The newsie's other job was to keep an eye out for troublemakers. On several occasions since the bookstore's grand opening, baseball-sized rocks had been thrown through the front window.

Alt Heidelberg contained a meeting hall where the Nazi flag was hung on the wall behind the podium. At the first meeting held in the venue, the Friends debuted their new uniforms, which of course echoed those worn by the Nazis in Germany, with brown shirts and black swastika arm bands. During the first meetings in that hall, speeches were sometimes interrupted by hecklers. The disturbances were quickly quelled by Pape's security guards, a.k.a. storm troopers.

Like any good proprietor, Pape worked the guests, making sure every glass was full, talking all the time in his thick-accented English. To anyone who would listen, Pape warned of the Jewish Communist conspiracy and predicted that the Jews would try to take over but would fail because the Nazis would rise as one and "save America." Pape regularly sent "progress reports" to Hitler and Goebbels.

Also walking around shaking hands was Hans Winterhalder, Pape's handsome power-hungry propaganda chief. Winterhalder was chiseled from stone: stiff, cold, without social graces, and insistent on being right. He was a rules-are-rules asshole of a man, and when he drank the Hitler Kool-Aid, he drank it hard. Hell, you'd be stiff, too, if you were taking orders directly from Joseph Goebbels, which he was.

Ideas and Ideals

The first open meeting of the Nazis of Los Angeles was held on the evening of July 26, 1933, at the Alt Heidelberg. On the industrial-gray walls were mounted electric fans, noisier than they were effective, blowing the hot air harmlessly around. For the first time, groups of men appeared in public in Los Angeles wearing brown shirts and red, white, and black swastika arm bands.

The meeting was designed to "get complete information of the Nazi ideas and ideals to all people of German extraction of Los Angeles in order that they might not believe that the new Germany has opposition to Jews as its object."

This description can at best be called bait and switch. At worst, it was a smug wink to the antisemites the Friends were looking for. Robert Pape was emcee. Standing along the wall was the Friends' secretary, Hermann Schwinn, with his little twitchy mustache, and a row of storm troopers eager for action, opening and closing their fists, thick-necked towheads with sadism in the cold fire of their crystal blue eyes.

Hitlerism in America

Winterhalder took the podium and proclaimed there were fifty German American organizations in southern California. What good was that? Unify, and they would be more than one hundred thousand strong, and Hitlerism in America would become a reality. The message played well.

Hermann Schwinn gave a speech entitled "Why Hitler Came to Power." Schwinn was a bespectacled chap, whose military cap hid the great height and width of his forehead. He was the only one of the California Nazi leaders to be a naturalized citizen of the U.S. Born in Hamburg, Germany, he grew up in Canton, Ohio, and, since 1928, had been in Los Angeles, where he worked in a German American bank. Schwinn carried himself like a man who thought himself in charge. Pape couldn't have liked him.

Dr. Hermann Meyer spoke on "Germany's Struggle Against Communism," and Dr. Clinton Wunder's talk was called "Communism in the United States." Author, inventor, and lecturer John H. Dequer delivered "The Jew in History." The thrust was that "the Jew" was not only the source of today's problems, but of problems throughout time as well.

Last at the podium was Dr. Rudolph H. Gerber, a nerve specialist and practitioner of "naturopathic" medicine. Born in Germany, Dr. Gerber came to L.A. in 1914. Dr. Gerber liked to say, "I've measured a great many craniums and Aryans, that is Germans, have the best brains." The audience cheered. Being superior was joyful.

The Friends were recruiting and advertised upcoming meetings in L.A. newspapers, and there was a reporter on hand covering the meeting, which is why we know the speakers and their topics. But the coverage brought controversy. On October 31, the *Los Angeles Evening Citizen News* caught flack for publicizing the Friends. A writer identifying themselves as ANTI-HITLER, wrote, "By giving publicity in your paper to meetings of that organization you are indirectly lending support to the growth of Hitlerism and all the intolerance and brutality it stands for."

During autumn 1933, the Friends grew popular—so much so that the meetings overflowed their meeting room. A larger venue was needed. If the growth in popularity continued unimpeded, L.A.'s Jews would be in trouble fast. Who would protect them?

The answer to that question was one man—Leon Lawrence Lewis.

CHAPTER 4

L. L. Lewis: "L.A.'s Most Dangerous Jew"

I don't see much future for the Americans. In my view, it's a decayed country. And they have their racial problem, and the problem of social inequalities. These were what caused the downfall of Rome.

—Adolf Hitler

L.A.'s Jews knew the ropes. Few were "fresh off the boat." More than half were born in the United States. The initial reaction to the resulting upsurge in antisemitism was to lay low—an attitude encouraged by B'nai B'rith, the Anti-Defamation League (ADL), and the American Jewish Congress (AJC). In L.A., Jews couldn't have been less conspiratorial. Outside those groups just mentioned, there was very little sense of an L.A. Jewish community. Individually, they soaked up the sun, put lights on their houses at Christmas, and kept their Jewishness to themselves. The urge to remain passive was especially strong in Jews who had relatives in Germany, where terror thrived the instant Hitler took power.

Not all Jews in L.A. chose to hang back. One man who wanted to fight was Jewish attorney Leon Lawrence Lewis, whom we met in the introduction. Lewis throughout his practice, fought tooth and nail for Jews who were down on their luck.

Lewis would become such a successful anti-Nazi warrior that in one correspondence, a Nazi named Rafael Demmler referred to the lawyer as "the most dangerous Jew in Los Angeles, the ringleader of all Jews here."

(Demmler was a character. He was chair of the Nazi Camouflage Committee, president of the pro-Nazi Steuben Society, and a former chauffer who told tales of seducing the daughters of the rich men he drove for. He would eventually reveal himself as a man prone to suggestion and blind with power hunger. Demmler was antisemitic but also considered himself an American, having come over when he was just a kid. That was the thing that bugged him about the Nazis in L.A. They hated America. "I grew up playing with American kids. I'm an American. Those swastika guys are never going to see it that way.")

Spy Squad

With Nazis moving into L.A., Lewis took it upon himself to do something about it. His idea was to assemble a squad of spies to infiltrate the Nazis. The nerve center for his operation would be his law offices in the Roosevelt Building. He had no idea that this would be his life for the next eight years.

The birth of Lewis's spy squad came on August 31, 1933, during a meeting of L.A. Jews that Lewis called at the home of Judge Isaac Pacht. The hostess was the judge's wife, Rose Pacht (nee Rudolph). The "advisory committee" appointed that day consisted of, among others, producer, director, and Palm Springs real-estate developer, Phil Goldstone, noted philanthropist Ludwig Schiff, J. Y. Baruh, whose home once appeared on the cover of *The Architectural Digest* in 1927, Columbia Pictures' general manager Sam J. Briskin, Tom May, Dr. Maurice Kahn, Irving Lapsitch, and a fellow who would later become a general in the Hollywood vs. Nazis war: entertainment attorney Mendel Silberberg.

The idea was to assemble a combination of men and women, Jews and non-Jews, to infiltrate the Friends of New Germany, the Silver Lodge of William Pelley, and the Ku Klux Klan. Lewis's Nazibusters would report back to him through the mails, on the telephone, or in clandestine meetings at remote places where they were unlikely to be seen.

Agent 11

By autumn 1933, the L.A. faction of the Friends of New Germany had grown to four hundred men. In their speeches, they openly recruited American veterans, who both had knowledge of military operations and might be disgruntled because the new president had cut back their disability benefits.

Lewis's first recruit fit that mold perfectly. He was U.S. Army Captain John H. Schmidt, child of a Bavarian military family, a career soldier who had served in the German army. Schmidt ran away from Germany when he was sixteen and came to the U.S. where he enlisted and joined the U.S. Army as a private. He first saw combat serving under John J. Pershing in Mexico. He also served in the American Expeditionary Forces (AEF) that fought in France in 1917, rising to the rank of captain. He received a medical discharge after contracting a "tropical fever," probably malaria.

Schmidt's strength was his appearance, which could not have been further from how we envision a spy. He was round and soft, with a face that smiled easily. He was five-eleven and had blond hair, blue eyes—physical attributes that made the Nazis swoon. And despite his years as an American, he still spoke English with a thick German accent.

Schmidt's weakness was his nerves. His time at war had left him sick and shell-shocked, a condition that caused him to be hospitalized for six years. He lived on his disability pension until 1930 when the Depression caused the U.S. government to discontinue unlimited aid to disabled veterans. When Schmidt wrote to an L.A. lawyer asking that he represent him in his effort to get his pension reinstated, that lawyer was Leon Lewis.

Lewis saw in Schmidt a guy who had every reason to turn on America, but by all appearances hadn't.

"You are a loyal American, correct?" Lewis asked.

"I am. I am a member of the Disabled American War Veterans,"

Schmidt said, referring to an organization commonly referred to as the DAV.

"In what capacity?"

"I am a member of the Americanism Committee."

Lewis said that he would fight to get Schmidt's pension reinstated, and until that time, he would give him money so that he could get back on his feet.

"But there is something I want you to do for me," Lewis said.

"Anything," Schmidt replied.

Lewis explained the setup. "I want you to join the Friends of New Germany. Tell them the truth. Tell them that you fought for the United States, and in the long run, they screwed you. Tell them you are looking for a better way, a German way. And then you report back to me and tell me everything you hear and see."

"It's a deal," Schmidt said. In Nazibuster files and communications, it was agreed, Captain Schmidt would be referred to as Agent 11.

Wanted: Anti-Nazi Gentiles

To solidify anti-Nazi sentiment, Lewis went to work at DAV and American Legion meetings, getting the L.A. chapters of both groups to pass resolutions condemning the Nazis and everything they stood for.

Rather than recruit Jewish people who could pass as Aryan, Lewis used non-Jews. Although it was not common for Christians to be willing to risk their lives to battle antisemitism, those brave people were out there, and Lewis found them.

There were lots of reasons to be anti-Nazi, including the fact that many felt the U.S. was going to end up going to war in Germany all over again, an idea that angered those who'd crawled in the gassy trenches of the Great War.

Pasadena Rally

In early August 1933, the Los Angeles Nazis took their dog-and-pony show, their recruiting mission, for the first time to the outskirts, to Pasadena, most famous for the eleven-year-old, hundred-thousand-seat Rose Bowl stadium, and its Tournament of Roses Parade each New Years since 1890.

It was headline news. That night, the Friends of New Germany was opening a "new chapter" in Pasadena and would accept initiates at the Athletic Club.

As the *Pasadena Post* reported, "The Swastika of Adolf Hitler will fly in Pasadena tonight at 8:30." The paper noted that not just anyone could attend the event, as it was exclusively for German Americans or those of the Aryan race and their families.

At the Pasadena rally, the big room was festooned with one hundred swastika flags and one American flag. Initiations were held. Eight new members endured a ceremony that would've made a Freemason proud. Afterward, there was lager quaffing from ornate steins, and plans were made to hold a midnight torchlight parade through Pasadena in two weeks. That would show the Jews what was what.

Now here's the weird part. As you might expect, the thought of Nazis carrying torches and marching at midnight through Pasadena was chilling to a large segment of the community, and there were howls of protest. In response the Friends denied, denied, denied—to an absurd level. There was no rally. No initiation. Plans for a torchlight parade? No way!

Whatever. An LAPD detective said there was no way the Nazis would have been allowed to march, anyway.

Later that month in an unpublicized meeting in Chicago of German American leaders, it was decided to affiliate the Friends with as many organizations as possible and to provide five million dollars to "fight the lying propaganda in the American press."

The Mission Begins

Fifteen days after the Nazi flag flew for the first time in Pasadena, just west of downtown L.A., on August 17, 1933, Agent 11 stood, heart thumping, on the South Alvarado sidewalk, outside the Alt

Heidelberg. He took a deep breath and walked in. A bell above the door tinkled. He was in the Aryan Bookstore.

Above the front door was a sign that read:

ARYAN BOOK STORE
Truth Brings Liberation

A phonograph record was playing a Hitler speech. There was no musty smell that bookstores sometimes have, no sense of organized chaos. There was no chaos as all, just a stifling sense of order. The air smelled of liquid soap and Aqua Velva. Where there should have been shelves, there were bare walls. On tables, books and leaflets were on display, perfectly spaced and T-squared into right angles.

Sitting on a stool behind a counter and a *ca-ching* cash register was a beautiful young woman, lips too red for the time of day. She flashed Schmidt a toothy smile. He nodded without changing expression.

Schmidt sensed other eyes upon him as he moved slowly up and down an aisle, looking at the titles. A man stepped through a doorway and gave him the once-over. Schmidt lifted a book from the table, looked at it, tossed it up and down in his hands to gauge the weight and closely examined the binding. The book was called *The Nazi Party Song Book.* Schmidt slowly and deliberately paged through it and stopped at a song called "Death to Jews." He laughed. He repeated the name of the song aloud and chuckled again.

With that bit of acting, he turned to the man and said, "I am John Schmidt, a proud German. I would like to talk to the man in charge. I am eager to learn more about the Friends of New Germany."

"You can talk to me, I am Paul Themlitz. I run this store."

The men shook hands and the thirty-one-year-old Themlitz began to show books and pamphlets to Schmidt.

"This is literature written by Germans for Germans," Themlitz said. "It expresses the goals that Friends of New Germany hold so dear."

Schmidt nodded approvingly. He glanced over at the woman behind the counter. She was examining red fingernails and reading a copy of *Movie Mirror* magazine, a platinum blond Bette Davis on the cover, while a headline promised an intimate feature on "Hollywood's Greatest Lovers."

Among the titles that Themlitz showed him were a newspaper called *California Staats-Zeitung*, Joseph Goebbel's book *Der Angriff*, and Julius Streicher's book *Der Stürmer*.

Themlitz felt he had a hot one. John Schmidt found himself being treated very nicely.

Great Strides

Schmidt was taken to Obergauführer Robert Pape, who in turn introduced Schmidt to Friends secretary Hermann Schwinn. There was back-slapping and declarations of the "great strides" Hitler was making in correcting society's ills.

"What is your organization's primary goal?" Schmidt asked.

It was Schwinn who answered. "We exist to combat Communism."

"Where do you get your orders?" Schmidt asked.

"Overseas," Pape said. Schmidt was visibly impressed.

Schmidt told the Nazis he was both German by birth and a naturalized U.S. citizen.

"We trust you, of course, but we have regulations," Themlitz said.

"What do you need?" Schmidt asked, with a note of understanding.

"Your American army papers, your American Legion membership, your DAV papers," Themlitz said.

"I will bring them the next time I am here." It was so easy. He had infiltrated the Nazis by using his own bio as his cover story.

"We are interested in recruiting as many American veterans as possible," Pape said.

"I will see what I can do," Schmidt promised.

CHAPTER 5

Agents on the Job

All warfare is based on deception. There is no place where espionage is not used. Offer the enemy bait to lure him.
—Sun Tzu, 500 B.C.

Schmidt came to be trusted by the Nazis. He reported to Leon Lewis that the Friends believed Jews were the source of all the world's problems, should be removed from American government and replaced by German Americans.

Schmidt wrote, "I have no sense that they are lying, but rather that they truly believe these things."

L.A. Führer Robert Pape told Agent 11 that patriotic groups such as the American Legion and the Veterans of Foreign Wars were anti-Nazi because they were misinformed by Jewish lies. (Well, yeah, that and the fact that American veterans of the First World War still hated Germany's guts.)

Upstairs Verboten

Schmidt's wife, the lovely Alyce, was the only person other than Lewis to know her John was a spy. Her reaction was unexpected.

"I want to be a spy, too," she said brightly.

"Why?"

"I can learn things you can't."

"Because you're a woman?"

"Because I'm a woman."

And so, John Schmidt did return to the Alt Heidelberg. He brought his papers—and Alyce. After a brief conversation with

Pape, showing him his bona fides, Mr. and Mrs. Schmidt strolled into the restaurant to eat.

During their meal, Alyce announced she needed the powder room and, without asking where it was, headed up a flight of stairs. She didn't make it all the way, however, as she ran into a woman coming down.

"Ladies?"

"Not up here. It is *forbidden* to come up here," the woman said sternly. Softening her tone as Alyce apologized, she gave directions to the *toilette*.

The next day, Agent 11 reported to Leon Lewis that there was something going on upstairs at the Alt Heidelberg that customers were not supposed to see.

"I suspect they may be storing weapons up there," Agent 11 said. "I will try to find out. Thanks to Themlitz, I think, word has gone out that I am to be given special respect.

"They are talking unity not just with other German American associations but with non-German groups as well. They talked of merging with the Silver Lodge."

Schmidt quoted Themlitz as saying, "We will form an anti-communist supergroup. There are a hundred like-minded groups. One day we will join and become one group, under the command of Adolf Hitler."

Rather quickly, Mr. and Mrs. Schmidt were invited to dinner with powerful people, some of whom were secretly in cahoots with the Nazis. The Schmidts were surprised to see police captain "Red" Hynes at one dinner. He was head of the LAPD's anti-Communist "Red Squad." Hynes was a complicated guy, liked to work the angles, sometimes more than one angle at a time.

William Francis Hynes was neither a Nazi nor a sympathizer. He and the Nazis had a common enemy in Communists, that was all. When Hynes thought of Communism, he thought of unionization. Religion didn't necessarily come into it. Hynes didn't seem to like the Nazis. He didn't just observe them; he criticized, pestered, and annoyed them.

Hynes told the Friends, "You should cut out this brown-shirt bullshit. It's too much like Hitler. It's scaring people."

The Friends leaders to a man thought he was out of his mind. But he was a cop, so they had to play nice.

Nazis Seeking Extra Work

One of Agent 11's first reports revealed that a small crew of Nazis were applying daily at the studios for "extra" work; that is, to play people in the background of movie scenes. Extras, because there was so much time hanging around between takes, could be useful if they kept their eyes and ears open. Already those spies had reported back valuable information concerning the way the Jews at the studios were "ruining white girls."

Schmidt, without his wife, was one of eighty men who attended the next Friends meeting at the Alt Heidelberg. Many of the men at the meeting wore military-style uniforms: white shirts, black ties, riding pants, tall leather boots. A flamboyant few went with a monocle. Several clasped riding crops in their hands, as if they were about to dish out discipline. When asked why they were dressed that way, they said they were emulating the uniforms of the Silver Lodge.

The main speaker was Friends secretary Hermann Schwinn: "It is our goal to see to it that the German government will provide all interested Americans with a free copy of *Mein Kampf*, translated into English."

The audience applauded. Schwinn apologized for delivering his comments in English, explaining that he had been away from the Old Country for so long that his German had grown rusty.

Schmidt Takes the Podium

Schwinn asked if anyone wanted to share any feelings with the group.

Schmidt raised his hand.

"Please," Schwinn said.

Schmidt took the podium and solidified his cover: "I know how many of you feel about the Jews. When you and I get to know each other better, I will tell you what I think should be done about those who come to America and abuse its trust and confidence. Thank you."

Applause.

Schwinn beamed with joy.

Schmidt smiled sheepishly and retook his seat.

When the meeting was over, chief propagandist Hans Winterhalder, with set jaw and face grim, vigorously shook Schmidt's hand.

"Well said, Captain Schmidt. Well said," Winterhalder said.

Again, Schmidt was urged to recruit. He would have to take Pape up on his offer to bring like-minded Americans to the next meeting. He reported this to Lewis and together they searched the DAV for other men willing to attend Friends meetings and report back to Lewis.

Carl Sunderland, Agent 8

The first of these men was Carl Sunderland, born in Fort Wayne, Indiana, in 1884, a longtime soldier, who had served three stints with the Thirteenth Cavalry and fought in the Great War. His time on the battlefield ended with a severe wound. Following months of hospitalization, he left the army in February 1919 as a captain. He was now forty-nine years old and steamed over his shrunken disability payments. He was head of the L.A. chapter of the DAV, and thus in a position to recruit. He was a member of the Veterans' Congressional Coordinating Committee. He was also an American, with grandparents who came over from Germany—a perfect résumé for the Friends.

And although he told Friends leaders that he spoke no German, he'd taken three years of German in school, which turned out to be enough for him to report things they said in front of him that they thought he didn't understand.

Sunderland recited the oath during his initiation and later reported back to Lewis the wording. "I was asked to say, 'I belong to no Semitic organization. I am of Aryan stock and have neither Jewish nor colored blood in me.'"

Bert Allen, Agent 7

The other new Nazibuster was C. Bert Allen, a former U.S. Army major, thirty-six years old, also wounded in action during the Great War and a DAV bigwig. He became Agent 7. (In written communications, Leon Lewis was designated Agent 1.) One of Allen's first conversations on the inside was with the undistractable Hans Winterhalder, who had consolidation on his mind.

"A merger of the DAV and the Silver Shirts would make a lot of sense for both organizations," Winterhalder told Allen, eyes fierce and without humor.

It's clear from their initial observations that Agents 7 and 8 had not known what they were getting into. Agent 8 thought the Nazis would be all bluster, "grown men playing dress up," having some "lively political conversations" and that was about it. The harsh reality quickly sunk in.

Agent 7's first report read: "These people are smart, systematic, and highly educated. They are a dangerous mob."

Sunderland said to his friend Schmidt, "They are serious and dangerous. If they find you out, they will massacre you so that your own mother won't recognize you."

Agent 8 wrote the kicker, "The Nazis are not just against the Jews. They are out to overthrow the United States."

Lewis read this and repeated that they must be careful to maintain their cover. If they were to visit Lewis's offices in person, they should not be observed. To be caught as a spy could be hazardous.

"We do not know what they will do if they catch you," Lewis said solemnly.

Regulars at the Alt Heidelberg

Sunderland's task was to investigate the Aryan Bookstore. During his first visit there he met the men who ran the bookstore, Hans Winterhalder and Paul Themlitz.

Lewis's three-man spy team became regulars at the Alt Heidelberg. Agent 7 was a favorite of Robert Pape's, whose backslapping good nature seemed simultaneously sincere and awkward.

"You are a lot like Hitler," Pape told Allen, the ultimate compliment.

"How so?" Allen asked, flattered at the reference.

"You are eager to have like-minded Americans join our group," Pape replied.

Schwinn, on the other hand, took a liking to Schmidt, who he knew had recruited the others. Schmidt told Schwinn that the Great War had been difficult for him, not just physically, but emotionally, as he had to fight against his homeland.

"You are a German at heart," Schwinn said. "You must have been terribly persecuted by the Jews. We must work together to drive those sons of bitches from this country."

In his report to Lewis, Schmidt noted that when Schwinn said that, he felt like "busting Schwinn's head in." But he stayed cool, certain his health depended on it.

Schmidt performed his part, and the next time he, Sunderland, and Allen visited the Alt Heidelberg, they brought the wives. Blanche Sunderland socialized with Mr. and Mrs. Robert Pape and Mr. and Mrs. Paul Themlitz. The couples became friendly and went out for drinks after Friends meetings. Laughter grew louder. Lips loosened.

Alyce Gets Inside

Robert Pape took a liking to Alyce Schmidt, the same woman who'd been told to halt while heading up the Alt Heidelberg stairs in search of the powder room.

"Alyce, my dear, would you be interested in doing some clerical work for me and the Friends?" Pape asked one evening over drinks. Alyce looked to her husband.

"John, is it all right?"

"Of course, if you want to help the cause," Schmidt said.

Alyce smiled broadly.

"Excellent," Pape said. "We cannot pay you, but as the wife of a German, you'll be working for a holy cause."

Now both Schmidts glowed with pleasure.

Schmidt notified Leon Lewis of this development. He hadn't thought of using women Nazibusters, thinking the work too dangerous, but as Alyce had volunteered, and was already in, he assigned her the designation Agent 17.

Beginning in October 1933, Alyce reported daily to a small office behind the Aryan Bookstore where she typed letters and clipped stories about the Friends from L.A. newspapers to make a scrapbook. (The scrapbooks Alyce made are in the National Archives in Washington, D.C.)

She purposefully avoided the appearance of curiosity, doing as she was told, but she listened to everything the men said.

"They are urgent and intense. Very military," she reported. "There is always a military salute when someone enters the room."

Der Tag

As the men grew used to Alyce at her typewriter, they spoke freely in front of her, and what she overheard was deeply disturbing. The Friends were planning an "offensive" against Jews. They would incite labor union tumult, a revolt that could then be stomped by the Friends. The plan seemed to Alyce to be a half-step too complicated.

The man most enthused about this offensive, which they referred to as *der Tag* (the day), was commander of the Friends' security detail, a fellow named Dietrich Gefken.

"He talks of joining forces with American veterans and defeating the Jewish communists who run America," Alyce reported.

Alyce confirmed that the men seemed always to believe what

they said, even though their conspiratorial plans seemed, to her anyway, delusional. She overheard men discussing receiving orders from "over there," which she understood to mean Germany.

"They strut like peacocks when they talk of this," she wrote.

"We will start in Los Angeles, and *der Tag* will spread to Chicago and New York," Gefken said. "We will work with the Lutheran and other Protestant churches, and spread the word to buy gentile, drive the Jews out of business. That will take care of the goddamned Jews."

"Vee Go Vay Back"

Alyce heard Gefken bragging that he'd been with Hitler at the Beer Hall *Putsch*, in Munich, 1923.

"What will you do on *der Tag*?" John Schmidt asked Gefken.

Gefken replied, "I am looking forward to shooting Jews on sight."

Alyce learned the requirements for working at the Aryan Bookstore. No one was hired without having read *Mein Kampf*. There was a written test that needed to be passed proving their familiarity with "Hitler's bible."

Even though the bookstore operators were men, the rapid-turnover employees at the cash register were all young American women. Alyce reported, "The Friends want their bookstore sellers to be knowledgeable *and* pretty."

"Get Out There and Foment Some Goldarn Discord"

Leon Lewis instructed his Nazibusters to note any rift or disagreement within the Friends, any crack that might be pried open with dirty tricks, a well-placed rumor, a carefully timed character assassination.

In response, Schmidt reported that the Friends, from top to bottom, didn't agree on the best way to increase their numbers. Some thought they should stick to German Americans, immigrants who could be counted on to feel patriotic toward the Old Country. Others thought the movement couldn't get off the ground until non-Germans were recruited, perhaps not as zealous but far more plentiful.

They also disagreed on how to present to new recruits the antisemitism that was a lynchpin of their philosophy. Some felt that calling a Jew a Jew was the only way to go. Others felt that, for new recruits, the enemy should be referred to only as Communists. After they were initiated, it would be revealed layer by layer that "all communists were Jewish and vice versa."

Agent WC

The next spy recruited by Leon Lewis was William C. Conley (Agent WC), a Jew, who agreed to pose as a pro-Nazi meathead. Conley had contacts inside the LAPD, which he used to get an undercover cop to monitor Friends get-togethers.

Like Schmidt, Conley recruited his wife, Emma, into the operation. As it turned out, the Conleys were the only Jewish members of Lewis's spy crew. Conley was a B'nai B'rith member, a national DAV commander, and now in charge of keeping an eye on "Red" Hynes, head of the LAPD's anti-Commie Red Squad.

During Conley's first days on the job, he met Dietrich Gefken who, as the Schmidts had learned, spoke plainly of Hitler's ultimate goals. One of Conley's first reports contained chilling information: There were German military vessels docked at San Pedro, just south of L.A., and ships of the Hamburg-American Line were docked as well, releasing Gestapo agents into L.A., their missions unknown.

When John Schmidt next spoke to Hermann Schwinn, the talk turned to nuts and bolts.

"Hermann, what is the Friends? You know, really."

Schwinn laughed. "You suspect subterfuge, John?"

"We are, how should I put it? We are up to something, no?"

"We are not just about the Nazis, John. We are *of* the Nazis." Schwinn replied. And that was as far as he went.

Talk turned to how the Friends cleverly used language to say different things to different groups.

"And we do it both in English and German," Schwinn bragged.

"Give me an example, Hermann."

Schwinn's example was their use of *Sportabteilung* as opposed to *Sturmabteilung*—that is, "sports troops" instead of "storm troops"—when referring to the security detail. It made the goose-steppers seem less threatening, almost wholesome.

"We always emphasize that in our Führer's world, good physical health is necessary," Schwinn said, his puny mustache twitching. "We Germans are stronger and healthier than any other race. We are tall, beautiful, strong people. We run faster and jump higher."

"How many sports troops have you, Hermann?"

"As of today, thirty-six."

"Ah, but they aren't doing jumping jacks, are they?" Schmidt asked.

Again, Schwinn laughed. "It is an innocent bit of public relations. At the Turnverein Germania, our new building, they perform military drills. They go to the Lake Hollywood reservoir regularly and shoot, real guns, real bullets. And of course, they know how to parade."

"I heard you keep recruits in the basement."

"I'm surprised you didn't smell them," Schwinn said.

Skid Row Recruiting Center

Then as now, L.A. was a city with a conspicuous homeless problem. The State Senate had just proposed a bill that would "prohibit all paupers, vagabonds, and indigent persons" from entering the city. The bill, had it passed, would have allowed authorities to kick out anyone who was likely to one day need public assistance. The bill didn't pass, so the LAPD took charge of keeping the number of bums in the city to a minimum. If you wanted to sleep under a bridge, a cop might give you "the bum's rush."

The Friends decided to tap into that homeless population. The large Turnverein basement was being used to feed and bed homeless German American men. Some were showbiz wannabes who didn't cut it. Others were Dust Bowl refugees, with the haunted expression of long suffering in their eyes. There were alcoholics, the mentally infirm, all with bad teeth. Thanks to the Friends, they were fed, deloused, and clothed in brown.

"Such men can be mentally malleable," Schwinn told Schmidt. "They will be valuable for their numbers if nothing else when *der Tag* comes."

The basement project swiftly grew unmanageable, and the ragtag crew of homeless recruits was released back into the wild. Schwinn had the Turnverein basement fumigated.

Patriotism, Americanism, and Loyalty

Eventually, all three of Lewis's secret agents, 7, 8, and 11, were briefed by their Friends associates on *der Tag*. Leon Lewis planned to use the Friends' recruiting mode to work additional spies into the organization.

When Pape gave a speech asking all members to go out into L.A. and search for the like-minded, and to bring them into the fold, all three Nazibusters agreed to be part of the recruiting process.

Schmidt told Pape that he had an idea.

"What is it, John?" Pape said.

"You know that I am a member of the DAV, right?"

"I do. Your faith in America was destroyed by their inability to take care of you even though you were harmed in their service."

"Yes. But I am also the member of another organization as well. The PAL. It stands for Patriotism, Americanism, and Loyalty."

There was no PAL, but Pape didn't know that. In fact, he smiled approvingly.

"I believe our organization and the Friends of New Germany are very similar in our mandate," Schmidt said.

"Do you think you could get your PAL associates to come to one of our meetings?" Pape asked.

"It couldn't hurt to try. I think we will find men there who are understanding of our viewpoint," Schmidt said.

To help sell PAL as a real organization, Lewis had letterhead printed so that the agents could show the Nazis hard evidence that it was real. An empty office was given some mismatched furniture and a PAL sign attached to the door. That office was then bugged with a Dictaphone machine hidden in a desk drawer to record the Nazis who came to visit.

In the meantime, Schmidt became a trusted companion of Friends leaders and witnessed funny business both at Friends HQ and in San Pedro, on the docks.

CHAPTER 6

The National Guard Heist

The tyrant, who to hold his power, suppresses every superiority, does away with good men, forbids education and light, controls every movement of the citizens and, keeping them under a perpetual servitude, . . . is obliged to make war in order to keep his subjects occupied and impose on them permanent need of a chief.

—Aristotle, 350 B.C.

One fall day, Schwinn, Winterhalder, Themlitz, and Schmidt drove south to San Pedro in an empty milk truck where, with toothy grins, they watched the German steamship *Este* dock.

"You and I shall go aboard," Schwinn said to Schmidt. Aboard the *Este*, Schmidt saw several shipmates snap to attention and give Schwinn the *Sieg Heil!* salute.

Schmidt was introduced to a cruel-mouthed member of the Gestapo, a chilling moment. His name was Kurt Waldman, and he gave Schwinn a progress report regarding national recruiting efforts. The Friends had made great strides in San Francisco, Portland, Seattle, and Vancouver. Hundreds of new recruits in each of those cities.

Burlap Bundles

In the *Este*'s cargo hold were several large bundles wrapped in burlap and labeled FROM: JOSEPH GOEBBELS, TO: HANS WINTERHALDER. Schmidt couldn't believe his eyes.

Back ashore, Schwinn demonstrated his knowledge of the

docks. He knew the names of the battleships in the harbor and commented that the Nazis could easily "blow them all out of the water."

As Agent 11 quietly watched, Winterhalder ceremoniously displayed his ID for a man on the pier, and signed a form. The men then loaded the bundles into the milk truck for the drive back to L.A.

"Are we worried about customs?" Schmidt asked.

"No," Winterhalder said. "Customs is easily bribed—a bottle of champagne and a twenty-dollar bill."

Back at Alt Heidelberg, Alyce Schmidt was there to witness the celebration. The milk truck had been filled with propaganda leaflets, grotesquely antisemitic, printed in Germany but geared for an American audience. At the bar, schnapps was flowing.

Both Alyce and her husband noted the leaflets in their next report to Leon Lewis. John wrote that there should be more rigorous customs inspections at the pier. Alyce was pleased to report that she had become president of the Friends of New Germany Ladies Auxiliary.

Schmidt quoted Winterhalder as saying, "Time will not be so long before there will be armed revolts and uprisings against Jews. We will overthrow the current form of government."

Robert Pape on one occasion pulled Alyce away and said to her privately, "Your John is becoming the backbone of this organization."

John, emphasizing how repugnant he found all of this, "It is up to me as an American citizen and lover of this country to use every possible effort to bring these men to the end they deserve."

Alyce wrote: "Winterhalder is a very dangerous man. He has the eyes of a fanatic."

In the meantime, Lewis was recruiting new spies so that John Schmidt could fulfill his promise regarding the fictional PAL organization.

Turnverein Hall

When the Friends outgrew their meeting hall at Alt Heidelberg that fall, they moved their Thursday night lectures to Turnverein Germania Hall, a two-story building at 936 West Washington Boulevard. (As noted, the building was already being used by "sports troops" for military drills, and homeless recruits in the basement.) The new room sat four hundred people. The Friends took over the building, and soon it had its own Aryan Bookstore.

Pape gave the first lecture at the new hall. His presentation was entitled "The Political Significance of the Hitler Movement."

Lewis asked his Nazibusters for a transcript of that and any future speeches. Trouble was, none of his agents knew shorthand and were imprecise in their synopses. Lewis demonstrated his ingenuity. He hired several stenographers out of his old legal pool to attend Friends events at Turnverein.

"Be obvious that you are taking shorthand. They will think you are working for them. If you are confronted, say you are keeping a written record of the great cause," Lewis said.

The ploy worked. No one asked. No one spoke to the stenographers at all.

Jews in the Crowd

Lewis's stenographers captured the Q&A as well as the speeches, which is how Lewis learned that members of the L.A. Jewish community with no connection to the Nazibusters, were boldly attending Friends meetings and asking tough questions.

The Nazis put on their saccharine grins and pretended they welcomed the questions from the rude Jews. Pape knew public relations. He said the tough accusations from the Jews gave an opportunity to correct the false news that was being printed in Jew-run newspapers.

"Are Jews in Germany being persecuted by Nazis in Europe?"

"Nonsense."

"Are Germans antisemitic?"

"Ridiculous. Germans are anti-communist!"

"Is Hitler an enemy of the United States?"

"Preposterous. Hitler is America's greatest ally in the fight against communism."

After several meetings worth of transcripts, Lewis found that three themes were being impressed upon those interested in joining the cause: (1) Jews started the Great War, (2) Jews caused the Great Depression, and (3) Jewish communists were in control of America.

Pape said: "For centuries, the Jews have been a landless people. That is why they take over the countries where they live. America is just as threatened by Jews as Germany. Americans must wake up and follow Germany's example. America must purify itself, or it will die."

Sunderland Delivers a Message

Captain Carl F. Sunderland, deemed unusually competent by the Friends hierarchy, was assigned a very important mission by Schwinn.

"I want you to deliver a message to the head of German espionage in southern California," Schwinn said.

"It would be my honor," Sunderland said.

"You will meet him at a location in Ensenada. You will wear a white carnation in your lapel so he will recognize you. He will give you an envelope and you will return it to me."

"You can count on me."

Agent 8 carried out the mission, but didn't learn the name of the espionage king, or what was in the envelope. Just the fact that there was an "espionage king" was terrifying.

"I would know him again if I saw him, of course," Sunderland reported.

Gefken's War

Dietrich Gefken was a hot one. To discuss Gefken, Lewis called a meeting with his undercover crew. Get this guy comfortable and loose and he might spill key info. So, they set up Gefken. The plan included the wives.

That night's Friends rally was shifted from Turnverein to the Patriotic Hall, an auditorium at the base of a ten-story building on South Figueroa Street. The big room was supported near its walls by chunky pillars connected at the top to one another by climbing arches. Dedicated as Patriotic Hall in 1925, it was designed to serve war veterans, including those of the "Indian wars," the Spanish-American War, and the Great War. (The building still stands. In 1959, it was renamed Los Angeles County Department of Military and Veterans Affairs. It was rededicated as the Bob Hope Patriotic Hall in 2004. It has been named a county historic landmark and is under consideration for the National Register of Historic Places.)

The couples watched as Gefken gave a strong speech to an SRO audience.

Afterward, the Conleys, the Schmidts, and the Sunderlands invited Gefken out for drinks. Sweaty, his face aglow with adrenaline, he eagerly agreed.

They went to the Lorelei Inn, a German bar on Washington Boulevard. The plan worked like a charm. Gefken drank . . . and blabbed.

"We are going to take over the government of the United States," he said. "Just as the veterans did in Germany." And: "We won't be happy until every Jew is where they belong, six feet under the ground." And: "We Germans must be ready to fight shoulder to shoulder with American veterans when the war against the Jews begins."

"How long have you been in the United States?" Conley asked.

"Ten years," Gefken said. "In 1923, I was at the Beer Hall Putsch. I saw Hitler being arrested!"

"That must have been some experience," Emma Conley said.

"I saw the great Hitler being led away and I knew what I

needed to do. I became a Jew hunter. I carried a pair of pistols in my pocket and let the Jews have the lead." He shot at the wall with his fingers a couple of times. Then, not as loud, but serious, conspiratorial: "I would like to ask for your help in what we are planning now."

"Tell us," John Schmidt said.

"I have joined the California National Guard. Company K, 159th Infantry. I have used my position to gain blueprints of the San Diego Armory, not just floor plans but where various types of weapons and ammunition are kept."

"You are planning a heist?" Sunderland asked, slurring a little bit, feigning intoxication.

"We will steal—get this, we will steal coastal artillery weapons, machine guns, and enough rifles and bullets for a full regiment of patriots."

"Once you have the weapons, what will you do with them?" Schmidt asked.

"We will launch a double-prong offensive, attacking simultaneously in San Francisco and San Diego. The Big Plan is already in place. We will be joined by the Silver Shirts in San Diego. We will be joined by the crews of every German ship that docks in San Pedro. We will kidnap the American officers and toss them in the clink."

"What will you do with them?" Conley asked, with a sick smile on his face. He hoped that some of his plentiful revulsion was not showing.

"They will be taken one by one to me, and I will demand they pledge their allegiance to Hitler. Those that do will join the storm troopers. Those that don't will be shot on the spot."

A Chilling Peek into an Evil Man

Schmidt quickly reported to Lewis that Gefken did not seem like a blowhard and a braggart, but rather like an evil man offering a chilling peek into what he liked to do and how he thought. There was no doubt, Schmidt wrote, the plans to rob the armory were real, as were the attacks planned for San Diego and San Francisco partially in conjunction with the Silver Shirts.

"What should I do?" Conley asked.

"Better tell Two Guns," Lewis said, referring to the LAPD Chief James "Two Guns" Davis, who would pose for photographs with a gun in either hand or do trick shots, shooting cigarettes out of a volunteer's mouth. Lewis added, "I presume he is interested in potential sabotage on the West Coast."

As Conley did that, Lewis called "Red" Hynes of the LAPD. Lewis explained what Gefken was planning and the men decided they should set him up, entrap him. Lewis planted a microphone in Gefken's hotel room. When Gefken spoke, Hynes listened in.

"Red" Hynes, Quintuple Agent—but Who's Counting?

Lewis sent Sunderland and Allen into that room to ask what they could do to help the planned attacks. Gefken, as hoped, told them he needed them to help with the stealing of the weapons and ammunition.

Schmidt subsequently visited the hotel room and told Gefken that he'd spoken to key members of the San Francisco National Guard, and they were with him if he decided to take over. Gefken was beside himself with joy.

"You will be welcomed back to your National Guard unit with open arms," Schmidt said.

It was LAPD's "Red" Hynes who was supposed to brief the National Guard to seal the entrapment of Gefken. But Hynes, if he did this at all, did it imperfectly, and when Gefken asked the commander of his unit how he knew John Schmidt, the commander said he didn't know any John Schmidt, and Gefken realized that he'd been fed a tale. Gefken returned to Los Angeles seething mad.

For Lewis and his team, it was not a complete failure. Lewis's next phone call was to an officer he knew at the Office of Naval Intelligence (ONI). He detailed Gefken's plan, and the Navy launched its own investigation, one that resulted in the arrest of two Marines who were selling weapons and ammo to local Silver Shirts.

Suspicion

There was good news and bad news: Gefken had been foiled. But he now knew that Schmidt was, at the very least, a liar. When Gefken took his suspicions to Themlitz and Winterhalder, they said they had their suspicions as well.

"He is a sick man, virus from the war, a veteran on a pension. Yet he buys many books and dines out frequently," Themlitz said.

"Where does John Schmidt get his money?" Winterhalder said. They did not know.

The men called in other trusted colleagues, two of whom were Lewis spies, Sunderland and Allen. The men were informed that John Schmidt was a spy. It was now a fact in their minds. Sunderland and Allen took this news gravely—no doubt concerned about their own cover.

Winterhalder thought the situation through. A spy, yes. "But for whom is John Schmidt spying? If he is spying for America, I can understand it. He is an American patriot. If he is spying for the Jews, he is a traitor."

Sunderland and Allen were uncertain how to react to any of this.

"It never occurred to me that he wasn't true to the cause," Allen said crisply.

"I do not believe it," Sunderland quickly added.

Winterhalder shot Sunderland and Allen an icy look and said, "We don't know about you fellows, either. Do you have anything to die for, or not?"

They assured him with wide-eyed sincerity that they did.

When Winterhalder told Schwinn that Schmidt was a spy, Schwinn responded oddly. He said he'd known for months, that Schmidt was not as smart as he thought he was. Winterhalder held his tongue, but the idea that Schwinn knew there was a spy but neither did anything nor told anyone was absurd.

Gefken hadn't said anything in a while, but now spoke up. "We need evidence to demonstrate that he is a spy and determine whether he is an American patriot or a Jewish traitor."

Winterhalder said, "We could feed him lies and set his bosses on the wrong track."

Allen and Sunderland, thinking on their feet, volunteered to shadow Schmidt and see what he was up to.

Pape said, "We can use him—just as he would use us."

The Nazibusters pinpointed weaknesses in the Friends' upper echelon. No one was clearly in charge. Pape had mentally checked out, his mind back in Germany, or somewhere. Schwinn wanted to be alpha but had weaknesses. Being a bad liar was only one of them.

"If you catch Schmidt doing something, you should do away with him," Gefken said. Dead serious.

"Don't worry," Sunderland said. "If we catch him, he is a dead man. We will make mincemeat of him." He worked up his most reptilian smile.

Of course, once the meeting broke up, Sunderland and Allen rushed to tell Schmidt that his cover was blown. Schmidt could have pulled the plug then and there, but decided his best defense was a little offense.

Next day, Schmidt marched with chin high and chest out into the Aryan Bookstore, thrust his hand in front of Themlitz.

"Shake hands with a spy?" he said loudly.

Themlitz was startled.

"Your friends suspect me of espionage. They are mistaken. I will continue to attend meetings, and I will continue working on behalf of the Friends of New Germany," Schmidt said, with an extra edge of defiance. (In his later report to Lewis, Schmidt mentioned that he'd also gotten a gun permit and planned to be packing if trouble came.) Schmidt turned on a heel, very Nazi-like, and marched back to the street.

When Themlitz's nerves calmed, he was struck by a thought. How did Schmidt know they thought he was a spy?

Themlitz's suspicions led to another meeting of the Nazi leaders. Who tipped off Schmidt?

Thinking quickly, Sunderland said that he knew. Allen and he had followed Schmidt just as they said they would and hadn't had a chance to report what they'd learned.

"We found out right away that he was a spy, but he wasn't spying in any of the ways we'd thought of," Allen said.

"He was spying for U.S. military intelligence," Sunderland added.

"I thought of that! I knew he was an American patriot," Winterhalder said.

"We have nothing to fear from him. He was here to find out if the Silver Shirts were in cahoots with the PAL. It had nothing to do with us. In fact, he insists he still supports us."

"He seemed irritated that we would suspect him when he came into the bookstore today," Themlitz said, not satisfied with the explanation.

Sunderland said he loved a story with a happy ending and suggested they hit the bar for a foamy lager. They agreed. But Sunderland could read the body language. He, Allen, and Schmidt were still suspect.

Schmidt's value as a spy shrunk. Nazis kept tight lips when he was in the room. He lost access to the leaders. It came to a head one morning when Schmidt went to the mailbox to get his mail and found a letter from Robert Pape.

"Due to your peculiar conduct, your membership in the Friends of New Germany is suspended."

Schmidt ran to L.A. German consul Georg Gyssling and showed him the letter.

Georg Gyssling

The bespectacled Gyssling was forty years old and stood six-three. He was born in Walzen, in Imperial Germany (now known as

Walce, Poland), and had earned a doctorate in German law before joining the Nazi Party in 1931. Gyssling was also an Olympic athlete, having competed in the four-man bobsled the previous year in Lake Placid, New York. The German team finished last.

As L.A. consul, Gyssling was the primary liaison between Goebbels and the Hollywood moguls. He'd been assigned by Goebbels himself to keep an eye on the studios and prevent them from making any film that "defamed Germany."

Gyssling's job was made easier when the Motion Picture Producers and Distributors Association (later called the Motion Picture Association of America or MPAA) established the Production Code Administration, regulating what could and couldn't be in a Hollywood movie. This was done because conservative politicians were giving loud speeches in which they talked about how "licentious" and "uncontrolled" Hollywood was. Sometimes they added the word "un-Christian."

The code's Section 10, Article 15, said films had to fairly portray foreign countries. What a complete pain in the ass that was.

Gyssling: Tone Down the Anti-Jew Thing

Gyssling was quietly of the opinion that the Nazis' intense antisemitism was making it harder to recruit in the U.S. This fact came to light when MGM released the previously discussed picture called *The Prizefighter and the Lady* starring real-life boxer Max Baer. The movie was approved by Gyssling as being harmless to Germany, yet it was banned and condemned by Goebbels because in real life Baer whupped the German champ while wearing a Star of David on his boxing trunks.

Gyssling, because of the Production Code, had Hollywood under his thumb for a time. Screenplays that were originally sharply critical of Nazism were filed down, their edge dulled into tepid romances in Anycountry, "Somewhere in Europe." If a film refused Gyssling's demands, members of the cast and crew would each receive a threatening letter from Gyssling.

Those letters were scary but a mistake on Gyssling's part, as one was reproduced in newspapers throughout the U.S. It didn't look good. American editors called Gyssling a bully and a lousy Nazi.

Despite the occasional bad press, Gyssling was considered a man of great charm, a true-blue German, and a thorn in Hollywood's side, yet by all accounts not much of an antisemite. He answered to Nazis, sure, but wasn't hateful. His job was to represent Germans living in or near L.A. and didn't particularly care what religion anyone was. Because of this he wasn't well-regarded by the Friends of New Germany, either, who considered him weak. (It later turned out that Gyssling thought antisemitism was the Nazis fatal flaw and went so far as to report Friends activity to the U.S. National Guard.)

It was John Schmidt who'd reported that there were Friends who wanted Gyssling out, replaced by a "real Hitlerite." Now it was that same John Schmidt who stood before Gyssling with something akin to panic in his eyes.

"He says I can't be a delegate to the German-American Alliance either!" Schmidt complained.

"Who?"

"Pape!"

That sent Gyssling screaming at Pape. This led Schmidt to report that Gyssling seemed to be Pape's superior.

After jawing at Pape, Gyssling came back to Schmidt with a question.

"Pape says you told him you were some sort of federal spy," Gyssling said.

"That's a lie!" Schmidt said.

"You have no connection to the U.S. government?"

"I do not," Schmidt said, his chin up. "Only the minuscule pension they give me."

In reaction to this exchange, Gyssling doubled down on his trust of Schmidt. He ordered Pape to put Schmidt on his executive committee and to get rid of the idiots who were there now, "those friends of yours."

Gyssling also intimated to Schmidt that he had his own team of clandestine agents who were investigating the leaders of the Friends. It occurred to Schmidt that Gyssling's trust seemed too pure to be real. He told Lewis he no longer knew where he stood and felt that there was trouble coming.

Lewis agreed. When John and Alyce next attended a Friends meeting at the Turnverein Hall, they were accompanied by a friend, a plainclothes police officer named Frank Irvine. Unfortunately, there was a Nazi at the meeting who knew both Schmidt and Irvine and quickly scoped out the arrangement.

"A bodyguard, eh, Schmidt?" the Nazi said. "Well, you may need one."

Demanding Changes

Even as he made anti-Friends moves, Gyssling obeyed his orders from Goebbels. When Warner Bros. planned to make a Great War picture called *Captured* (1933), which depicted Americans being ill-treated by German POW guards, Gyssling went into action.

Before production began, Gyssling demanded changes in the script. After it was made, without any of his changes, Gyssling demanded that it be banned. It wasn't, but the controversy he stirred hurt business.

Gyssling repeated the process later in the year with Columbia Pictures and one of their Great War movies, *Below the Sea*. This time, when Gyssling demanded changes in the script, the changes were made. This continued the trend of Warner Bros. standing up to the Nazis while other studios backed down.

New Assignment

In October 1933, Lewis summoned Agents 7 and 8, Carl Sunderland and Bert Allen, to his office in the Roosevelt Building.

"I have a new assignment for you," Lewis said. "I want you to join the Silver Lodge."

CHAPTER 7

William Dudley Pelley

Jesus was the first Silver Shirt.
—William Dudley Pelley, 1933

The Silver Lodge was the 1933 creation of William Dudley Pelley, who was already an accomplished man in several fields, including confidence games, before he created the Silver Shirts. Unlike the Friends of New Germany, where being German seemed a prerequisite, the Silver Lodge accepted anyone, man or woman, if they were white and Protestant. Their theme music was "The Battle Hymn of the Republic." A paramilitary wing known as the Silver Rangers was organized into armed brigades.

Pelley had a long face and long fingers, and he was a con man through and through. His face breaking into a huge three-dollar-bill smile, he used the weight of his unnatural charm to lean on his believers. (Think John Huston in *Chinatown*.) Always kempt, in later years, he sported a devilish goatee.

The Man, the Myth

Truth and Pelley had a hate/hate relationship. Thus, it's difficult to distinguish bio from myth.

Born in New England to a Methodist minister and his wife, Pelley rebelled against his dad and, while still a teenager, started his own magazine, *The Philosopher*, chockful of iconoclastic and anti-religious messages. The magazine was short-lived, but Pelley remained a "journalist," editing country newspapers in Vermont.

He claimed that, during the summer of 1918, when U.S.

President Woodrow Wilson ordered American troops in Siberia to fight the Bolsheviks, he was just a boy and volunteered to go. He claimed that he learned the "virtue" of antisemitism from a man named Dr. Toisler, whom he met in Siberia. The mysterious doctor told him that his life goal should be to keep Jews out of elected office.

Despite his eccentricities, or maybe because of them, Pelley's weird stories earned him a decent magazine-writing career, publishing adventure stories with a strong romantic angle in the *Saturday Evening Post* and *Good Housekeeping*. As a magazine writer, Pelley was respected, even lauded. He won an O. Henry Prize for a short story called "The Face in the Window" (*Redbook* magazine, May 1920).

He grew into a novelist, most famous for *The Fog* (1921), from which a silent film was made in 1923, and *Golden Rubbish* (1929), about an abandoned girl who grows up to be a great Manhattan businesswoman. In all, Pelley wrote sixteen scenarios for produced movies, from 1917 to 1929.

Like much of Hollywood's talent, Pelley stopped getting work after silents turned to talkies. Suddenly playwrights from "back East" were all the rage and scenario creators like Pelley were shown the door. Pelley blamed his setback on the "Jew moguls," too stupid to understand his greatness.

Unlike some fascist leaders who couldn't keep it in their pants, Pelley was sexually repressed and a hostile prude toward Hollywood's sexual excesses. The studios were an orgiastic cesspool, he decided.

Pelley was nothing if not resilient. Given the Hollywood boot, he moved on to writing nonfiction about his bizarre conversations with the dead—and politics. He was a new man. He now wrote mystical and spiritual prose, enlightened as if struck on the head with a divine hammer, not just a man of vision but of visions, having conversations with Jesus.

Pelley's Claims . . .

Pelley claimed that, at 3:30 A.M. on May 28, 1928, while living in a suburb of L.A., he woke from a sound sleep and heard an urgent voice echoing, "I'm dying!"

Overcoming a fear that he might be suffering cardiac arrest, he sensed an unearthly substance enveloping him, plunging him into a "mystic depth of cool blue."

He was naked, splayed upon a marble slab, a sacrificial altar. Flanking him were men who called themselves "Spiritual Mentors."

"You are a man of destiny," they told him. "One day you will lead a great spiritual movement."

For the rest of his life, Pelley claimed his mentors were steering his every move. He called the episode in his life "The Great Release," which was also an expression used in that era's smut.

"The Mentors told me to give up smoking and the next time I picked up a can of tobacco a mysterious force knocked it from my hand," he wrote ("Seven Minutes in Eternity: The Amazing Experience That Made Me Over," *The American Magazine*, March 1929).

For a time, he argued in public against Christianity, claiming Jesus was not Jewish, but rather from Gaul.

"Jesus hated the Jews," Pelley would declare, fist clenched, an evil grin creasing his face.

Then he switched sides and became pro-Christ. His eyes bright with zeal, Pelley formed his own church, the Church of Christian Democracy, of which he was the High Priest. He formed an organization called Fraternity for Liberation. His messages to followers were always based on communications from the great beyond.

Neither venture quite clicked, but it was during this time that Pelley became fascinated by the up-and-coming Adolf Hitler and worked Nazism into his philosophy. His claims evolved from the spiritual to the political. He'd been "given a sign" in 1929 that a man named Hitler was going to rise to power in Germany, and that he himself would become the leader of Hitler's movement in the United States.

When asked about his antisemitism, he always gave it a wholly inadequate sugar coat: "We are not against the Jews as a people, but because they are the slaves and serfs of their rabbinate who want to see communism come in and close all the Christian churches." Oh.

The American Jewish Committee once commented: "To Pelley, Jews are the root of all evil. Whenever he is against anything, it is because Jews are connected with it—and if he can't find Jews, he creates them."

In 1933, Pelley formed the group for which he'd be best known, the Silver Legion, dedicated to politically and spiritually transforming the United States. His followers were called Silver Shirts, although the uniforms were actually light blue.

Pelley's group understood Americans better than the Friends of New Germany ever could. In the U.S., the xenophobes and religious zealots were the same folks. His Silver Lodge always portrayed itself as a *Christian* organization.

"Jesus was the first Silver Shirt," Pelley said.

(One wonders if the Nazi movement, stringently anti-religion, would have done better in America had they, publicly at least, embraced Christ as their savior.)

Pelley praised Hitler in his speeches but never claimed to be affiliated with him, and he wasn't. The Silver Lodge was true-blue American.

The Scarlet L

Pelley's blue army uniforms had a scarlet *L* embroidered over the left breast. The *L* stood for "Love, Loyalty, and Liberation" (later shortened to just "Liberation").

His speeches always focused on recruiting Christian patriots to purge the nation of Jewish vermin and were punctuated by statistics designed to frighten: four million Jews in America in 1920, eight million in 1930.

“They are replacing us,” he said, “at a rate of fifteen thousand Jews a week for ten years.”

He spoke like an exterminator but, early on, anyway, came just shy of calling for extermination. Pelley offered detailed plans to herd Jews into tightly restricted neighborhoods. He called them “Jew zoos.” As time went on, he let it slip that killing Jews was probably the inevitable solution, either by having living Jews sterilized to prevent breeding, or by mass execution.

Hollywood remained one of Pelley’s favorite targets: “The Jew moguls have a slogan,” Pelley said. “‘Don’t shoot until you see the white of their thighs.’ For the sake of white womanhood, we must usurp Jew control of Hollywood.”

Pelley would eventually form nine divisions of the Silver Legion, stretching across the country. Each was under orders to “be prepared for action.” He carried a gun in a holster at his left hip and enjoyed it when his minions called him “Chief.”

Although headquartered in the East, Pelley had high hopes for his L.A. branch. He ordered an encampment to be built just outside L.A.— a fortress, really, in Rustic Canyon in what is today part of Will Rogers State Historic Park. At the time they called it Murphy Park, and Pelley called that fortress the Silver Shirts’ U.S. headquarters. (Today, all that remains of the camp are a cluster of derelict buildings.)

Pelley’s L.A. operation was up and running for only days when it was infiltrated by John Schmidt. Formerly Agent 11, for his new assignment, he became Agent 74, and in his first report wrote that the Silver Lodge had a map of Los Angeles that showed all of the houses in which Jewish celebrities lived. Pelley’s organization, Schmidt wrote, was anti-Jewish and anti-Catholic, but not vocally pro-Hitler.

In subsequent reports, Schmidt noted that members of the Friends, whom he recognized and who recognized him, were attending Silver Lodge meetings, boldly singing Hitler’s praises. None of the Silver Shirts were gung-ho for Hitler, but many acknowledged that the Lodge and the Nazis had things in common.

Surprisingly, Pelley went at the Friends like a corporate raider. Many Friends joined up. He easily talked the Friends' chief propagandist Hans Winterhalder into becoming the head of a Silver Lodge post in L.A.

Wires

You had to be careful about wires in 1933. Electronic surveillance was in its infancy, but very popular—and the mere threat of it kept many lips zipped. The technology was energized and pushed into the future, *especially* in L.A., because of Hollywood's still recent conversion from silent to sound pictures. Sound technicians were everywhere. People who knew how to build (and hide) microphones were a dime a dozen.

You couldn't talk in a restaurant, and you couldn't talk on the phone. It was better to be a moving target to avoid being picked up by a microphone. Men who kept secrets would meet on the street and walk together as they conferred, confident that no one could listen in.

Searching for the Good Guys

Leon Lewis, looking to expand his Nazibuster operation, sought a sanctioning body capable of providing funding. The City of Los Angeles was out. Many members of the LAPD could not be trusted to defend Jews against antisemitic attacks, either physical or psychological. Same with the government. There were too many elected officials who thought the Jews in Hollywood were the problem.

Lewis met with Joseph Dunn, then the Southern California chief of the Justice Department's Secret Service, who said he couldn't help until the Nazis committed an "overt act."

Lewis did find one potential ally in the police department, "Red" Hynes, the cop who'd helped the Nazibusters in the Gefken investigation. He was no Nazi-hater, nor a Nazi-lover, for that matter, but he was easily bribed. For a fee, Hynes (now designated in Lewis's files as Agent M) would provide Lewis with copies of LAPD files regarding Nazi activity.

"One other thing," Hynes said.

"What's that?" Lewis asked.

"If you learn anything, and I mean anything, about Communist activity, you let me know."

"Deal."

Hynes also suggested Lewis talk to "Two Guns" Davis. "My boss will listen to you," Hynes said.

Lewis met with Davis and explained that the Nazis in L.A. were plotting to overthrow the U.S. government and replace it with a fascist system. Davis listened but promised nothing.

"I do not think the Nazis pose a threat to Americanism," Davis said. "It is the Communists we should be worried about. Germans cannot compete economically with the Jews in Germany. They have been forced to take the actions you talk about. You only think this way because you are Jewish." Davis concluded the meeting by telling Lewis, "Submit to me any reports you like, but I can't promise I'll ever do anything about them."

Lewis's next stop was B'nai B'rith, which had offices in L.A. He explained his mission and was promptly scolded for being a troublemaker.

"Those of us with relatives in Germany are particularly fearful. What if our activities here were to hurt our families over there?" they said.

Though B'nai B'rith as an organization was against what he was doing, Lewis was able to find within the organization individuals who thought monitoring the Nazis was important.

Joseph Loeb

One such individual was Joseph Loeb, a Jewish attorney who was a second-generation Angelino, and a member of one of L.A.'s most prominent Jewish families.

"I will gather up top Jews," Loeb told Lewis, "Present your case to them. Rest assured they will listen."

That meeting was again held at the home of Superior Court Judge Isaac Pacht, and the "top Jews" did listen, for a while. Lewis laid out the information he had gathered so far through his undercover operation, and the powerful men pledged $5,000 to the cause, money that would go to help his agents—particularly the Schmidts, who were impoverished—as well as to pay "Red" Hynes, his spy inside the LAPD.

At the meeting it was moved that they form a new antidefamation organization, one that fought back against antisemitism. When B'nai B'rith learned of this, it was seriously angered. B'nai B'rith leaders said, "It is hard enough to fund our activities during these hard times without competition from among ourselves."

Lewis was again horrified. B'nai B'rith seemed more comfortable attacking him and his efforts than it was in attacking the real enemy.

As it turned out, B'nai B'rith had nothing to worry about. The new antidefamation organization (which never had a name) turned out to be a bust. When it came time for Lewis to collect the promised money, the rich men pulled their pockets inside out and shrugged. Times were tough all over, they said. Lewis was going to have to continue funding his efforts out of his own pocket while searching for rich friends.

Nazi Means War

Americans might've been naive regarding events in Europe, but they had to duck and twist in order to stay that way. One strong attempt to warn America about the militarization of Germany came in October 1933, *Nazi Means War*, a book by *New York Herald Tribune* reporter Leland Stowe. The book vividly warned of the holocaust to come. Stowe described the indoctrination of "Hitler youth," one and a half million children goose-stepping, and wrote eloquently of the terror he felt at a nation where conformity was expected without question.

The book sold miserably, and Stowe was criticized as an alarmist

In L.A., Leon Lewis saw the futility of raising public consciousness regarding the Nazi menace without a rock base of credibility. To hurt the American Nazis, Lewis concluded, he'd have to get them in court.

CHAPTER 8

Friends on Trial

I will refuse to answer any questions asked by a Jewish lawyer.
—Mrs. Maria Griebel

The first Nazi in America to be arrested was Heinz Spanknöbel, busted on October 28, 1933, in New York, for claiming to be a German diplomatic agent when in fact he was a Nazi spy.

Julius Hochfelder, attorney for the Jewish War Veterans, wasn't content with the arrest. He saw Spanknöbel's deception as the tip of an iceberg. Hochfelder asked New York State Attorney General John J. Bennett to hear sworn witnesses regarding Spanknöbel, his Friends of New Germany, and their influence on other well-meaning German American groups. The attorney general took him up on it, and more than a dozen anonymous witnesses were called. Testimony touched upon acts of terrorism instigated by "Spanknöbel and his lieutenants."

Witnesses spoke of an incident in Chicago in which Spanknöbel attended a congress of delegates of German American societies in the U.S., after which, all Jewish members were expelled, replaced by men "loyal" to the home country.

Representatives of German American organizations that refused to affiliate themselves with the Nazis testified that during meetings they'd received intimidating visits from Nazi agents who made threats and on one occasion assaulted the non-Nazi Germans.

Testimony claimed that many Nazis were in the U.S. illegally, skipping the immigration process, working as crew members on German ships, then hopping ship at U.S. ports.

There were discussions of sabotage upon American-owned concerns in Germany and the establishment of six pro-Hitler, intensely antisemitic newspapers. Nazi storm troopers were used to break up American labor strikes. There were attempts by Nazi agents to merge the KKK with the Friends.

In New York City, consciousness re the Nazi threat was raised. A little. Mayor John P. O'Brien said, "It seems we have unearthed a secret invasion of the country." People paid attention. For a minute.

Pro-Friends Witnesses

The other side was heard in court as well. At the hearing, the boots-on-the-ground leader of the Friends was Ignaz Griebl, who was in court with his Johnny pump of a wife, Maria. She wasn't along as his date, but rather because she'd been subpoenaed, too.

Maria made the papers when she told a reporter, "I will refuse to answer any questions asked by a Jewish lawyer. As an American citizen, I have the right to be questioned by a gentile District Attorney or judge. I will not take any oath with my hand on the Bible, because that's the Jewish Old Testament."

She was all bark. When the time came, she was asked questions by a Jewish lawyer and she answered them.

In the retelling, Maria added drama. She claimed she refused to take the oath with her hand on a Bible but rather with her hand over her heart while gazing adoringly at an American flag. In reality, none of the witnesses were sworn in with their hand on a Bible, and there was no American flag in the courtroom.

Following the hearing, federal authorities began deportation proceedings against Spanknöbel and his lieutenants.

The Nazi trial in New York was only small-print news in L.A., but it certainly may have encouraged Leon Lewis's idea. There were all sorts of advantages in getting the Nazis in court and hanging perjury charges over their heads. The problem would be in keeping witnesses secret and free from tampering or retribution.

The New Plan

The leadership of the L.A. Friends of New Germany were thinking big. Over cocktails, it was decided they should take over and rule the largest non-Nazi German American organization in southern California, that being the *Deutsche Amerikanische Stadt Verbund* (translated in contemporary news reports and court documents as "German-American Alliance" but also referred to as the "League"), an organization that linked many smaller German American clubs. It held meetings and conventions which had a reputation as wild parties. The Verbund's outdoor activities were held at Crescenta Valley Park in La Crescenta, seventeen miles out of L.A., north of Pasadena and Glendale, where bands were booked to play German tunes and men drank draft lager from colorful steins. (The following year, the site would be re-named Hindenburg Park.)

Schmidt overheard Themlitz and Winterhalder discussing the plan. They would "join" the organization, and come election day, October 13, 1933, they would elect their own men to run it.

"I only know one thing about the Verbund. It is rich," Themlitz said.

"In a matter of days, we will control that bankroll," Winterhalder replied.

The Nazis later did the math and realized getting new members elected as officers in the Verbund was unlikely no matter who or how many they leaned on. So, the plan was revised. The organization's president, a political man named Max Socha, might be convinced to do as the Nazis pleased. So, they got him alone and braced him. They stood uncomfortably close to him and Socha could feel and smell the tobacco-and-peppermint Nazi breath on his face.

"Be with us, and we will make sure you are reelected as president," Themlitz said.

"With you?"

"You're either in all the way or you are not in at all. Make up your mind. You want power. We are here to *help* you."

One stumbling block to winning the election was getting the Friends accepted as a member organization. There was a pesky legal loophole: New members needed to be incorporated and the Friends were not.

"We need you to waive the incorporation clause, so we can join," Winterhalder said, and again Socha agreed to this.

The guy running against Socha for president was John Vieth, who said out loud he feared the Nazis would end up hurting all German Americans with their hate talk. He and his secretary, Philip Lenhardt, ran for office on a strong anti-Nazi platform.

The elections were held in Turnverein Hall on a Friday night. Socha and his Nazi pals won by a single vote. That led Lenhardt to do something unexpected. He wrote a letter to B'nai B'rith exposing the corruption that had led to the Verbund being taken over by Nazis.

"The election was fixed, full of illegal votes, members of a group that illegally joined the Alliance," Lenhardt wrote. "We have worked so hard to repair Germans' reputation after the war, and the Nazis are ruining it for all of us. We feel that something should be done."

B'nai B'rith, upon receiving the letter from the group's outgoing secretary, informed Leon Lewis. Lewis, of course, knew all about the plan to take over the group, but this was the first he heard that the defeated parties weren't taking it lying down. Lewis met with Vieth and Lenhardt.

"You understand that to challenge the Nazis publicly could put you physically at risk?" Lewis asked.

The men insisted they understood. They did not want to be bullied.

"Have you spoken to anyone else about this?" Lewis asked.

"Yes," Vieth said. "We went to see the police commissioner."

That was Barry Munson. "We told him that there might be trouble and he assigned us a plainclothesman to keep the peace."

Lewis's mind was already working. This might be the case he was looking for, something that would put the Friends on the front pages of all of L.A.'s papers.

Congressman Samuel Dickstein

Back East, in November 1933, Congressman Samuel Dickstein, a Democrat representing the Lower East Side of Manhattan, investigated claims that Nazi organizations within the U.S. had committed acts of espionage and counterespionage. Dickstein, a Jew, was born in Lithuania in 1885, son of a rabbi and his wife. When he was two, he crossed the ocean with his parents, and they settled on the Lower East Side, where he grew up. He attended City College and earned a law degree at NYU.

Dickstein was far more interested in the threat presented by the Nazis than were his fellow non-Jewish congressmen. Dickstein's "investigation," like Leon Lewis's, was largely coming out of Dickstein's pocket.

"I had to pay the train fare for witnesses to come to Washington and testify," Dickstein later recalled. He was terribly limited. He could neither subpoena unfriendly witnesses nor force anyone to testify truthfully under fear of perjury.

Lewis traveled east to visit Dickstein and was allowed to review the anti-Nazi evidence Dickstein had gathered up to that point. Lewis was disappointed to find that it was all hearsay. He urged Dickstein to stop his investigation and to restart when he had some solid evidence to present. (Dickstein halted his hearings just two days later.)

Lewis agreed to allow Dickstein to use a portion of the evidence his Nazibusters had gathered, but just the stuff that could've been learned without a spy in place. Dickstein wanted it all, but Lewis held firm.

"A premature release of the evidence could jeopardize the safety of five families, including my own," Lewis wrote.

Dickstein agreed. He explained to Lewis that his goals for his investigation were modest. He hoped merely to convince Americans that the Nazis were not just a problem for the Jews but for everyone.

On the other end of the congressional stick was Representative Louis McFadden (R, Pennsylvania) who loudly denied that Jews were being persecuted in German, and said it was fishy that FDR had appointed Jewish men to his cabinet.

League for American Principles

While back East, Lewis went to New York and visited the leaders of the American Jewish Congress. Lewis proposed that a nonsectarian organization be formed to fight Nazis at a national level. He said that the group should consist of men of good character, not just liberals, but those everywhere on the political spectrum who could agree that a Nazi takeover should be avoided at all costs.

"We will call it the League for American Principles," Lewis said. "They will preach equality and tolerance—and if necessary, go to war."

The idea pleased the AJC leaders in general, but when it came to specifics, namely who would pay for it, plans fell apart, and the League for American Principles was never formed.

The meeting was not a complete waste of time, however. The AJC and the ADL agreed to work with Lewis's Los Angeles operation, exchanging and pooling information. The man who would be the depository for the gathered intelligence would be Frank Prince, a former reporter for the Hearst newspapers. Lewis would be their man in L.A.

Lists of Nazis and Nazi sympathizers were made. Five years later, when Jewish gangsters and other tough guys were busting up Nazi meetings and belly-punching Nazis on the street, those lists helped identify targets. A few years after that, the lists would help finger potential saboteurs.

Mr. X

A witness known publicly as Mr. X told Dickstein that Nazi agents in New York City were sending messages back to their superiors in Berlin. Mr. X said that his source was a document on genuine Friends of New Germany letterhead from W. Haag, a Friends leader.

"The envelope was sealed with a genuine Friends seal," X said.

When the Friends hierarchy, Spanknöbel and others, learned that the damning message from Haag to Berlin had been intercepted by a mole, an emergency meeting was held at the George Washington Hotel to determine what to do about it. They decided to take no action.

That meeting, X revealed, was attended by Representative Hamilton Fish, a New York State Republican and staunch anti-Communist. "I, myself, will present documents showing that Fish has been aiding Nazi propaganda," X said.

Phooey!

Back in L.A., the Verbund met on November 11, 1933, the first meeting since Socha was reelected with the Friends of New Germany at his back. John Schmidt, at Lewis's instruction, accompanied the opposition, Vieth and Lenhardt, to the meeting.

At one point, Lenhardt stood and said he refused to recognize Socha as president of the organization, as he had been elected illegally. He was shouted down before he could complete his statement.

"Phooey!" the Nazis cried out, according to Schmidt. (The word, back then, meant something smelled bad, roughly the equivalent of "Bullshit!")

After the meeting, Schmidt pulled aside Vieth and Lenhardt, along with anti-Nazi German leader Otto Deissler.

"This is the idea. You are to file a lawsuit against the Friends, accusing them of stealing the election. Then hire a Christian lawyer. This must not be seen as a Jewish battle. These are good Germans calling out bad Germans," Schmidt said.

"But we don't know how—"

"Don't worry, the lawsuit has already been written," Schmidt said.

Written by Leon Lewis, of course. It would be entitled *Otto Deissler and Philip Lenhardt v. Max E. Socha et al.* The lawsuit claimed that the Friends existed solely to distribute insidious propaganda, spread Nazism, and to "undermine the government of the United States."

The suit said that the Friends had been organized by Adolf Hitler himself, that the Friends had infiltrated several smaller German American clubs and had transformed them overnight from social to political groups, and that the Verbund was now completely under the control of the Friends.

The lawsuit was filed a few days after Christmas, 1933. Those Christian lawyers turned out to be Hugo Harris and David Field. Lewis agreed to pay for the legal fees out of Nazibuster funds and his own pocket.

Unfortunately, John and Alyce Schmidt's days as undercover agents within the Friends would have to end, as they would have to testify in court as to what they'd learned—and they would have to do it without exposing Lewis. The defendants mustn't learn the true origin of the lawsuit.

Widening Rift

In December 1933, the Nazibusters found that rifts between the three Friends leaders were widening, not to mention friction between the Friends leaders and the complicated German consul, Georg Gyssling.

In whispers rather than shouts, the Nazibusters sewed dissension among the Nazi leaders and then poured gasoline on it.

"Winterhalder is your enemy."

"Do not trust Winterhalder."

"Pape and Winterhalder are out to get you."

The product of the campaign was anger, an anger turned inward. Plans to conquer California stalled.

Winterhalder wrote a speech that Pape considered "too antisemitic," and told Winterhalder not to give it, but Winterhalder gave it anyway. That pissed off Pape, who threatened to beat Winterhalder up. Winterhalder didn't bother to threaten. He reached back and punched Pape in the face, knocking him to the floor. Word of the fight reached New York, and Pape was officially removed as West Coast Führer, replaced by Hermann Schwinn.

So, there was high drama among the Friends hierarchy, but it would be equaled and then some by what was about to occur in an L.A. courtroom.

CHAPTER 9

The Civil Trial

I will prove to the American people that there exists and is being conducted an insidious, traitorous country-wide propaganda and conspiracy aimed at the peace and security of our country.

—Samuel Untermyer

The lawsuit against the Friends came to trial in January 1934, in L.A. Superior Court, with the Honorable Guy F. Bush presiding. The newly dethroned Robert Pape was in the courtroom. Sitting on the other side of the gallery was New York lawyer and leader of the Non-Sectarian Anti-Nazi League, Samuel Untermyer.

Asked what he was doing there, Untermyer said, "I'm an observer. I have no official connection with the case but flew here from my winter home in Palm Springs because of the case's probable international importance."

Untermyer further used the occasion to sound the alarm regarding the Nazi menace: "I wonder how the thirteen million loyal American citizens of German birth or ancestry will react to the knowledge that Hitler organizations such as the 'Friends of Germany' [sic] and others have been planted and are actually functioning on our shores, in which our citizens are at the same time German citizens with a divided loyalty and are not only so encouraged but actually recognized by the German government."

He asked true-blue German Americans to rise as one against "the impudent attempt to convert them to the cruel and despicable

Hitlers of bigotry and race hatreds and join their American brethren in driving these traitors our of our fair land."

There were other celebrities looking to get in on the anti-Nazi action. The British aviatrix Lady Isobel Clayton, with her husband, Sir Edmund Clayton, sat in the gallery. They were visitors to L.A. and appeared gussied up for the theater.

Gyssling's No-Show

L.A. German consul Dr. Georg Gyssling released a statement. "I have no interest in the proceedings." Gyssling thought that through for two hours and amended the message with a second, more carefully worded dispatch: "My government, the government of Germany, has no connection, officially or otherwise, with the local organization. Also, there are no members of the Nazi party enrolled in the Friends of New Germany."

No Jury Trial

Lewis's plan was working almost perfectly, it seemed. One hitch: He would've preferred a jury trial, but at the insistence of the defendants, Judge Bush would determine the outcome. If the trial did not proceed as hoped, Leon Lewis, ever the troubleshooter, had already taken detailed affidavits regarding the election from plaintiffs Otto Deissler and Philip Lenhardt.

Lewis gave copies of those affidavits to the plaintiffs' attorneys, Harris and Field. "If something goes wrong, give these to Sam Dickstein," Lewis said.

Agent 8 on the Stand

The first witness was Agent 8, Captain Carl Sunderland, who identified himself as a member of the Friends of New Germany. Sunderland testified as to a conversation he'd had on October 2, 1933 with Dietrich Gefken: "He told me he was a member of the Hitler party and was devoting his entire time in L.A. to the furtherance of its principles. He told me he wanted to form some connection between the Friends of New Germany and the disabled veterans.

"He said the veterans had received a raw deal under the economy bill and that he felt they would welcome a change. He said that the Jews had been removed from control in Germany and that he believed it his life duty to carry out that work here.

"He told me he had enlisted in the 159th Infantry, California National Guard, and had obtained blueprints of the San Francisco armory, precisely locating the ammunition supply and arms. He said that when the time came the armories of L.A. and San Diego would be seized, and that materiel used to overthrow the government of the United States.

"He told me that it was his purpose to foment unrest, that sooner or later the communists would gain control and then the people would wake up. He said they would be without leadership and that the veterans would then step in and that the Friends of New Germany would march shoulder to shoulder with them.

"I asked him what would happen if the veterans did not get control by votes. Gefken said that it should be done by force.

"He told me that there was going to be a parade preceding the annual picnic of the German society, and that swastika flags were to be displayed. He told me he'd brought in storm troopers to protect those flags with their lives. I told him that I knew there were members of the Disabled Veterans who would try to break up the parade if there was an attempt to display the swastika.

"He scoffed so I went with Captain John H. Schmidt to their headquarters on West Washington Boulevard and I asked for Captain Robert Pape. They told me he wasn't in. I spoke to Hans Winterhalder instead. He said he would call the German Consul. He dialed the phone and spoke for some minutes in German. He then hung up and said the German Consul insisted flags be flown.

"Captain Schmidt and I left and on our way out we ran into Paul Themlitz and Hermann Schwinn, who had just returned from a German ship in the harbor, the steamship *Schwaben*. I told them about the threat to break up the parade if the flags were flown and Themlitz said, if necessary, he would bring fifty storm troopers from the German ship and guard the parade. I said it would be a mistake, that they had no right to come on American soil. He said the men would defend the flags and fight to the limit and he was ready to die for his country."

Captain Sunderland was asked if the parade was ever held.

"I don't know for certain, but I do not believe so," he replied.

At another point in his testimony, Sunderland said there were members of the Friends of New Germany who were getting their U.S. citizenship without renouncing their German citizenship.

"It is my understanding," he concluded, "that the organization in Los Angeles gets its instructions from New York as relayed from Berlin."

He said that members of the Friends, like those in a military organization, were required to obey orders: "I remember a time when Captain Schmidt failed to appear at a Friends of New Germany picnic. Winterhalder told him that orders were orders and must be obeyed to escape punishment. Winterhalder said that two men had been severely beaten for taking down the swastika at the picnic and that Schmidt's mother in Germany might not fare so well."

Sunderland was cross-examined by H. H. L. Carnahan.

"Isn't it true, Mr. Sunderland, that you joined the Friends of New Germany as a spy?"

"No, sir."

"Isn't it true that you joined as part of an investigation by someone or some organization?"

"Not at all. I went on my own accord."

Schmidt Testifies

Captain John Schmidt was called next to the witness stand. Schmidt took the oath and testified that he'd served in the German army before coming to the United States thirty years before and becoming a U.S. citizen.

"I served in the A.E.F.," he said. "That is, the American Expeditionary Forces that fought in France in 1917. I was made a member of the Friends in September of last year. I remained a member until I was suspended several weeks later."

"During the time you were a member, did you determine how the leaders of that group were chosen?"

"I did. The leaders were appointed by Hans Spanknöbel of New York under authority of Dr. Goebbels, chief of propaganda under Adolf Hitler."

There was a gasp from the gallery.

"You are testifying against the Friends of New Germany today. Are its members your enemies now?"

"Not at all, sir. I feel a strong affection for many of the members, but as a group I find them best defined by what they are against. They are anti-United States, anti-Jew, and anti-Catholic."

"I understand that, while gathering information about the Friends, you kept contemporary notes?"

"Yes, sir," Schmidt said, and he pulled from his pocket a "small memorandum book." Referring to it, he told the court about visiting German ships in the harbor. He overheard German officers discussing "the progress being made in America." He saw several bundles of pro-Nazi pamphlets being unloaded from the ship to the shore. "The material was written both in English and German," he added. He also saw a mysterious attaché case being handed off from one officer to another with the whispered message, "Be careful, don't lose it." Schmidt assumed the case contained money. It, too, was going ashore.

"Did you attend an event of the Friends of New Germany on the night of October 11 last, and if so, what did you observe?"

"Yes, sir. I observed it to be a secret caucus to nominate the Nazi slate for the Alliance election. Nearby there were military-type operations. While there I heard commands in German being uttered to men drilling in another room. Later, I caught a glimpse of the drilling men and they were all lined up and standing at attention."

"What was the tenor of the meeting?"

"The thrust was, and I quote, 'Once a German, always a German.' The idea was to wake up the patriotic pride in old Germans who had been in America for a long time."

"You had conversations with Captain Pape, then the leader of the organization?"

"I did. He told me he was still a captain in the German army and was receiving three hundred marks a month for his work in the U.S. The money, he said, was deposited to his account in a German bank."

"Did you discuss with him any intentions he might have to become a U.S. citizen?" asked attorney H. H. Harris.

"Yes, sir. He told me he would never take out citizenship papers in a rotten country like the United States run by Jews and Catholics."

"You once had a conversation with one of the defendants in this suit, Hans Winterhalder, in which he threatened a prominent U.S. citizen, is that correct?"

"Yes, sir. He was angry with a man named Tony Entenza, who was at one time the national commander of the United Spanish American War Veterans. Entenza had given a public speech in front of a high-school group in which he attacked Nazi activities in the U.S. I was speaking with Winterhalder and Paul Themlitz, and they asked me if I knew Entenza. I said I knew of him but didn't know him personally. I said that I had heard him talk and I thought he was a good old United States fighter and stood for justice and right. I told them he was a national character and that I would be glad to contact him for them. Themlitz remained calm when I said this, but Winterhalder became nervous, and said, 'You bring him down here and I shall whip him. I shall whip him.'"

Schmidt testified that during his time with the Friends, he frequented the organization's headquarters, first in its home on South Alvarado Street, the old HQ, and then the current site on West Washington Boulevard.

"I just wanted to see what was going on," Schmidt said.

On cross-examination, Attorney Carnahan seemed to suggest that the "terrible literature" was a figment of the witness's imagination. "You say you read this literature, that you say was so terrible, and yet you bring nothing here to show the court?"

Schmidt calmly replied, "Everything that I picked up, all this literature I studied, translated and sent to my government in Washington. I sent about twenty pounds in all. If I had known this trial was coming up, I would have taken two copies of each pamphlet."

"And how often did you see this terrible literature?" Carnahan inquired.

Schmidt stuck to his new cover, spy for the feds: "Right up until the day I was discharged as a spy against Hitler in the United States. I was trying to find out what was behind Hitler. All these men," Schmidt gestured at the defendants, "are very likable men, just in a bad spot. I went slow. I didn't want to hurt them."

"So, you didn't want to hurt these men?" Carnahan was incredulous.

"As long as the interests of the United States government are not at stake, I will not hurt my friends."

Schmidt's time on the witness stand was over. As he walked up the aisle, he saw men he recognized as friends of Themlitz in the gallery.

"Themlitz is a dirty pig who lives in the gutter," Schmidt muttered as he passed.

"You'll pay for that," one of them replied.

Defense Case

The next day it was the Carnahan's turn to make the defense case, and his big witness was twenty-nine-year-old Hermann Schwinn, L.A. leader of the Friends of New Germany. Keeping his tiny mustache as still as he could, Schwinn testified that he was born in Hamburg, Germany, and came over to the U.S. on the boat in 1923.

"I became a naturalized American citizen two years ago," he added.

Carnahan led Schwinn through his direct testimony: "First of all, Mr. Schwinn, tell us about your relationship with the Friends of New Germany."

"I helped organize it, and I have been its leader here in Los Angeles since December."

"You took charge about three weeks ago?"

"Something like that, yes."

"Does the organization hold allegiance to the government of Germany?"

"It does not. We sympathize with the new German government. But first, we are loyal American citizens, standing fairly and squarely behind the man who has given this country a New Deal, just as Adolf Hitler has given Germany a new deal."

Someone clucked with disgust from the gallery and earned a glare from Judge Bush.

"Tell us how the organization came to be."

"We had a common interest in informing people in Los Angeles what is really going on in Germany."

"What is really going on?"

"We are in a terrible struggle against Communism, but the world is being fed lies about it."

"Lies? Who is spreading lies?"

"There is a certain minority group made up of Communists who spread malicious propaganda and atrocity stories from Germany."

"And how did this organization, the Friends, start?"

"It started when myself and Captain Robert Pape, first leader of the local group and a German citizen, Paul Themlitz, and a man from San Francisco drove to Chicago last July to discuss forming a local group of Friends."

"And what were the original aims of the organization?"

"We believed it necessary to keep up the friendly relationship existing between the United States and Germany. To stop the lies."

"You have spoken about a boycott."

"Yes, sir. There has been a boycott of German goods that has been instigated by the same small minority. It might cause a break in the friendly relationship existing between the two countries and that it was easy to see that a German boycott of American goods would be harmful to the United States."

"Your organization has a message regarding Communism?"

"Yes, sir. We want some of the experiences that we had in Germany with Communism to be made known to Americans for their benefit."

On cross-examination, Schwinn was confronted with Nazi literature he'd been caught with. How had those materials been brought into the United States?

"Some came through regular mail channels and some were obtained from officers of German ships."

"About how many leaflets were brought into this country off of German ships?"

"Thousands."

"And was any duty demanded or paid?"

"Not that I know of."

Themlitz Takes the Oath

Paul Themlitz took the witness stand and was asked by his attorney if he had been surprised that John Schmidt had testified for the plaintiffs.

"Not at all," Themlitz said.

"And why not?"

"Schmidt blew his cover long ago," Themlitz said. "He got drunk one night and admitted what he was. A mole. A little mole. Secret Service man investigating the Friends of New Germany. He really made a fool out of himself."

"Did you believe him when he said he was with the Secret Service?"

"No. I figured there was no way a buffoon like that could be

Secret Service. I am certain the U.S. Government has much better men to do that sort of job if they feel it is necessary."

"That's a lie," Schmidt called out from the gallery.

Judge Bush banged his gavel somewhat wearily.

"You are a traitor, Themlitz!" Schmidt screamed.

"Silence in my court," Judge Bush admonished.

Schmidt looked across the aisle and saw the friends of Themlitz who'd earlier threatened him. One drew a finger across his throat. With that, Schmidt got up and left the courtroom with a hurried step. Themlitz's friends got up and followed. As they left the courtroom, they held their arms down but away from their sides, fists clenching and unclenching. They followed Schmidt into the hallway. Blood drained from Schmidt's face.

One of the tough guys gave Schmidt a solid push that rocked him back a few steps. Schmidt didn't charge back, but stepped forward to show he planned to hold his ground.

"Get a cop!" someone yelled, so loudly that it could be heard inside the courtroom. Judge Bush, a man of action, flew off the bench with robe billowing, hopped down to the courtroom floor, and hightailed it up the aisle. A guard opened the door so the judge could get into the corridor without breaking stride.

"Here, here. There will be no fighting here," the judge said, and the physical altercation ended. The tough guys slunk from the hallway and left the courthouse, although they would return later in the trial.

Pape in the Hot Seat

Eager to quit California and return to the Fatherland, a visibly weary Robert Pape took the witness stand and testified that he was a retired German army officer and the "Western Leader" of the Friends of New Germany.

This stretched the truth in two ways. Pape had told Sunderland that he was still on active duty for the German army, stationed in Los Angeles. Also, Pape was no longer the West Coast leader, replaced by Schwinn after being socked in the face.

On the stand, Pape admitted that he was a German citizen and had been chosen to lead efforts in California by Heinz Spanknöbel, the former national head of the Friends who was awaiting deportation hearings.

"I was appointed to my post last summer in Chicago," Pape said. "My task was to organize the western sections." He denied that the Friends had a political or military agenda but admitted that Jews were not eligible for membership.

Good, Clean Exercise

The next witness was Karl Specht, leader of the Friends' *Sportabteilung*, the storm trooper unit pretending to be the Friends' physical-fitness component.

To counter claims that there was militaristic drilling in the Turnverein, Specht said that the Friends did use drill regulations of the German *Sturmabteilung* to keep their greatest athletes in shape.

"But these exercises are not militaristic," Specht added.

"We'll Kill You"

There were more fireworks on the morning of January 19, 1934. During testimony, the Schmidts, John and Alyce, listened from the back row of the gallery. A man in a yellow jacket plopped himself down next to John Schmidt and softly said, "We'll kill you, Schmidt, you son of a bitch."

The man got up and left the courtroom. Sitting just in front of the Schmidts was Leon Lewis, there in his capacity as a veteran, not as a lawyer—and certainly not as leader of the Nazibusters.

"Major Lewis, my life has just been threatened," Schmidt said. He got up and left the courtroom.

Alyce told a high-ranking member of the American Legion sitting near her about what had happened.

"I'll see if I can catch that guy," Lewis said, working his way past others in the gallery and leaving the courtroom in time to see the yellow jacket moving smoothly at the end of the hall.

Sensing the commotion, Judge Bush looked out into the gallery and asked, "What's going on now?"

"My husband's life has been threatened," Alyce called out.

"How many fights must I break up?" the judge muttered, and again zipped down the aisle with long strides. In the corridor, Bush was surprised to see Schmidt squared off against a small and shabbily dressed man.

"What's going on?" Judge Bush asked.

"I have been threatened once more," Schmidt said.

"I make threats *not*," the little man said.

A bystander chimed in, "Yes, he did, I heard him!"

The little man turned to the bystander with a look of betrayal, and said, "You are a gentleman. I am but a miner. But I make no threats. I punch him in the nose."

Somebody said the little guy had a friend who was also all mouth. "There he is!" they shouted.

Judge Bush looked at the second man, who was not in a yellow jacket, and commanded, "You! Come over here."

But the little man didn't like that and tried to alibi his friend: "No, not him. I am the one."

The judge for a moment seemed lost for words. Finally, he managed, "Well, you can't block the passageway. Everyone on their way now. Disperse!" To the second man he said, "Beat it!" and pointed toward the door.

The judge grabbed Schmidt by the sleeve of his jacket. "You, come with me!"

Judge Bush ordered Schmidt onto the witness stand: "You're already under oath. Sit!" Schmidt sat.

"What just happened out there?" Judge Bush asked.

"Since the start of these proceedings I have been threatened several times. I expected trouble today. I received a telephone call this morning, telling me to stay away from the courtroom and that if I took the witness stand again I would be treated like the Jews who were killed in Germany."

Members of the gallery laughed. That angered the others. Judge Bush pounded his gavel as hard as he could.

Attorney H. H. Harris for the plaintiffs said, "Your Honor, please remind the gallery that witnesses being threatened is serious business."

Judge Bush admonished the gallery: "This is not a laughing matter. If there is one present who believes perjury has been committed, let him go to the District Attorney. Stop these threats. And if you want to fight, hire a hall!"

"Your honor, I request a bodyguard for the remainder of the trial," Schmidt said.

Judge Bush visibly sighed. "All right, to prevent a tragedy, I appoint Deputy Sheriff V. D. Agnew to remain at Captain Schmidt's side to protect him from further attack, verbal or otherwise." (The next day, a photo of Judge Bush, Schmidt, and Agnew having a discussion appeared in the L.A. papers.)

Attorneys for the Nazis didn't like any of this. It made them seem like the bad guys. When Judge Bush finally made it back behind the bench and order was restored, they said that the threats had gone both ways and that several members of the Friends of New Germany had received "letters of a threatening nature."

That evening, again thinking ahead to possible trouble, Leon Lewis took detailed sworn affidavits from both John and Alyce Schmidt regarding the threats they'd received and the incidents in the courthouse.

Lock the Doors

The next morning, as soon as Judge Bush sat down at the bench he said, "Bailiff, lock the doors."

Faces in the gallery opened as one—high eyebrows and gaping mouths. Wha—?

"There has been a threat against this court. Last night, I received a threat. I am deputizing Bernard White, photographer for the *Los Angeles Times*. Mr. White, I would like you to photograph everyone in the gallery to help us determine who the culprit was."

As this was being done, the photographer for the *L.A. Examiner*, not about to be scooped, took a picture of White taking pictures. Four members of the gallery, all Friends—Dr. Konrad Buchardt, Hermann Schwinn, Ludwig Leithhold, and Hans Winterhalder—gave the Nazi salute for their photo.

Those images, when eventually published, cemented in the public's mind that the Friends were Nazis—which had been Leon Lewis's goal when he wrote up the lawsuit in the first place.

Getting to the Point

The courtroom activity couldn't be seen and heard without the glaze of global tensions. But the proceedings did eventually get around to the charges of the lawsuit: that Friends leaders tried to illegally intervene in the elections of the German-American Alliance.

The defense called Alliance President Max E. Socha to address the point. Predictably, Socha said there was nothing irregular about the election or the delegates.

Hugo H. Harris, attorney for the plaintiffs cross-examined aggressively: "Did you at any time ask Captain Robert Pape, organizer and leader of the Friends of New Germany, if he was an American citizen?"

"No, sir."

"You say you were interested in the aims of this new group and yet you weren't interested enough to ask the leader if he was an American citizen?" Harris asked wide-eyed.

"I was not. I believed Captain Pape to be a man of honor. I understood that his organization was eligible for membership in the Alliance."

Esoteric Soviet Symbolism

The defense team took the offensive. Accused terrorist and saboteur Dietrich Gefken, from whom the Nazibusters had learned plenty, took the stand. He didn't talk about plans to start a war in southern California. Instead, he presented "evidence" that the NRA (National Recovery Administration), a New Deal organization set up by FDR to alleviate the pain of the Great Depression, was actually part of an insidious Soviet Russian plot.

Gefken's "proof" was the NRA's symbol, a blue eagle. "It is full of esoteric Soviet symbolism," Gefken said. "The seven feathers of the eagle's left wing stands [sic] for one of the geographical divisions of Soviet Russia. The ten feathers on the right represent the nation's ten political divisions."

Judge Bush looked at Gefken like he had two heads. "Let me point out," Bush said, "that secret symbolism cannot be considered evidence of anything unless it ceases to be a secret. I doubt highly that the man who designed that eagle on behalf of the government agency had esoteric Soviet symbolism in mind."

Poised to Step In

On cross-examination, Dietrich Gefken denied ever plotting to make war against the U.S., after which, the defense rested.

Plaintiff's attorneys requested permission from the court to call one more witness, and Judge Bush okayed it.

The witness was C. Bert Allen (Lewis's Agent 7), who testified as to things that Gefken had told him: "He said the Friends were just a cover organization for the storm troopers. He said they had arms, they had supplies, they had thirty men training weekly to fight, street fighting, making and detonating bombs. He said America was on the brink of revolution and when it came the Friends were poised to step in and take command."

The trial ended with a whimper not a bang. Judge Bush declared the election of the Friends representatives as officers of the German-American Alliance perfectly legal. The Nazi menace was unaffected. There had been a slump in attendance at meetings when the trial first began, but things quickly improved into a boost in recruiting because of the publicity.

Alyce Grows a Shadow

John Schmidt had no further problems with the Nazis, but his wife, Alyce, was not as lucky. One day near the end of the trial she was walking on Wilshire, just northwest of MacArthur Park, when she sensed she was being shadowed. Stopping and looking back she saw a large man, German in appearance, stopping and looking around.

After making him duck into a few doorways by starting and stopping, she picked up her step and stretched out a slight lead on the guy, before entering the art deco building at 3050 Wilshire Boulevard. It housed a branch of the luxury department store called Bullocks Wilshire (opened by John G. Bullock in 1929). The main Bullocks was in downtown L.A. Alyce spent thirty minutes pretending to shop and then went out the way she came in, only to find that her shadow was waiting for her, smoking a cigarette and leaning disinterestedly against a streetlight. Coming out of the building she took a left, looked back to see her tail flicking away his cigarette into the street and walking toward her. She again walked as fast as she could, two and a half blocks to Vermont Avenue, where she hopped in a cab waiting at the curb.

"On break, lady."

"Please, I'm being followed by a man I don't know. Take me anywhere."

"You bet," the hack said, snapping to. Thank goodness, a gentleman. And that was the last Alyce saw of her shadow. What he intended for her, she would never know.

Looking to the Future

Leon Lewis had hoped that his mission against the Nazis was about over, that the Alliance trial would spark a grassroots anti-Nazi movement among gentiles, and Hitler's plots would be foiled. But the outrage over the uncomfortable truths outed by the trial never happened.

Lewis's work was nowhere near finished. And he was in a poor position to rekindle his efforts. He'd lost much of his team. John Schmidt, Carl Sunderland, and C. Bert Allen had been exposed. New operatives would have to be recruited, and they would need to be compensated. The mission for those undercover agents would be more dangerous than ever.

To carry on, he would need money, and the rich Jewish bankers and businessmen that had promised to fund Lewis's anti-Nazi efforts hadn't come through.

What to do? Snap. There was another group of rich Jewish men in Los Angeles who might be willing to help, Russian immigrants, many of them. Jewish but in denial, some of them. They ruled over a rowdy colony of beautiful people. They made motion pictures.

CHAPTER 10

The Hollywood Branch

In show business the key word is honesty. Once you've learned to fake that, the rest is easy.
—George Burns

During his private practice, one of Leon Lewis's favorite clients was a pop-eyed entertainer named Eddie Cantor, who'd been around the block a few times. He was born in New York to a fiddle player and his wife, and was performing in and winning talent contests with his broad comedy and piping voice by the time he reached puberty. When Cantor was a young man, Flo Ziegfeld cast him in his show *Ziegfeld Follies of 1917*, doing his "Banjo Eyes" bit. He was known as Izzy Cantor until his future wife decided it too ethnic. When the talkies converted Hollywood, Cantor was a natural for musicals, and by 1933 he was a major movie star, either playing himself or thinly fictionalized characters named "Eddie." Lewis had gotten Cantor out of a few scrapes.

Lewis said, "I need to cash a chip."

"I'll make a few phone calls," Cantor replied.

The Last Tycoon

A few hours later there were three men calling and schmoozing, arranging for the head Nazibuster and the moguls to have a major sit-down. The second man working the phone was the Brooklyn-born MGM production chief, the powerful but sickly Irving Thalberg.

Born in Brooklyn, Thalberg was the "boy genius" of Hollywood known for his literary adaptations, transforming books he'd read as a bedridden kid into motion picture art. He began at Universal, working for Carl Laemmle, but was hired away by Metro Studios (soon to be MGM). Thalberg believed that pictures could be made in assembly-line fashion like Henry Ford made automobiles. Unlike other men, he had the imagination and the judgment to control the budgets and creative elements of multiple projects. He was a mass psychologist, instinctively knowing what audiences wanted, and what turned them away, a gifted diplomat, smoothly moderating disputes between the volatile Louis B. Mayer and "New York"—which was how Metro's executives tended to refer to Marcus Loew and Nicholas Schenck, of Loew's Inc. which owned MGM. Thalberg knew everybody, and everybody wanted to be his friend.

Rabbi to the Stars

The third man calling important movie people was Rabbi Edgar Fogel Magnin, forty-three years old, son of a San Francisco department store owner, ordained at Hebrew Union College when he was twenty-four.

Since 1915, Magnin was head of the Wilshire Boulevard Temple. He was known as "Rabbi to the Stars," and quietly reinforced the moguls' urge to completely blend themselves and their product with Americana, an objective that meant sublimating their Jewishness. Mayer was one of Magnin's best friends.

Mendel Silberberg

Also recruiting was Mendel Silberberg, who'd been at the meetings to form the Nazibusters and was very optimistic. The moguls and the Nazibusters seemed like a match made in heaven. When it came to public relations, Silberberg had something Lewis lacked, roots in L.A. In fact, he was a lifelong Angelino, born in Los Angeles in 1886, son of a pioneer couple who were among the first Jews to go west. By 1933, Silberberg was one of L.A.'s most powerful attorneys.

His firm—Mitchell Silberberg & Knupp (MSK), it's still around and thriving—represented several of Hollywood's top studios, including the biggest of them all, MGM. He, too, was a close friend of Louis B. Mayer. Silberberg qualified for the op in other ways. He was Jewish by blood but raised Christian Scientist. He was very smart, very charismatic, and was ever mindful of how his Jewishness was presented in public. He was a veteran, like Lewis, served in the Army Air Corps during World War I and afterward was the founder of American Legion Post 8. As a Nazibuster, Silberberg's job became recruiting powerful Jews (and their money) into the fold, which required a certain knack.

There was the old line: No one in Hollywood is Jewish, but everyone seems to be. Aware of America's intrinsic xenophobia, the moguls and their families prioritized assimilation. They even dabbled in other faiths. Louis B. Mayer studied Catholicism and had a portrait of a Catholic cardinal on his office wall. Harry Cohn worked on Yom Kippur and converted to Catholicism to marry one of his wives. Paramount's Jesse Lasky and his wife were "spiritualists" and received messages through "automatic writing."

For them, Silberberg was the perfect Jew. This denial on the part of Hollywood's super-successful Jews was responsible for at least some of their feet-dragging when attacked for their Jewishness. "What Jewishness?" they might have asked themselves.

All of that illusion, all of that assimilation, melted away like candlewax. Hitler's propaganda agents in America pummeled the moguls with antisemitic hooey: "They're raping Christian girls!" the leaflets said.

The moguls had to face facts. The world knew they were Jews. At best, there was a trust issue. At worst, people wanted them usurped.

Silberberg suggested to Lewis that they better use their

military veteran status to move the anti-Nazi message away from Jewish persecution and toward patriotic duty.

Lewis told Silberberg he'd been in touch with foreign correspondents, working press in Germany: "They say that Hitler is encouraging Germans in America to form active cells."

Walter Wanger, Independent Producer

The Nazibusters' relationship with the American Legion grew cozier. They had members in common. Lewis, Silberberg, and independent filmmaker Walter Wanger belonged to both organizations, including the L.A. American Legion's Americanism Committee, the Legion wing that led the battle against Nazism. Wanger (born Walter Feuchtwanger), thirty-nine years old in 1933, was an independent film producer who became the first to make pictures in defiance of America's state of neutrality in Europe.

During the silent era, Wanger had worked for Paramount. When talkies came, he reinvented himself as an indie, working from contract to contract, making smart pictures with provocative messages and an occasional melodramatic romance.

(During the last few years before Pearl Harbor, Wanger served as President of the Academy of Motion Picture Arts and Sciences.)

End of the Pre-Code Era

In 1934, the Silver Lodge's William Pelley was arrested for draining his publishing company dry and declaring bankruptcy. He was indicted in North Carolina and charged with defrauding stockholders. He ended up serving parts of 1934 and '35 in jail.

As that was going on, Hollywood was bending to pressure, agreeing to work under the Production Code Administration—Joseph Breen, head code master—monitors of all that is decent and good and *Christian*. Breen was a foaming-at-the-mouth antisemite. Jews, he once reportedly said, were "like lice."

Breen dictated to cowards. Hollywood should not be making anti-Nazi propaganda. "Though it may be entertaining," he said, in real life the Nazis were scary. As late as 1938, the PCA and Breen would tell RKO they couldn't make a movie called *The Mad Dog of Europe*, because it was "too controversial" and "might cause a spike in antisemitism."

The skid-row studios, which often operated outside of PCA rules anyway, made some anti-Hitler films during the 1930s (see Appendix) but found it difficult to find theaters in the U.S. willing to show them. Eventually, the subject of Nazism was understood as taboo. Bargain-basement filmmakers moved on to other things.

The House of Rothschild

In 1933, Joseph M. Schenck (Nick's brother) and Darryl F. Zanuck started a new studio, Twentieth Century Pictures. Their second feature was *The House of Rothschild*, starring George Arliss, Loretta Young, and Boris Karloff. It is best remembered for being a black-and-white picture with the final sequence in Technicolor. The film showed wealthy Jewish bankers enduring violent antisemitic attacks in 1850s Europe. The parallel to current events in Europe couldn't be ignored.

This was the first Hollywood picture to be blatantly anti-Hitler. *Time* magazine said it out loud in their review. The picture was "shrewdly timed to touch obliquely on current Jew-baiting in Germany." (Six years later, scenes from *The House of Rothschild* were included, obviously without permission, in an antisemitic propaganda picture out of Nazi Germany called *The Eternal Jew*.)

The House of Rothschild managed to offend both L.A.'s German consul, Georg Gyssling, and head-Nazibuster Leon Lewis. Gyssling's reasons were obvious, Lewis's more complicated. Lewis felt that, because it was about ultrapowerful Jews, it would perpetuate the myth that Jews controlled everything and were responsible for the Great Depression. Obviously, the film was not shown in Germany.

Meeting at Hillcrest

Lewis held his big secret meeting on March 13, 1934, only weeks after the conclusion of the Friends trial, at the toney Hillcrest Country Club on Pico Boulevard in Cheviot Hills—also the golf course where the Three Stooges would film *Three Little Beers* in 1935. Other L.A. clubs had restricted memberships, so wealthy Jews had opened their own club, Hillcrest, and Hollywood bigs like Sam Goldwyn, Louis B. Mayer, Al Jolson, and the Marx Brothers were members.

Present at the meeting were the bigwigs recruited by the team of Eddie Cantor, Leon Lewis, Irving Thalberg, Rabbi Magnin, and Mendel Silberberg. Hillcrest employees were used to celebrities, but to have moguls from all major studios there at once brought attention. These guys weren't tall but they had trouble moving in mysterious ways. It was a stunningly impressive crowd. A banquet was catered in the club's kosher dining room.

A sizable contingent from MGM was first to arrive, including the studio's top dog.

Louis B. Mayer

MGM's chief executive, born in Ukraine on July 12, 1884—although he later claimed it was July 4. Came over on the boat as an infant, his family settling in Saint John, on the Bay of Fundy in New Brunswick, Canada. As a heavily muscled boy, he dove into bay waters, where the changing tides are legendary, to retrieve scrap metal from shipwrecks for his junk-dealer father to sell. He quit school at twelve to help dad full-time.

In 1904, Mayer married the daughter of a cantor, and the couple had two daughters. In 1907, Mayer purchased a dump of a theater in Haverhill, Massachusetts, called the Gem Theater, fixed it up and changed the name to the Orpheum. It opened as a cinema on November 28, 1907. By 1910, Mayer opened a second theater in Bradford, New Hampshire, the Colonial Theater, seating capacity sixteen hundred.

After becoming a U.S. citizen in 1912, Mayer moved to Boston and in 1914 founded the American Feature Film Corporation, the idea being that he would make his own pictures to show in his own theaters. In 1915 he teamed up with Pittsburgh promoter Richard Rowland, to form Metro Pictures, which cranked out a picture per week. And that was where Mayer was when in 1919 Marcus Loew bought Metro. Metro was the first M in what in 1924 became MGM. Mayer was the second.

MGM Contingent

Sitting beside Mayer was the previously discussed Irving Thalberg, MGM production chief, and next to him Larry Weingarten, production supervisor.

Also on hand from MGM:

Producer David O. Selznick, who was working his way up. (In 1939 he produced what would become MGM's greatest film, *Gone With the Wind*. His dad, Lewis, had been a movie-making pioneer, cranking out silents in Fort Lee, New Jersey.)

Ernst Lubitsch, director, who understood better than some the horrors Jews would face with Nazis in charge. He'd been born in Berlin in 1892, became a filmmaker in Germany, moved to Hollywood in 1922, and earned his first of three Oscar nominations in 1928 for directing *The Patriot* at Paramount.

George Cukor, director, who was currently working on *Little Women* (1933) with Katharine Hepburn and Joan Bennett.

Harry Rapf, producer of silents for Metro dating back to 1917 and, in 1934, producing shorts.

Sam Marx, story editor, who later became known as the man who discovered Elizabeth Taylor.

Edwin Justus Mayer, former reporter and playwright from back East who came west to work for Sam Goldwyn and became a busy screenwriter, often working with Lubitsch.

Harry Wardell, actor, best known as the narrator for the Warner Bros. talkie trailer announcing the gimmick that would allow audiences to "hear Al Jolson" in *The Jazz Singer* (1927).

Henry Myers, silent actor, best known as the lead in the 1921 version of Mark Twain's A *Connecticut Yankee in King Arthur's Court* and as the eccentric millionaire in Charlie Chaplin's *City Lights* (1931).

The Warner Bros. Crew

From Warner Bros. came Jack Warner, studio chief. Jack and his brothers started their movie business with one projector and a tent that they moved from town to town. But the business grew. Harry and Albert stayed in New York and handled finances, Jack and Sam moved to Burbank and handled production.

Missing, but there in spirit was Harry, the oldest of the Warner brothers, born in Poland to Polish parents who came to America in 1883 to live in a place where they wouldn't have to practice their religion in secret. Harry and his sister Anna made the trip. The other Warner brothers were born in the U.S. Parents Benjamin and Pearl Warner settled in Youngstown, Ohio, where Benjamin became a cobbler, teaching his sons in turn how to make shoes.

Of the brothers (Harry, born 1881, Albert, 1884, Sam, 1888, and Jack, 1892), Harry was the only one who seriously practiced his religion, understood the importance of his parents' move to the U.S. in search of religious freedom, and understood how fragile that freedom could be. And Harry was the brother who took on the role of conscience for the Jewish Hollywood community, doing the right thing rather than the most profitable thing.

Harry learned of Hitler's impending danger even before Hitler assumed power, having traveled to Germany in 1932 to make a deal to purchase a prestigious German film studio. After seeing the antisemitic slogans, and the troubling presence of Nazis in uniform everywhere, he backed out of the deal and hurried home. Harry later wrote that Hitler's own words helped make up his mind not to invest in Germany. Hitler not only talked about removing Jews from Germany but urged America to do the same, with no sense at all that non-Jewish Americans might come to the rescue of their Jewish neighbors.

Even as Harry Warner was maintaining his strong moral stance regarding business with Germany, he was having a miserable year. In 1934, there was a fire at the Warner Bros. studios in Burbank, causing millions of dollars in damage and wiping out twenty years of films. To pile on, the government went after Harry and busted him for an antitrust violation, charging him with trying to enforce a theater monopoly in St. Louis, Missouri.

Columbia Pictures

The leader of the Columbia Pictures attendees was Sam Briskin, Harry Cohn's second in command. One day soon, Columbia would be considered a major player in Hollywood, but not yet. Briskin brought along Henry Herzbrun, his attorney. The movie that would elevate Columbia was *It Happened One Night*, already in preproduction and slated to star Claudette Colbert and Clark Gable.

Also in attendance from Columbia were writer/producer Albert Lewis and Howard Green, writer of *I Am a Fugitive from a Chain Gang* (1932) and soon to be the first president of the Screen Writers Guild.

Radio-Keith-Orpheum Pictures (RKO)

Heading the RKO crew was Pandro Berman, producer of 115 films. Years later, Berman would receive two awards named after other men in the room, the Irving G. Thalberg Award from the

Academy and the David O. Selznick Lifetime Achievement Award from the Motion Picture Producers Guild of America.

Also there:

Adolph Ramish, theater mogul, building theaters for the legitimate stage and vaudeville dating back to 1907. Partnered with Joseph Schenck to build a series of California theaters under the name Wesco.

Jacob Walter Ruben, who directed nineteen pictures during the 1930s.

Universal Studios

To represent him at the meeting, Carl Laemmle sent:

Henry Henigson, a producer, most recent success a haunted-house picture called *Secret of the Blue Room*.

Edward Sloman, a silent actor who transitioned well to talkies by directing pictures like *Puttin' on the Ritz*, *Hell's Island* (both 1930), and *Gun Smoke* (1931).

John Stahl, director. Not as famous today as he should be because some of his best pictures were remade in the 1950s and because he made non-horror pictures for Universal, which tend not to be shown on TV as much. Most famous for *Leave Her to Heaven* (1945).

Others

From Twentieth Century, Joseph M. Schenck, president. One of Hollywood's top producers. During the silent era he made superstars out of Roscoe "Fatty" Arbuckle, Norma and Constance Talmadge, and Buster Keaton. In two years, the company would merge with Fox Studios to become Twentieth Century-Fox.

From Fox, producer Sol Wurtzel, one of the founding fathers of Hollywood. He discovered director John Ford and Western stars Will Rogers and Tom Mix. After Fox merged with Twentieth Century Pictures, Wurtzel produced Mr. Moto and Charlie Chan pictures.

From United Artists, Harry Brand, a writer of scenarios for the silents who moved into publicity with the talkies, and would soon thereafter move to Twentieth Century-Fox as director of publicity.

Also at the Hillside meeting were primary recruiters Rabbi Edgar Magnin and Mendel Silberberg, whom we've already discussed, two L.A. judges, Lester Roth and Isaac Pacht—and of course, Leon Lewis.

After Dinner

After eating, the men were led into the Club Room. They lit cigars as Lewis introduced himself as the chairman of the Los Angeles Jewish Community Committee, and distributed copies of William Pelley's antisemitic periodical, *The Silver Ranger.*

The men were easy with one another, not an act. True they were in direct competition with one another for theater money—but they competed in other more personal ways as well, on the golf course, and at the card table. For a time, they were all breeding Thoroughbred racehorses.

As the men looked at the Pelley newspapers in disgust, Lewis gave them a blow-by-blow synopsis of how he had infiltrated and exposed the Friends.

"You will note, gentlemen, that this propaganda singles you out, saying the 'Jews of Hollywood' are the enemy of Christian America," Lewis said, picking up one of the papers. "Let me read you a passage I've marked. 'Protestants and Catholics should be terrified that the powerful Hollywood motion picture industry is in the hands of former pants-pressers and button-holers.'"

"I owned a drug store and an amusement park. This is a crime?" Joe Schenck said.

"That is how the antisemites write their propaganda, Joe," Thalberg said. "Dehumanization by reducing us to stereotypes."

"What is this 'ruined white girls' stuff?" Henry Henigson asked, looking at the paper.

"They think we are all Harry Cohn," Thalberg quipped, and that got a laugh. Cohn had a rep as being rough on the starlets.

Lewis told the gathering about the brave work of John and Alyce Schmidt. The men had read about the civil trial but had been unaware of the undercover operation that preceded it.

"But you lost your suit," one of the men commented.

"Not really," Lewis said. "Our object was not to win the suit but to expose the Nazis, which we did—and that effort cost seven thousand dollars," Lewis said, "most of which I have paid out of my own pocket. Now my pockets are empty, and I am seeking your help. Frankly, without your help, this effort to combat antisemitism and fascism is over."

Lewis told them that Nazis had invaded the studios, sometimes in supervisory capacities. Sure, the money men, the men who ran the joint, were Jewish, but try to find a Jewish gaffer or seamstress. The reason was, the Nazis had people in place in all studios and they were *preventing* Jews from being hired.

"There are some departments in some studios that, the Nazis claim, are approaching one-hundred percent Aryan," Lewis said.

This was clearly news to the other men in the room. There were even a few snorts of disbelief.

Lewis upped the ante: "My people have also exposed death plots against the studio heads, you very gentlemen. I daresay we must stop them before they stop us."

Lewis told them he wanted to "create a war chest" for his already trained and in-place spies within the California Nazi scene.

"I come to you today for money, gentlemen. Money to continue my efforts not only to keep track of how the Nazis are trying to influence the studios but also to dismantle plans for sabotage and murder in southern California. Can you help?"

Thalberg, the MGM wunderkind who didn't have long to live, said, "I'll help with fundraising. I've been squeezing money out of people for years. I can do it to fight Nazis. I had a fucking heart attack in Bad Nauheim last year. I have witnessed the Nazi repression. There is great tension. A lot of Jews will lose their lives." Thalberg's brain went straight to the great finish of this real-life movie plot: "But I'll bet that Hitler and Hitlerism will pass, and the Jews will still be here."

Thalberg said MGM would give $3,500 to the anti-Nazi effort. Then he volunteered to be liaison between Lewis and the studio heads, some of whom were in the room.

Mayer said, "There can be no doubt as to the necessity of carrying on, and I for one am not going to take it lying down. As I see it, two things are required, namely money and intelligent direction. It is the duty of the men in this room to help in both directions."

Harry Rapf noted that the decision to combat Nazism was not easy for the moguls, because there were so many damn movie theaters in Germany, and Germans loved Hollywood movies.

"Some of these men," Rapf said with a broad gesture, "have been deeply wounded by the economic doldrums we're in and rely on Germany for their very existence. If they contribute money to combat the Nazi groups in L.A., it will have to be a secret."

No problem, Lewis said. "I guarantee one hundred percent confidentiality."

"Of course, we're already getting out of Germany, so attack away, I say," Jack Warner bragged.

"That's your brother Harry's work, he's a Communist," Mayer said, laughing pleasantly.

"I signed off on it," Jack Warner said defensively. "And Harry is not a Communist. He is merely a good Jew with a conscience."

"Kidding! I'm a kidder," Mayer said.

Rapf then suggested that one man be appointed from each studio to form a subcommittee, the "Community Relations Committee," to monitor and, when necessary, supervise the anti-Nazi activities.

"There should be one person from each studio," Sam Briskin interjected.

"Volunteers?" Lewis asked.

Everyone raised their hand. Briskin ran to make a phone call. He returned saying Mr. Cohn wanted to rep Columbia personally.

In addition to Cohn, it was decided that Irving Thalberg would represent MGM, followed by Joseph Schenck (Twentieth Century), Sol Wurtzel (Fox), Pandro Berman (RKO), Henry Henigson (Universal), and Jack Warner (Warner Bros.).

Eventually all studios kicked over with money. Lewis walked out of the meeting with $24,000 pledged for the anti-Nazi campaign. That's almost a half-million dollars today.

Lewis went home and wrote a letter to a friend at the Anti-Defamation League. "For the first time," Lewis penned, "we have established a real basis of cooperation with the motion picture industry, and I look for splendid results."

The money helped pay for Lewis's ops but came with strings attached. Not only was the source of the cash to remain secret but also Lewis had to promise that his spies would help keep Nazis out of the studios.

To disguise the paper trail between the moguls and Lewis, the studios formed the Community Relations Council (CRC) of the Jewish Federation of Greater Los Angeles, under whose auspices the checks were written to Lewis. And it is through that committee's archives that we know the details regarding Lewis's anti-Nazi activities. The CRC met at noon on Fridays in the offices of the Jewish Welfare Federation of Los Angeles from March 1934 through the end of World War II in 1945.

CHAPTER 11

Spies at Work

It's the oldest question: Who can spy on the spies?
—John le Carré

On May 28, 1934, the biggest news story of the year occurred, when the Dionne quintuplets were born in Canada. For the next few years, it was hard to find a newsreel that didn't include the latest shots of the five identical girls, who were considered by many Americans, particularly women, as magic. They weren't, but they were a very cute distraction from the news of the day, which was almost completely bleak.

In the meantime, if Captain Carl Sunderland had been spooked by his experiences as Agent 8, he didn't show it. In the middle of June 1934, at Patriotic Hall, he gave a speech before the Third District of the DAV and the Women's Auxiliary. The speech was entitled "Americanism," and was advertised in the *Los Angeles Times*. Sunderland wasn't hiding.

Agent 33

With his coffers freshly flush, Lewis hired a new Nazibuster, fifty-four-year-old Walter Clairville, designated Agent 33. Clairville was an American, born in Oakland, served in the Fifth Field Artillery during the Great War, and survived eight pitched battles. He was an American Legion commander and for years presided over meetings at the Patriotic Hall.

His assignment: infiltrate as many fascist organizations as he could. Lewis instructed: "Root out plans involving violence, and determine if you can the connections between the Nazis and the Silver Lodge."

Clairville was also an investigator for the L.A. city prosecutor's office who often worked undercover to expose corruption in city offices. He figured he could approach the fascist organizations as himself and offer them his skills as an investigator. One of the first organizations he joined was the Silver Lodge's Metropolitan Post. His line was simple: He hated Jews, loved the Silver Shirts, so here he was.

One Silver Shirter who bought into Clairville was Eugene Case, and he invited Clairville to help out at Silver Lodge headquarters on South Grand Avenue. Agent 33 was a busy fellow, working all day at HQ and attending meetings in the evenings. Then one day Case approached Clairville and asked him to become the Post's investigator.

"What would I investigate?"

"Investigate all new members of the Post, Walter. Make sure no Jews or spies get in."

"Right up my alley," Clairville said.

He became a close friend of the Metropolitan Post's secretary, a fellow named Mark White. Clairville took White out drinking and learned there were Metropolitan Post members who thought the upper echelon of the Lodge was corrupt and were determined to do something about it.

"What are the complaints?" Clairville asked.

"They gouge us with dues. They gouge us with the uniforms, which they mark up a thousand percent."

White told Clairville that the Lodge attracted two distinct types. As it was a Christian organization ("Jesus was the first Silver Shirt"), there were conservative churchgoers who bought into the Communist menace propaganda, and then there were the haters, who wanted to rid America of anybody who wasn't a white Christian.

"Surely, you admire Pelley?" Clairville said, as he watched White drink.

"Him?" White said. "He is nothing to us. He is a slob. Sometimes I feel like I should go to Washington, D.C., and spill the beans!"

When Clairville introduced national politics as a topic of conversation, he was surprised when White didn't condemn FDR.

"The President is doing the best he can," White said. "And I'm a Republican!"

Flipping White

When Clairville reported back to Lewis that there was a post in L.A. that wasn't happy with Silver Lodge leadership, Lewis had an idea.

"See if you can get White to flip. Recruit him. Tell him why you are really there. See if he comes along with you."

"If he turns out to be one guy when he's sober and another when drunk, my cover is blown."

"That's a good risk—easy for me to say—but I think he's ready to unburden himself of being a Silver Shirt. And even if he doesn't flip, he won't report you. To whom? The slob? He likes President Roosevelt more than William Pelley."

And so Clairville approached his friend White, more than a little the worse for wear from the previous night's binge, and said that he was investigating fascist activity in Los Angeles on behalf of a lawyer who had the ear of Samuel Dickstein. As Lewis had hoped, White agreed to come to Lewis's office and "spill the beans."

It was like a dream come true for Lewis. White outlined the interactions between the agents of Hitler and the Silver Lodge. White knew all the top guys from the Friends of New Germany and revealed that the no-nonsense Hans Winterhalder had been recruited into the Silver Lodge.

"He's leading his own post," White said. Winterhalder's post was different, White explained. It was the Nazi post. They wore swastika pins on their silver shirts. American citizens were not allowed to join Winterhalder's post. Lewis asked White about Dietrich Gefken and White corroborated previous reports that the Nazis and the Silver Lodge post in San Diego had been plotting together to attack the U.S. military.

White and Clairville were sent back undercover to learn more about the Nazi–Silver Lodge alliance and reported back that "militant leaders" in L.A. were plotting an organized effort to "kill Jews and Communists."

White volunteered to help the Lodge's military operation. Case was happy, thinking White to be an exceptionally competent man. He told White to put together a team of four men, who while heavily armed could go to war in the same automobile.

"After you have thoroughly trained them, send them out to train four men, and so on and so on. That is how you build an army," Case said.

White thought Case was nuts but nodded eagerly.

American White Guard

During the summer of 1934, members of the Lodge's Metropolitan Post broke off from Pelley's organization and formed their own group called the American White Guard, led by experienced military men who'd said phooey to Pelley.

They were Major W. C. Fowler and Colonel Walter McCord, combat veterans, and they knew how to prepare for war. McCord was a sharpie, led a machine gun battalion during the Great War, and Fowler was a huge man with great slabs of muscle crossing his upper body. Brains and brawn.

White Guarders were instructed to play it close to the vest if asked about White Guard business. The instructions were: "Tell them that we are peaceful. Tell them we are anti-Communist. Then shut up."

Lewis instructed Mark White to introduce Case to Gus Price, a Ku Klux Klan leader, and listen to the exchange. Accomplishing this, White reported that Case told Price, "We are militant, eight hundred strong, all veterans, the first line of defense when the war comes—and it will." Price replied he already knew that because there were Klansmen in his group who were Silver Shirts.

"We have Klansmen everywhere. Hundreds of Klansmen are also police officers," Price said. At the end of the meeting, Price said, "I have a word of warning for you. There are Jews who are monitoring our activities. Beware."

Case, whose smugness led him to believe he could smell Jews, merely laughed.

Potentially Crippling Rifts

As frightening as these plans reported by White were, Clairville's next report was surprisingly optimistic. He said there were internal rifts, fatal flaws, in every fascist organization he'd seen.

A focused troublemaker could cause devastation. Case and Pelley could barely be in the same room. Plus, the Silver Shirts remaining in the Metropolitan Post were steamed at the American White Guardsman who'd split off to do their own thing.

Lewis sent Clairville and White back into the fray with instructions to be catalysts for discord.

One of the first things they did was plant a stranger at the next Lodge meeting, one who would heckle Case. In his speech that night, Case said that the Silver Shirts and the Nazis were becoming as one. The stranger—actually White's brother—stood and said that he was a veteran who'd fought the Germans in the Great War and he didn't want to have anything to do with Nazis. A surprising number in the audience agreed.

News of the troubling exchange during the meeting reached Pelley, who immediately got on a train heading west to see what he could do to smooth out the Nazi problem, as well as to get the White Guarders to rejoin the Lodge, perhaps as their own post.

A Weaponized Pen

Lewis became an active member of the divide-and-conquer plot. He anonymously wrote a series of magazine articles that exposed the Hans Winterhalder connection between the Friends and the Silver Lodge. The articles were a call to action, asking all red-blooded Americans who were in the Silver Lodge, to join the fight *against* Nazism.

The articles caused a sharp reaction from the Friends. Schwinn told reporters it was all lies: "So what, we sell Pelley's newspaper in our bookstore. We sell many magazines and pamphlets and books. It's a bookstore. What of it?"

To Lewis's chagrin, the information the articles exposed was too specific. There were high-ranking officials in the Silver Lodge who thought items in the articles to be very similar, even down to the wording, of things they'd said in front of Walter Clairville.

Lewis's Agent 33 was in trouble, his mission just about through. But on his way out the door, Clairville convinced Eugene Case to tell what he knew. Lewis, always the troubleshooter, quickly collared Clairville and Case and had them give affidavits. He also arranged to have them interviewed by a Justice Department official, but that was a bust. The fed lawyer was oddly unimpressed with tales of Silver Shirts and Nazis working together to heist weapons and attack the U.S. military.

FDR's Tiny FBI

In May 1934, Lewis—at last!—found he had allies in high places, as FDR asked the Secret Service and FBI to evaluate for him the Nazi threat inside the United States. All agreed the Nazis needed to be investigated, so FDR put J. Edgar Hoover on the job.

As Goebbels noted to Hitler when he first broached the subject of conquering Hollywood, the Depression-era FBI was puny. It began the Nazi investigation with high hopes, only to find themselves spread oleo thin. That year, the FBI would prove to be deadly to bank robbers—John Dillinger coming out of the Biograph Theater in Chicago with the lady in red, Baby Face Nelson in Wilmette, Illinois—but harmless to Nazis.

When lack of results grew obvious, Hoover disregarded

Roosevelt's orders and told his agents to investigate Communism in the United States and let the Nazis be.

Dickstein's Spy

Sam Dickstein's new investigatory body, the House Un-American Activities Committee (HUAC), had a special investigator working for them by the name of R. Robert Carroll. After a briefing from Lewis, who was lingering behind the HUAC scenes, Carroll agreed to go undercover to investigate Nazis in America, beginning in southern California.

Carroll thought big at first: "For my spy team I'll need fifteen men and three women."

The committee countered with: "You'll get three men, one woman, but only if you break off communications with Leon Lewis."

The official explanation for this demand was that Lewis couldn't be trusted to hire the best people for the job, that he gave key assignments to his friends and wouldn't trust an outsider with superior clandestine skills. This was pure bullshit.

To his credit, Carroll agreed and then immediately disregarded the no-Lewis rule. Carroll could see that Lewis's drive to fight fascism was stronger than anything found in the U.S. Congress, and that the mission had a better chance of succeeding if Lewis remained in the mix.

The Angry Glare of Conservative Congressmen

Carroll quietly went to work during summer 1934, assigning one of his men, Emile Dormile, to infiltrate Silver Shirt HQ on South Vermont Avenue. During meetings, one of Dormile's duties was to wait until no one was looking and go out on the street and write down the Silver Shirts' license numbers. Armed with this, and a friend at the DMV, a list of names and addresses could be made.

Dormile, during his undercover mission, had dealings with Walter Clairville, Agent 33, but neither knew about the other. The government spy didn't last long. He was about as subtle as a bulbous schnoz. Within days he observed himself being photographed by surreptitious shutterbugs and vanished from the scene.

Planning a Putsch

Better at his job was another of Carroll's team: William Lucitt, who had a knack for being inconspicuous and filed detailed reports on who was at Silver Shirt meetings in L.A. and Pasadena and what was said by whom. He also gained trust and, while knocking back a few at a tavern, was told the Nazis were planning a *putsch*.

"Jews and Catholics will be stomped," the Nazis bragged.

Carroll's woman agent was Florence Shreve. Her mission was the most successful of all. Attractive and apparently alone, she was invited by wolfish fascists to attend parties where she met top dogs of the Friends of New Germany.

Shreve, who was paid less than either Dormile or Lucitt, spoke excellent German, and had previously done undercover work for Carroll, so he knew she was good.

(Shreve apparently stuck with undercover work long after she was through investigating Nazis. In May 1941, she was kicked out of a White House press conference when her press credentials were discovered to be forged. Who was she working for that day and why was she there? We don't know.)

Dickstein Comes to Town

In August 1934, Dickstein's HUAC completed its hearings back East and came to L.A. Frank Prince and Leon Lewis prepared a witness list and Lewis wrote out the questions that would need to be asked of each witness. At Lewis's suggestion, the L.A. hearings were held in executive session—out of the public eye.

Scheduled to testify first was German consul Georg Gyssling, but Gyssling refused to cooperate on the grounds that he had diplomatic immunity.

Paul Themlitz testified on August 2, Hans Winterhalder on August 3, and Hermann Schwinn on August 6. The men echoed the same message: deny, deny, deny. No, they had nothing to do with Hitler. No, they had nothing to do with the Silver Shirts. No, they didn't train storm troopers (they repeated the lie about those groups being sports troopers). No, they didn't know anything about Dietrich Gefken's plan to infiltrate the National Guard, rob an armory and attack the U.S. military. They admitted that the Friends had more than six hundred members, and yes, some of them were not yet U.S. citizens. What they *were* was anti-Communist!

"We know about Communism from our experiences in Germany," Schwinn insisted. "We are qualified as to the dangers of Communism."

Winterhalder testified, "We are un-Jewish, not un-American."

The L.A. hearings seemed like a waste of time until two U.S. Marines who'd listened to the Nazis' recruiting pitch testified. On August 7, Virgil Hayes and Earl Gray testified that they had observed the Silver Shirts performing militaristic drills, and more important, accumulating a stockpile of arms.

"We went along with them at the request of the Office of Naval Intelligence," said Hayes.

"We were told the Silver Shirts planned to remove Jews from political office, and remove them from the United States, violently, if necessary," said Gray.

The hearings then shifted their focus from the Friends to the Silver Lodge. The L.A. leader of the Silver Lodge, Frederick Beutel was called to the stand.

Beutel's Suspicious Connection

Interestingly, considering that Hitler was attempting to infiltrate the Hollywood film industry, Beutel was assistant trust officer at the Federal Trust & Savings Bank of Hollywood. The president of that bank was Joe Schenck, owner of Twentieth Century pictures, soon to merge into Twentieth Century-Fox, and the brother of Nick Schenck, who ran Loew's Inc., which in turn ran MGM.

The Schencks, Jewish immigrants from Russia, were the most powerful brothers in Hollywood history—and the subject of this author's book *Moguls*, written with acclaimed film director Craig

Singer. So, it is interesting that the Silver Lodge leader was an executive at Joe Schenck's bank, the bank that did major business with the Hollywood studios.

Beutel and his wife were into power genealogy. He was also an officer in the Los Angeles Colony of Mayflower Descendants. Mrs. Beutel was a member of Daughters of Founders and Patriots of America.

Did Schenck, when presiding over bank meetings, know that there was a man at the table who on weekends dressed like an evil boy scout and preached ultimate solutions to the "Jew problem"?

Nazibusters Under Oath

Next to be questioned by Dickstein's investigators were Nazibusters Mark White and Walter Clairville. The men identified themselves only as "veterans" and, to protect Lewis, were not asked how they had come to join the Silver Lodge in the first place.

John Schmidt was also scheduled to testify but, his nerves shot, was recovering in the Palo Alto V.A. Hospital. The L.A. hearings were completed without a mention of Leon Lewis or his spies.

Published Findings

The committee's eventual report stated that "an effort to spread the theory of the National Socialist German Labor Party had been underway in the United States for several years." Agents both foreign and domestic, were trying to inject Nazi ideologies into American culture. Nazism was every bit as big of a threat to the American Way as Communism. Racism and intolerance were perversions of Americanism.

The report recommended legislation be written to limit the ability of foreign propaganda agents from entering the U.S. (It wouldn't be until 1938, however, that Congress would pass the Foreign Agents Registration Act, requiring foreign agents to resister with the U.S. State Department.) The American press mentioned these findings but were far more interested in the handful of Hollywood stars who'd been caught contributing to "Communist causes," a.k.a. unionization.

Naziganda

In those days before television, movie newsreels showed the world how the news looked, something you couldn't get by reading a newspaper. But Hollywood newsreels were extremely limited in what they could depict. Because the big studios produced a global product, they practiced the fine art of offending no one, and the "news" was generally cheerful and adventurous. That said, they did want to cover stories that audiences were interested in, and Hitler was damned interesting, an angry dust storm one could see just beyond the horizon.

Covering Hitler was problematic, however. To get permission to film, they had to agree to include in their footage "some shots which are of propaganda value for Germany." The film crews called it *Naziganda*.

By agreeing to do this, the filmmakers were able to show American cinema audiences images that became part of the evil Nazi gestalt, like skulls and crossbones painted on Jewish shop windows, and the burning of books with Goebbels himself supervising like a conductor before a full orchestra. It was the work of these newsreel film crews that helped convince Americans over the next eight years that Nazism wasn't just a European problem or a Jewish problem but a danger to America as well.

Franz Ferenz

While Big Studio Hollywood was still hesitant to make anti-Nazi movies, pro-Nazi movies were alive and well in L.A. Lewis's spies, as part of their undercover activities, attended these imported films, and took notes. The films were screened in a theater managed by Franz K. Ferenz, a high-ranking member of a pro-Hitler organization called the Friends of Progress. Ferenz was a strutter, full of himself. Other Nazis were in awe of Hitler. Ferenz liked to brag that he was "better than Hitler."

Ferenz was born in Vienna, Austria, in 1889, as Francis Kotausek, and came to America as a young man. By 1919, he'd changed his name to Ferenz and was cofounder of the Ferenz-Martini Art Atelier in Greenwich Village, New York City. Ferenz made a nice living traveling to Europe, buying art, and then selling it in the U.S. On one of those trips, he fell under the Nazi spell.

He wasn't the only member of his family to turn Nazi. He had a sister-in-law who was in the Viennese Nazi Underground movement. Ferenz abruptly quit the New York art scene and moved to L.A. in 1928, opening the Los Angeles Academy of Modern Art in Hollywood.

By 1933, Ferenz was producing pro-Nazi events, including one in which the main speaker discussed Hitler's plans to "sterilize the unfit." The language was solidly pro-genocide. Another speaker gave a speech called "The Jewish Question in Germany" in which Jews were referred to as the "cancer of democracy," which when removed would result in a "resurrection" of Aryan peoples.

In Germany, the Nazis were making new laws, ignoring old ones, a fact lauded by Ferenz and his friends. On their home ground, the Nazis no longer had to wait for parliamentary approval before they acted. They could fire Jews and other political opponents with no other cause. Unions were dissolved, union leaders sent to Dachau.

Ferenz was owner of the Continental Bookstore on West Seventh Street, where Nazi propaganda was available. One pamphlet was entitled "Hitler—What Every American Should Know About the Man Whose Influence Is Felt the World Over." You could buy bronze relief plaques of Hitler and Nazi-themed phonograph records, and take classes in German on the state of the world.

The bookstore was so successful that Ferenz opened the Continental Cinema on West Twenty-fourth Street. When undercover Nazibusters attended the movies there, they were horrified by both the content of the films and the audience reaction. A movie called *Kosher Slaughter* showed a steer being slaughtered, causing a spectator to shout out, "Let's do the same thing to the Jews!" That got a laugh.

To expand his business and show more pro-Hitler movies, Ferenz leased several L.A. theaters, including the Mason Opera House. This turned out to be a mistake. The away-from-home movies drew the wrong crowd and became instantly controversial. After a few showings, the theater was raided, and a judge barred Ferenz from booking any movie houses in the future. Ferenz filed an unsuccessful lawsuit saying that his business had been illegally shut down.

The Wandering Jew

The first anti-Nazi movie to achieve distribution in America was *Der Vandernder Yid* (The Wandering Jew) (1933), a British film presented in Yiddish, which used Nazi Germany as a framework to present a history of antisemitism.

The film didn't perform well at the box office, not because of the subject matter but the bad acting and snail pace. Viewed today, it contains heartbreaking dialogue, such as, "The Nazis burn our books, but they can never extinguish the Eternal Spirit."

Mad Dog of Europe

It would be years before America would be ready for an anti-Hitler picture. In 1933, producer Sam Jaffee (not the actor), and legendary screenwriter Herman Mankiewicz (*Citizen Kane*) tried to develop an anti-Nazi picture called *The Mad Dog of Europe*, but weak-kneed execs made sure it never happened.

"Too inflammatory," was the verdict.

Even by 1935, America preferred to look the other way regarding Hitler's "anti-Jew thing." That year, Nick Schenck of Loews, Inc., imported another British film called *The Wandering Jew,* a remake in English, to exhibit during Yom Kippur in Loew's Theaters that served Jewish communities in the U.S. Big mistake. The film shows a Jew disrespecting a Christian icon. It was the Jewish communities that moved to suppress the film, afraid of what might happen if a gentile went to see it, which apparently none did.

There was great joy in the Roosevelt Building when news came that the Friends of New Germany were disbanding. Leon Lewis gave a mission-accomplished speech and was cheered.

Way premature. Turned out, the Friends were merely morphing into a new and even more dangerous animal.

CHAPTER 12

Birth of the Bund

We are each our own devil, and we make this world our hell.

—Oscar Wilde

The Nazis in Southern California regrouped during the early months of 1936 with a new strategy: They would hide as much as possible behind the American flag, while distancing themselves from Berlin. Any German activist in California who was not an American citizen was urged to become one ASAP. This new organization was *American*, Americans getting together enjoying a common heritage.

To boil it down, it was a rebranding effort. The Friends of New Germany would vanish, and when they reappeared, they'd be known as the German American Bund. The German Foreign Ministry made a public statement that this new Bund was not in any way associated with the Friends of New Germany.

New Leader

The Bund was organized into three regions, or three *Gaus*: East, Midwest, and West. The national Bund leader—who was new—was Fritz Julius Kuhn, a brilliant public speaker, but that was about it for his points of quality. He was a drunk, a womanizer, and a lone wolf. He took the money from recruits, money for dues and money for uniforms, but the uniforms were slow to arrive, ostensibly because he wanted to make sure the brown shirts were not touched by Jewish tailors, but in reality, because he'd spent the money on women and schnapps.

Under his leadership, Bundists now *Sieg-Heil*ed one another while saying, "*Sterbt ein Jude.*" Let a Jew die. They were playing God.

Kuhn had a protruding jaw, a low brow, and maintained a vainglorious yet grim countenance, like a general who regretted slaughtering his enemy, but, alas, it needed to be done. When he spoke in public, that jaw pointed upwards, a picture of arrogance and defiance.

Kuhn was born in Munich in 1896 and fought in the Great War as a German infantry officer. He was a big man, six-two, 240 pounds. After the war he earned a degree in chemical engineering at the Technical University of Munich.

Among Kuhn's uncorroborated boasts were that he'd been a charter member of the Nazi party and had fought beside Hitler at the 1923 Beer Hall *Putsch*. His Nazi heroics aside, his poor character leaped up and bit him on a regular basis. As a young man he'd been arrested repeatedly for petty theft and probably left Germany to avoid jail time.

He came to the U.S. in 1928, lived in Detroit, and worked for America's number-one fascist, Henry Ford. Kuhn became a naturalized citizen in 1934 for public relations purposes, and worked at the Henry Ford Hospital, no Jews allowed. He was always in trouble, usually for attempting to dally with the nurses.

He was also a con artist, frequently passing himself off as a physician even though he was merely an X-ray technician. The last straw came when he annoyed coworkers by practicing his Hitler impression at the top of his lungs in the hospital's dark room.

Out of work, Kuhn joined the Friends of New Germany and—because of his ambition, size, and booming voice—became a leader of its midwestern division, headquartered in Detroit. He put that Hitler impression to work and gave rousing speeches. Hitler's movement, he explained, may seem un-American to the Jews and liberals who'd taken over the U.S., but it was actually parallel to American principles as expressed by the Founding Fathers.

When the Friends became the Bund, Kuhn moved into the top spot. His Hitler impression was loved by Bund members but drew unwanted attention. While Hermann Schwinn was claiming that there were no Nazis in America, Kuhn was walking, talking proof that this wasn't so.

To be a card-carrying member of the Bund you had to demonstrate that you were neither of African nor Jewish descent. After that, you took a pledge and paid nine dollars a year in membership dues.

The Rosh Hashanah Distribution

Leon Lewis was blissfully unaware that the Nazi phoenix in L.A. was rising from the ashes—that is, until Rosh Hashanah, the Jewish New Year, on September 29, 1935, when someone at the *Los Angeles Times* placed a toxic leaflet inside each copy of the Sunday edition. The leaflet bore the title *The Proclamation* and was written in language that mimicked Thomas Jefferson's *Declaration of Independence*. The flyer called for a boycott of all things Jewish. In the clearest language yet regarding the "Jewish problem," the leaflet said that the only solution was to "eliminate" the Jews who had formed a "nation within a nation." Jews, it said, were conspiring against Christian decency. Again, the motion picture industry was singled out as a distributor of Jewish indecency. Hollywood *Judenfilm* was obsessed with sex and crime. The leaflet concluded, in all caps, "BUY GENTILE! EMPLOY GENTILE! VOTE GENTILE!"

In addition to the Sunday *Times* distribution, the leaflet was posted all around L.A., on trees and telephone poles. It wasn't just consciousness-raising. Terrorism was involved as well, as disseminators wallpapered areas near synagogues.

By Sunday afternoon, Leon Lewis's phone was ringing off the hook. Lewis realized he was going to have to restart his undercover operation, at the very least to find out who put the leaflets inside the Sunday *Times*.

Agents N2 and C19

To carry out the mission, Lewis recruited two new undercover agents. They were Neil Howard Ness, who would be known in written communications as Agent N2, and Charles Slocombe, Agent C19.

Slocombe was twenty-eight years old, and an undercover veteran, having infiltrated the Long Beach chapter of the Ku Klux Klan during the 1920s, reporting to the Long Beach police.

Ness, like any good spy, told multiple versions of his personal history. The most often repeated was that he was a mechanical engineer who traveled, in 1930, at age thirty-three, to the Soviet Union, where he was ostensibly, but not really, a supporter of the Communist movement. Returning to America, he became a journalist, writing pieces with a liberal slant. He spent four years as an undercover investigator in Chicago. He was not Jewish but fiercely anti-fascist. During his time in Chicago, he investigated Nazi infiltration into the Illinois National Guard.

In L.A., during his day job, Ness installed air conditioners.

Lewis contacted Ness's old boss in Chicago, received a gleaming reference, and put N2 to work on this new German American Bund.

"When all of this is over, I will write a best-selling book. The greatest spy story ever told," Ness said happily.

Reading the N2 and C19 reports, it becomes clear that though the men were working undercover for Lewis simultaneously, they did not know about each other.

On December 15, 1935, Ness walked into an El Monte, California, bakery known as a Nazi hangout. He glad-handed the Germans gathered there and said he liked the cut of their jib.

Ness had no trouble infiltrating the Bund. He was an American, spoke English without an accent, yet claimed to be a Hitler-phile without peer. Hermann Schwinn was thrilled. Ness could help the Bund seem American.

Americanization

Berlin had been slow to realize the intensity of American xenophobia. It was the foreign nature of the Friends of New Germany that sunk the mission. Other fascists in America distrusted them because they weren't *American* fascists. Thus, German American Bund. It had *American* in its name!

Meetings were now held only in English. American citizenship became compulsory. Schwinn explained, "As U.S. citizens we have the right to open our mouths and demand equality of rights." Schwinn rejected the "Sterbt ein Jude" salute that Kuhn preferred. In L.A., the salute mantra was changed to "Free America."

N2 Gets Inside

"I am a writer, very interested in learning more about your cause," Ness said to Hermann Schwinn.

"I will give you books and pamphlets to help you educate yourself," Schwinn replied eagerly.

Within days Schwinn was sharing inside information with Ness, including the fact that the Nazis had financed the printing of *The Proclamation* and arranged for it to be distributed in the Sunday *Los Angeles Times*.

As had the first round of Lewis's agents, Ness brought his wife along to socialize. She was Danish-born, Esther. The Nesses double-dated with the Schwinns, dining and drinking and gabbing.

Over cocktails, Ness pitched an idea, a German American Bund magazine for youths. Schwinn loved it. What a find this guy was. He was immediately given his own office in the new Deutsches Haus on Fifteenth Street.

New HQ

With the rebranding, the L.A. Nazis had a new HQ. They set up camp in an aging, brown, two-story mansion in the seedy Automobile Row neighborhood. The building previously housed the Ernest Belcher School of Dancing, which promised excellent students jobs in the movies and put on its own "revues" in a 700-seat arena that would become the hall for Nazi meetings.

The new arena also became a Nazi movie theater, where Franz Ferenz would come over from his Continental Theatre once a week and screen the latest pro-Hitler reels, fresh off the boat in San Pedro.

A shooting range was installed where men held target practice with air rifles. There was a restaurant and offices. Schwinn's office was accessed through the bookstore. The restaurant was known as the Gaststube (Restaurant), and was popular in a completely nonpolitical way, with its authentic German food, and red-and-blue checkered tablecloths. Customers loved the colorfully costumed serving wenches, sturdy and buxom, with just a touch of wiriness to their braided blond hair.

And oom-pah music. The bar, decorated with "Germany's Great" travel posters, was called Bierwirstschaft (Beer Bar).

Ness made himself valuable around the Bund, and within a few weeks, there was discussion of bringing Ness into the "inner circle." Ness had his run of the place and submitted to Lewis a precise diagram of the layout of each floor.

C19 and the KKK

Meanwhile, Charles Slocombe, Agent C19, went to the downtown L.A. headquarters of the KKK on Seventh Street and introduced himself as a member of the now defunct Long Beach chapter of the Klan.

"I received a copy of a flyer called *The Proclamation* in the mail," Slocombe said. "I was wondering if I could get more copies."

"Sorry, we're all out," they said.

"Who might have some?" he asked.

"Try the Deutsches Haus on Fifteenth Street."

"Thanks."

"Wait, one moment, why do you want copies?"

"I would like to distribute them. People need to know . . ."

"Oh, excellent. Be sure to put them where they will do the most good."

Hans Meyerhoffer

L.A. German consul Georg Gyssling repeatedly complained to the Foreign Office that the Friends/Bund were hurting more than they were helping. In response to the complaints, a good friend of Rudolf Hess named Hans Meyerhoffer was sent to L.A. to see what was up.

Ness could tell that Meyerhoffer was a high-ranking official of some sort. Bundists tensed up when he entered the room and treated the man with kid gloves. The visitor could toss off threats and everyone continued to be polite.

"Better shape up around here or we're moving the West Coast headquarters to San Francisco," he said. He had everyone beating to his drum.

When Meyerhoffer spoke at the next Bund meeting, the L.A. Nazis learned that, besides being bossy, he could drift into a white-eyed fugue state and exalt his praises for Hitler like a man in church rapture.

Klepto

N2 reported to Lewis that he'd spoken to the barkeep at the Bierwirstschaft.

"Schwinn's character is even weaker than at first suspected," Ness wrote. Schwinn had sticky fingers around the cash register, which was the reason the bar was losing money. He'd been "pilfering all along."

N2 whispered in a number of key ears that Schwinn's fingers

were frequently dipping into the till. This resulted in Schwinn being called out.

"Where does all the money go? You manage this Bierwirstschaft in a lousy way!" said a storm trooper named John Tippre.

Schwinn and Tippre took turns inviting the other to kiss his ass, and it was Schwinn who stormed out. N2 smiled inwardly.

Ingram Hughes, "Great" Writer

Charles Slocombe did get copies of *The Proclamation* and, though he didn't distribute them, he came back empty-handed and asked for more. He became a regular both at the KKK and Bund meetings.

"*The Proclamation* is so well written," Slocombe said to Hermann Schwinn one day. "Who is the author?"

"He is a great writer by the name of Ingram Hughes," Schwinn replied. "We plastered the city with his flyer."

Hughes, Slocombe learned, was a propagandist for the American Nationalist Party. He grew lustful when he thought of "removing Jews from American society" and considered the public execution of Busby Berkeley and Charlie Chaplin to be a natural launch for a national American pogrom against the Jews. Hughes wanted all like-minded men to carry maps at all times, showing the homes of Hollywood's prominent Jews.

Slocombe used his detective skills to trace the source of the flyers. The paper stock, ink, and typeface demonstrated that the flyers came from the Los Angeles Printing Company, where Ingram Hughes worked.

Ness, working independently, learned that among the Los Angeles Printing Company's other employees included a fellow named Joseph Landthaler, who was on the Bund's Political Committee.

Slocombe approached Hughes and offered his services. Hughes liked Slocombe's enthusiasm and took him on as his private secretary. They worked together out of Hughes's boardinghouse office on Fourth Street.

Hughes told Slocombe that he was working on a piece to run in a Nazi periodical called *World Service*. "It will be called 'Antisemitism: A World Survey.'"

As Hughes's right-hand man, Slocombe not only accompanied his boss to meet and woo potential donors, but also surreptitiously read Hughes's mail and reported on its contents to Leon Lewis.

Striking Fear

Hughes and the Bund planned another plastering of L.A. with vile flyers.

"They will be doing it on December 17 between four and six in the morning, when the LAPD is asleep," C19 wrote. "They will be concentrating on areas near synagogues. The emphasis will be on Americanizing the Nazi message, to pit true Americans against Jewish aliens. There is also a troubling legitimization of violence as a tool to achieve their goals."

The new flyer was designed to strike fear into Jewish hearts. It warned Jews that they'd best behave, as patriotic Americans were preparing a solution to the "Jewish problem." It was a thinly veiled reference to genocide.

"It is the duty of American citizens to join in the fight against the Jews," it said.

Another memo to Lewis corroborated that the Nazis were ready to graduate from plastering walls to shooting Jews. The Deutsches Haus shooting gallery replaced its targets with photos of the Jews the men most wanted to shoot. The favorite targets were images of Louis B. Mayer, head of MGM, Congressman Samuel Dickstein, and Samuel Untermyer, who was advocating an anti-German boycott back East.

Necktie Party

It got worse. Hughes told Slocombe that he had a dream.

"We will kidnap twenty of the most powerful Jews, and we will see the sons of bitches swinging from the end of a rope," he said.

"Where will you hang them?" Slocombe asked.

"In the oak grove at Hindenburg Park. There are many nice oak trees there. It is an ideal spot for most any occasion. There are no homes nearby. No one to disturb. A perfect place for a necktie party."

"Aren't you worried about getting caught?"

"Phooey. Every participant will have an alibi. Airtight!"

"How can I help?" Slocombe asked.

"Buy the rope, but not all at one store. Go to several stores, so that you do not arouse suspicion."

"Maybe it would be better if we tarred and feathered them," Slocombe offered.

"No!" Hughes said. "Tar and feathers will wash off. A rope will not."

Hughes went so far as to acquire eight-by-ten glossies of the twenty Jews he'd chosen for lynching. He put the photos up on the wall of his office.

"Memorize their faces!" he ordered his minions. "You must abduct the correct Jews when the time comes."

"Is it just us who will be holding the necktie party, or will there be others?" Slocombe asked.

"Hermann Schwinn's men will be with us. He will be supplying men who know how to keep their mouths shut. I have also discussed it with the Silver Shirts. They are in."

Hughes's plans didn't stop at the necktie party. He planned an all-out pogrom against Jewish businesses.

"We will smash the windows of all Jew businesses," he said.

"Do we have enough guns to do that?" Slocombe asked.

"We do not need guns. We can use slingshots and steel balls. Three shots and the windows will come crashing down."

Another Hughes plan was to have Nazis impersonate exterminators, the kind that fumigate houses and get rid of vermin. "But we will not be exterminating rodents. We will be exterminating Jew rats," Hughes said.

"But how?" Slocombe said.

"Exterminators are allowed access to cyanide," Hughes said, his eyes wild. "We'll make tanks with vents in the top for large hose connections. We can make a portable centrifugal blower. We'll put the hoses into air vents and drop cyanide into an acid solution. The mixture makes gas at a tremendous speed and, forced with a blower, will kill them instantly, thousands of Jew rats killed at once. Women, children, Jews of all sorts killed off. Exterminated! That's the way to get rid of them!"

It took all of Slocombe's acting skills to keep his horror from showing.

Call the Cops

Lewis talked to his connection within the Long Beach Police Department, Captain Owen Murphy, and they assured him that there was enough evidence to arrest Hughes, but Leon Lewis didn't want to go that route.

"Hughes is very good at scary talk, but he is all talk," Lewis said, unaware that what Hughes was describing, the cyanide and acid, was exactly what was to be used on Jewish prisoners in Europe with increasing efficiency. With C19 imbedded so close to Hughes, Lewis figured there would be plenty of time to stop any pogrom, should it materialize.

"Well, okay, but could you do me a favor?" Captain Murphy said. "Can you get me a set of Hughes's fingerprints?"

Lewis said he would. And so Slocombe took Hughes's typewriter to Murphy. The captain dusted it for fingerprints, and Slocombe returned the typewriter to Hughes's office without Hughes ever realizing it was missing.

The Times's Revenge

Using the *Los Angeles Times* as a vehicle to distribute Nazi propaganda turned out to be a mistake. The *Times* was a political force in southern California, an entity that prided itself on journalistic integrity, a noncorrupt island in a sea of corruption. The *Times* called L.A. County District Attorney Buron Rogers Fitts, who directed police detective A. C. Arnold to talk to Leon Lewis.

"We can help you, Lewis," Arnold said. "We can bug their homes and offices."

Lewis liked that idea. They discussed bugging the homes of Hughes and Hermann Schwinn, plus the offices of Silver Lodge head honcho William Pelley in the nine-story neoclassical Merritt Building at the corner of Broadway and Eighth Street in downtown Los Angeles (still standing).

To bug the Deutches Haus, Detective Arnold wore plain clothes and rented the hall for a private party. The Hollywood Branch footed the bill. The incident ended the days when the LAPD seemed to be working against Lewis. L.A. police commissioner Ray Kleinberger became a Nazibusters board member. (During the remainder of the decade, the relationship between local law enforcement and Lewis grew until, by 1938, Lewis was deputized.)

Though evidence had been gathered to prove that Hughes was the author of *The Proclamation*, he was never arrested, as his propaganda was protected by the First Amendment.

California Weckruf

While C19 was investigating Hughes and his plans to hold a necktie party, Neil Ness, Agent N2, was working from deep inside the Bund, cozying up to Hermann Schwinn, editing the German American Bund's newspaper, the *California Weckruf* (Wakeup Call).

Sometimes at meetings, Schwinn asked Ness to take the podium and work the crowd. When that happened, Ness avoided hate talk. Instead, he went on and on about German superiority, and the audience always ate it up.

In a memo to Lewis, N2 wrote, "Schwinn plans for me eventually to give recruiting speeches."

"They Are Talking About Putting Me in Charge"

N2 infiltrated the Nazis at the highest level. "They are talking about putting me in charge of the national Nazi youth movement," he reported.

Because of his position, Ness gathered intelligence of higher significance. Ness could prove that the Bund's antisemitic literature was coming directly from Berlin. The materials were written for an American audience, printed in Germany, and brought to L.A. via German tourist ships.

"The materials are smuggled past U.S. Customs and reprinted by the Bund to mask its German origins. I have been instructed to fill the *California Weckruf* with attacks on Jews, in particular the Jews of Hollywood," N2 wrote.

Ness related to Lewis a terrifying conversation he'd had with Schwinn. Ness asked if Schwinn was going to single out individual Jews for attack or would it be a general attack. Schwinn said it would be specific, the most important Jews.

"Who are you going to choose for your first victim?" Ness asked.

"We are going after Louis B. Mayer—and when we get through with him, he will know he got the works," Schwinn said.

"You better go easy on him. He is a pretty big shot around here," Ness said.

"Ha! Don't you know the bigger they are the harder they fall?"

No Limit to the Nazis' Treachery

With Schwinn, Ness attended secret meetings with German steamship captains in which Schwinn handed over reports to go to Berlin and received instructions from Berlin in return.

Schwinn's language, Ness reported, changed depending on whom he was speaking to. When around Bund members, he delighted in referring to himself as "*Der Führer des Westens.*" But when questioned by D.A. Buron Fitts, he said, "There are no

Nazis in America. They are a German political party and do not exist here."

When Ness asked Schwinn why he'd lied to the D.A., Schwinn replied, "What they don't know won't hurt them."

As consul Georg Gyssling was Hitler's man to govern the content of Hollywood movies, and Gyssling and the Bund didn't get along, Agent N2, from his lofty perch near the very top of the Bund, could foment discord and, maybe, take some of the Production Code heat off the very moguls who were financing Lewis's clandestine war.

We move now to the docks in the nighttime cool as the marine layer comes on big dog feet. A ship flying swastika colors blows her horn, a lonely echoing moan, and patiently enters the harbor . . .

CHAPTER 13

The Hollywood Anti-Nazi League

Propaganda does not deceive people; it merely helps them deceive themselves.
—Eric Hoffer

March 10, 1936. San Pedro, California. A group from the Deutsches Haus, including N2, stood on a pier at the docks, shivering in the chilly evening. They were there to meet the German ship *Oakland.* Docking the big ship was slow and noisy business, but eventually the gangplank dropped and the Bundists were escorted aboard and taken to the captain's quarters.

Schwinn handed the captain a briefcase. All Ness knew was that it contained "reports." In return, the captain gave Schwinn a package wrapped in brown paper and sealed in red wax that was labeled "Translation of Propaganda."

The captain served drinks, and the Nazis drank until they acted like pigs. The captain grabbed one of the women in the room and dragged her off somewhere. Schwinn made a pass at a woman and was punched by the woman's husband. When it was over, Ness needed to help the drunken Schwinn off the ship and into a car.

"He slept on my shoulder all the way back to the Deutsches Haus," N2 reported. Ness took the opportunity to open the brown package Schwinn received from the captain. "They were instructions on how to cultivate Americans into the Nazi movement, and how to push the upcoming Olympic Games in Berlin as proof of Aryan superiority. (Sports historians will recall that the Black American athlete Jesse Owens put a crimp on Hitler's plan.) After reading the contents of the package, Ness carefully resealed it and put it in Schwinn's office.

N2 was able to learn something about the chief of Nazi espionage in southern California that Captain Carl F. Sunderland could not, despite the fact that Sunderland was face-to-face with the man. His name. The "Espionage Chief" was Count Ernst von Buelow.

"He is funding both the Bund and the Silver Lodge. His home is in the hills overlooking San Diego. From his home he can watch every move the U.S. Navy makes in that port," Ness reported.

Schneeberger

Schwinn introduced Ness to a man identified only as Schneeberger, an Austrian Nazi leader who was in L.A. after visiting New York and Chicago, and who said he was on his way to Yokohama. Schneeberger was plotting an attack on the U.S. military in southern California. Ness took it upon himself to dish out some disinformation.

"I told Schneeberger that a small woods ten miles south of Long Beach was the planned site for a new fort. He asked how I knew. I told him I heard it from a friend in the U.S. War Department."

The men traveled together to San Diego where Schneeberger took photos of docked U.S. warships.

N2 reported real-life details that would eventually leak to studio scriptwriters and develop into movie tropes: "I was introduced to a man named Dr. Konrad Burchardi, who wore a monocle. He was called Scarface for the long scar on his cheek, a keepsake from a duel he'd won, he liked to say."

N2 reported that the Bund remained separated into two schools of thought: One consisted of killers and desperadoes who couldn't wait to begin the purge, and the other, moderate followers of Hermann Schwinn, wise enough to know recruiting Americans necessitated more tact than "Let's kill Jews." Schwinn preached moderation when discussing antisemitism, and many saw the wisdom in that.

N2 reported that Schwinn was easily manipulated because he maintained an affable reputation when in public, but in the privacy of Bund HQ, he wielded power in a clumsy and showy way, in a way some men interpreted as insecure. He tended to manufacture morale problems.

N2 reported that high-ranking officials of the Nazi party were "unhappy" with the Bund. Growth was minimal, and efforts to infiltrate the movie industry were sluggish.

A New Rift

Pitting one Nazi leader against another had been effective when defanging the Friends of New Germany snake. So, Leon Lewis was encouraged when N2 reported that Schwinn and Gyssling couldn't stand one another. "Exploitable," N2 wrote.

In fact, only a handful of men at the Bund, hardcore and moderate alike, liked Gyssling. Schwinn sought opportunities to embarrass Gyssling. Gyssling thought Schwinn was sloppy, crooked, degenerate, and in need of careful watching.

N2 reported that his situation had improved: "I have been officially initiated into the German American Bund."

"Insinuate yourself between Gyssling and Schwinn. See if you can cause trouble," Lewis instructed.

Ness, with some social awkwardness, assembled a small crew of pro-Gyssling men who wanted Schwinn out. Like a football team, they huddled.

"I have a plan," Ness said.

The plan was a little bit wacky. It called for the pro-Gyssling group to raise some money and purchase the lease to Deutsches Haus, which would give them the ability to oust Schwinn as the West Coast Nazi leader. Gyssling himself heard about the plan and said he was willing to write a check to purchase the lease but not until Ness verified that it was for sale.

Ness said he'd call the man who owned the building and picked up the phone. Instead of calling the owner however, he called Leon Lewis, who played along. Gyssling agreed to write the check.

Unfortunately for Ness, Gyssling gave the matter some thought and decided against it. He had to look at the bigger picture.

"Schwinn is bad with money and owes a fortune to some powerful Germans. There is no way he would be able to pay those people back if he were ousted," Gyssling said.

It didn't sound to Ness like a real reason, but that was it. And so, the plan fell apart. Ness tried to agitate in the other direction, informing Schwinn that Gyssling was plotting his removal. Schwinn seemed unbothered.

Gyssling had other duties to think about—following orders from Goebbels, for example. He was sending periodic letters to all movie studio heads, beseeching them to not make movies that portrayed Hitler in a poor light.

N2 Under Suspicion

Those were the high points of Ness's career as N2. Upon orders from Berlin, Gyssling and Schwinn agreed to put their differences aside and make up. Gyssling went so far as to call Schwinn the "real leader of the L.A. Bund." Soon thereafter, the Republican Party contacted Schwinn, promising favors if he could deliver the German American vote.

During the autumn of 1936, Ness's role as an informant became insecure. An article in an ADL paper had too many accurate details, reports on meetings held with few men in the room. For the first time, Ness was observed with suspicion.

Schwinn was the first to say it out loud. "Did you ever notice that he is always the first with the glad hand, always the first to ask questions. He is the number-one information seeker."

"He is a journalist, after all," someone suggested.

Schwinn would have none of that: "I think Ness is with the Jew Secret Service."

Ness had known the risks all along. He'd had enough chummy exchanges with storm troopers to know they were looking for an opportunity to execute a traitor. To add to the pressure, Ness's wife was under suspicion as well. Esther took notes during a speaker's lecture at the Deutsches Haus. Later, the speaker asked for a copy of the notes and Esther had to scramble for an answer: "I took them so my husband could review them," she said. "But they've been discarded."

Rather than face retribution, the Nesses withdrew from Lewis's operation during the autumn of 1936. Neil Ness showed up at the Deutsches Haus one last time to support his cover, telling them that if they thought he was a traitor, they could all go to hell.

Ness gave Lewis his last report, and also paid a visit to the director of immigration and naturalization in L.A., telling him that half the Bund members, for all of their talk of being American, were in the U.S. illegally.

Ness's contributions to the anti-Nazi cause were huge. He was the one who'd proven the Bund was getting instructions directly from Berlin. Lewis organized Ness's written reports and saved them for a rainy day, when the U.S. government would be willing to listen. (See the Epilogue for Ness's end story.)

In the meantime, Lewis still had Agent C19. But he would need to recruit another undercover operative to replace N2. It wasn't going to be easy.

Hollywood Anti-Nazi League

June 1936. Hollywood, California. Harry and Jack Warner formed an organization called the Hollywood Anti-Nazi League for the Defense of American Democracy, although the name was quickly truncated to HANL. It was inspired by the Untermyer group back East. They sought to "let the world know the truth about the Nazi regime and their plans" and to fight for the release of what they called "political prisoners" in Germany.

HANL headquarters was on Hollywood Boulevard, next door to Grauman's Chinese Theater, where, out front, movie stars

Within days of Adolf Hitler's rise to power in Germany, his agents began arriving in LA. Their goal: to conquer Hollywood and turn it into a Nazi propaganda machine.

The idea of turning Hollywood pro-Nazi was Dr. Paul Joseph Goebbels's. He was a small, weak-chinned, and clubfooted man who had Hitler's ear and became his Minister of Propaganda.

Leon Lawrence Lewis was the Jewish lawyer who put together a team of spies to disrupt the Nazis in Hollywood. The Nazis called him "LA's Most Dangerous Jew." Like any good spymaster, he was rarely photographed. This is the best image there is, taken circa 1918.

Harry Warner, oldest of the Warner Brothers, was the voice of Hollywood's conscience during the Great Depression, and an early warrior in the fight against the Nazis. *Wikimedia Commons.*

Louis B. Mayer, who managed Hollywood's largest studio, MGM, was also Target #1 in the Nazi plots to kill Hollywood's "big" Jews.

Carl Laemmle, the head of Universal Studios, was the first filmmaker to set up camp in Hollywood, at Sunset and Gower, in 1912.

Movie star Eddie Cantor was a key liaison between the Hollywood moguls and the Nazibusters of Leon Lewis. *Library of Congress, Prints & Photographs Division, LC-B2- 4740-2.*

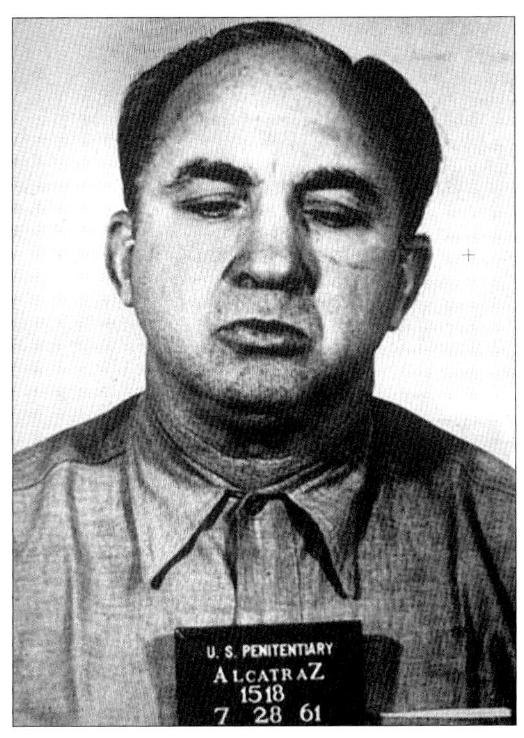

Herman Schwinn, from his twitchy mustache to his penchant for robbing the till at the Bund restaurant, combined a somewhat foolish persona with tremendous ambition to became LA's top Nazi. *Courtesy Community Relations Committee Collection, CRC316, Special Collections & Archives, University Library, California State University, Northridge.*

In 1938, when gangsters across the country were busting up Bund meetings, Hollywood's number-one gangster Mickey Cohen was a hurt machine, letting the Nazis know that Jew-hating was less fun with a broken nose.

Joseph Roos was only thirty years old and working as a script doctor at Universal when he joined Leon Lewis's team. He would quickly become Lewis's co-spymaster, responsible for organizing the information gathered by the spies and getting it to the masses. *Courtesy Community Relations Committee Collection, CRC265, Special Collections & Archives, University Library, California State University, Northridge.*

Nazis smash windows and put up posters outside Jewish shops during the boycott.
Wikimedia Commons; creativecommons.org/licenses/by-sa/4.0/deed.en.

Hollywood newsreels showed a Nazi book burning, images that horrified Americans in a way that crimes against Jews could not.
National Archives and Records Administration, College Park/ United States Holocaust Memorial Museum/Wikimedia Commons.

WANTED

William Dudley Pelley

DESCRIPTION

Age, approximately fifty years; height, five feet, seven inches; weight, 130 pounds; has black hair mixed with gray; heavy eyebrows; wears mustache and a vandyke; has dark gray eyes, very penetrating; has straight Roman nose; wears nose glasses; dresses neatly; distinguished looking; good talker; highly educated; interested in physic research.

Capias has been issued by the Judge of the Superior Court of Buncombe County for the arrest of the above-named party for sentence on conviction of felony, making fraudulent representation, and also for violating the terms of a suspended sentence on another charge by failing to remain of good behavior, and by engaging in, among other things, UN-AMERICAN activities.

Arrest and notify

LAURENCE E. BROWN, Sheriff

Asheville, N. C.

William Dudley Pelley, fascist leader with the soul of a con man.
He went to jail a few times, but he always landed on his feet.
Courtesy Community Relations Committee Collection, CRCms175, Special Collections & Archives, University Library, California State University, Northridge.

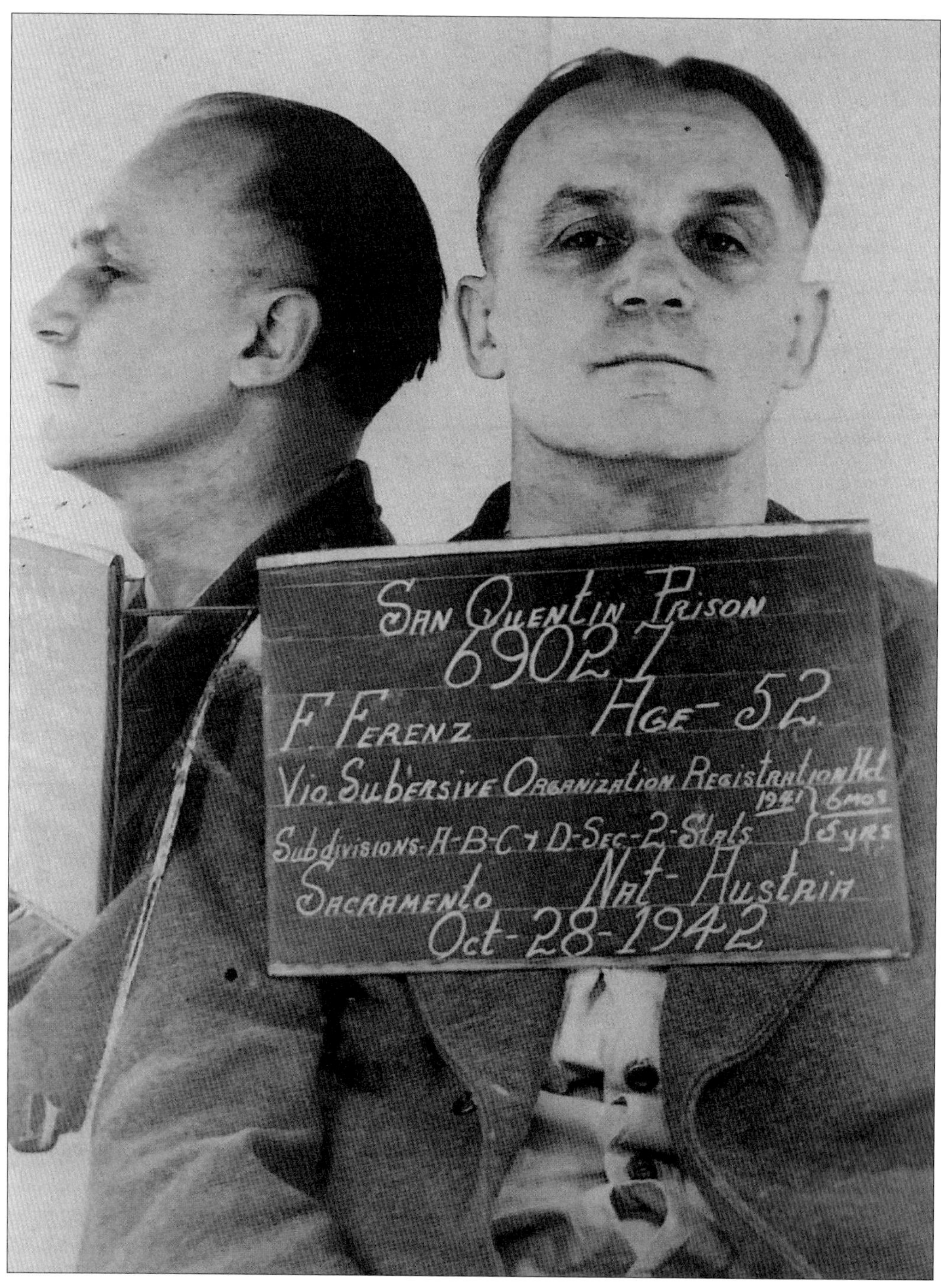

Nazi films were screened in an LA theater managed by Franz K. Ferenz, a high-ranking member of a pro-Hitler organization called the Friends of Progress. He was also assembling a brigade of well-armed Nazi soldiers on motorcycles that could roam Hollywood and "respond to any emergency."
California State Archives.

Leon Lewis tried to get this man, Texas Democrat Martin Dies, and his House Un-American Activities Committee to out the Nazi menace in California, but Dies was more interested in finding communists in the woodwork. *Library of Congress, Prints & Photographs Division, photograph by Harris & Ewing, LC-H22-D- 8425.*

That nice lady on the far left was known for a time as Mrs. Leslie Fry, a Nazi spy who conspired to kidnap Leon Lewis's young daughters. Standing next to her is Henry Allen, whose briefcase was taken by the Nazibusters and contained damaging evidence of a plot to kill Hollywood's top Jews. *Courtesy Community Relations Committee Collection, CRC261, Special Collections & Archives, University Library, California State University, Northridge.*

Aviation pioneer Charles Lindbergh, America's most popular fascist.
Library of Congress, Prints & Photographs Division, LC-USZ62-68852.

William Francis "Red" Hynes was head of the LAPD's anti-communist "Red Squad." Hynes was a complicated guy who liked to work the angles—usually more than one at a time.
UCLA Charles E. Young Research Library, Department of Special Collections/ Los Angeles Daily News/Wikimedia Commons; creativecommons.org/licenses/by/4.0/deed.en.

How close did the Nazis get to the Hollywood moguls? Joseph M. Schenck of Twentieth Century-Fox might've had a Nazi on his lap. (See below.)
UCLA Charles E. Young Research Library, Department of Special Collections/ Los Angeles Daily News/Wikimedia Commons; creativecommons.org/licenses/by/4.0/deed.en.

The starlet Mary Maguire was getting along swell with Joe Schenck, and he might've offered her a contract and bought her a fur, as he so often did for young actresses, but then he learned Maguire was engaged to a Nazi and out the door she went, never to be hired in Hollywood again.
Wikimedia Commons.

Only known image of Julius Sicius, a detail from a group shot, the only one of Lewis's spies to die for the cause. He was caught writing down license plate numbers outside a Bund meeting and soon thereafter was killed on Hollywood Boulevard by a blow to the head.

Ellis O. Jones and Robert Noble were both arrested on information supplied by Nazibuster Sylvia Comfort. While in jail, they were beaten up by Jewish gangster Mickey Cohen. *Courtesy Community Relations Committee Collection, CRC326, Special Collections & Archives, University Library, California State University, Northridge.*

Helene Bertha Amalie "Leni" Riefenstahl was Hitler's personal filmmaker, but when she came to Hollywood in search of a production deal for her new film, she received the iciest of all shoulders. Speaking of shoulders, here are Leni's, along with the rest of her, as she appeared during her acting career, in the Roman bath scene of the German film *Wege zu Kraft und Schoenheit,* or *Ways to Strength* and *Beauty* (1925). And how she appeared all buttoned up. *Wikimedia Commons.*

Charlie Chaplin as *The Great Dictator* (1940). Some complained that he gave Hitler too much style and grace.

Captured image from *You Nazty Spy!* (1940), the groundbreaking Three Stooges satire from Columbia Pictures. Moe Howard embodies the intense anger that was key to Hitler's charisma. (And Jerome "Curly" Howard was pretty good as Mussolini, too.)

regularly pushed palm prints into wet cement. Leon Lewis made sure to attend every meeting. The Nazibusters and HANL, Lewis insisted, would be most effective if working together.

Screenwriters on the HANL called first dibs on intelligence coming from inside the Nazi and fascist groups, information that would inform the screenplays of the first of a thousand anti-Nazi pictures and, later, TV shows that Hollywood was destined to produce.

The beauty of the HANL was that it was not a secret organization. It was a competing force, crosshairs on the Nazis, openly recruiting new members, scheduling rallies at large auditoriums.

Lewis's troops reported that the Bund was calling emergency meetings: What to do about the HANL rallies? One suggestion was to gas the hall with cyanide and take them all out. Another suggested fountain pens that shot hypodermic needles filled with poison. All suggestions were too complicated.

Members of the Hollywood Anti-Nazi League included:

Director Ernst Lubitsch, who fled Germany to work in Hollywood.

Paul Muni, a Jewish actor, considered one of Hollywood's finest.

Mervyn LeRoy, who was married to Harry Warner's daughter.

Suave leading man Melvyn Douglas.

Jewish screenwriter Howard Koch, who came to Hollywood via Columbia Law School (and would be blacklisted as a communist in the 1950s).

Boris Karloff, king of the Universal monsters, starring in both Frankenstein and Mummy pictures during the 1930s.

Donald Ogden Stewart, screenwriter, Yale graduate, friend of Ernest Hemingway, said to be the basis for the character Bill Gorton in *The Sun Also Rises*—and member of the Algonquin Roundtable. (Stewart would go on to win a 1941 Oscar for writing *The Philadelphia Story).*

Other HANL members were Dorothy Parker and Robert Benchley, also Round Table veterans, and Eddie Cantor, the banjo-eyed performer who we've met. Cantor addressed an HANL meeting held in July 1936 and talked about his pictures being banned in Germany because he was a Jew.

"I'm glad it happened," he explained, "because I don't want to make people laugh who make people cry."

Glorifying Hitler

Over the next few years, the HANL raised relief money for Jewish refugees, organized boycotts against German and Japanese goods, and fought without success for the release of those "political prisoners."

At one meeting before the HANL, Harry Warner said that Warner Bros. would no longer show newsreels before their features containing footage of Adolf Hitler that might be construed as glorifying. No goose-stepping, or Sieg-Heiling. No cheering crowds. (The rule would fall apart in 1938 over a March of Time newsreel called "Inside Nazi Germany." See chapter 16.)

Stars Shine at the Shrine

The first HANL rally at the Shrine Auditorium drew seventy-five hundred people. Because it was a group of Hollywood folks holding the rally, there were another thousand people outside the auditorium hoping to get a glimpse of Fredric March, Ray Bolger, Fanny Brice, Fred MacMurray, Sophie Tucker, and Joan Crawford.

The speakers inside didn't just rail about Nazi activity in Europe, but right there in L.A. as well. The meeting did not go unchallenged, as a paltry twenty-four members of the Bund held a protest outside. One of them was Hermann Schwinn, who didn't need to carry a sign to let people know which side he was on. His mustache told the story.

The Bundists had friends in the arena's security and had no trouble sneaking inside. When one speaker began to harp on Nazi evil, it was Schwinn himself who stood to heckle: "We don't want to hear from this Communist murderer!"

It was a mistake. About a hundred anti-Nazis fell upon the Bundists and beat them to a pulp. One of Schwinn's men was bed-ridden for a week with injuries. Schwinn didn't understand any of it. From New York to L.A., Bund meetings had been attacked by small groups of Jewish men, thugs, and the meetings were always terribly disrupted, and the Jews got the better of it in the resulting fistfight. How could that be? It seemed, by the Nazi way of thinking, against the natural order.

What Schwinn didn't know was that the Jewish men who fought so well when breaking up Bund meetings were chosen for that purpose, powerful men who could kill with their hands: pro killers, bouncers, and boxers, some of them men who'd worn a championship belt and now loosened Nazi teeth.

The Nazis, being smug and unquestioning, always assumed that any Jews they might fight would be soft. Aryans were superior—except, it seemed, when real fights broke out.

"Unheil Hitler!"

HANL protested an article in *Liberty* magazine with the title "Hitler Planning to Be Kind to the Jews?" The answer was no, but you had to read the article to know that. The organization sent the magazine a strongly worded letter, and in response, *Liberty* published a fiercely anti-Hitler article in its next issue.

At its peak, there were approximately forty-two hundred members of HANL, and one thing they all understood was show-biz. So, they produced anti-Nazi radio shows, ideological satire, broadcast on Saturday evenings from 7:30 to 8:00 in L.A. over

KFWB, the L.A. radio station owned and operated by the Warner brothers.

Donald Ogden Stewart was the host of the show, saying things like, "Our cause is genuine democracy and its battle against its one true enemy, Nazi fascism. Our slogan is 'Unheil Hitler!'"

The programs were designed to teach Americans about the evils of Nazism, and to agitate the Nazis as much as possible. The agitation worked, too. During the early morning hours of April 16, 1937, Bundists broke into the HANL HQ next to Grauman's and trashed the place. The LAPD could not have cared less. HANL was a bunch of Hollywood sissies playing politics. Another organization doesn't like you? Ho-hum. Welcome to L.A.

As more celebrities joined the ranks, the HANL exploited the glitz of their fundraisers and get-togethers. They allowed stars to become anti-Nazi spokespersons, which was a bit of a precedent in Hollywood. Hollywood stars were expected to do their jobs and allow the studio-fed movie magazines to tell their stories. They had no real opinions, ever. Now the HANL was going to get actors to do the talking for them.

Not everyone liked it. For the most part the opinionated thespians were ignored, but the *Hollywood Reporter* proclaimed them dim bulbs whose politics would hurt their bottom line.

Using their intensified star power, the organization lobbied for the support of President Roosevelt himself, asking him to call a massive peace conference to promote "the collective defense of democracy throughout the world."

Only late at night, when the HANL hard-cores were hanging out after most had left, did the topic come up: Why were they making radio shows in Hollywood? Why can't Hollywood make anti-Nazi movies?

The answer, of course, was economics. Alienate a group of people and you could measure the dip at the box office. Give them Jeanette MacDonald and Nelson Eddy. Don't mention the nasty business in Germany.

Others called the opinionated actors worse names than stupid. Conservative journalists were quick to speculate that the actors were being manipulated, puppets on a dirty Commie string.

As Hitler completed his third year in power, American films directly criticizing him came exclusively from Poverty Row and fringy studios, none of which could muster much distribution.

CHAPTER 14

Summer Games

In 1940 the Olympic Games will take place in Tokyo. But thereafter they will take place in Germany for all time to come.
—Adolf Hitler, 1937

While Hollywood's moguls remained gun shy about making anti-Nazi pictures, in 1936 the Russians released one called *Der Kampf* (an answer to Hitler's *Mein Kampf*), which documented the rise of Hitler. It was cheap and crude by Hollywood standards but did show scenes inside a concentration camp. The studios, all of which ran their own chain of theaters, were interested in showing the Russian film, with cheaply done subtitles, in American theaters, but first had to get it past the Production Code—which it couldn't.

There were theaters in America that showed pictures that weren't approved by the Production Code. One such theater in St. Louis, Missouri, booked *Der Kampf*, but the local German consul had a fit, screamed at the mayor, and the mayor shut down the movie.

William Bockhacker

The new Nazibuster, brought on to replace Ness was William A. Bockhacker, born in New York City, and thus a U.S. citizen, to German immigrant parents. When he was an infant his family moved back to Germany, and Bockhacker grew up there, not returning to the U.S. until after the Great War, an adult on his own. In America, he worked as an undercover investigator for the William Burns Detective Agency.

Bockhacker was introduced to Lewis by Eddie Cantor. Bockhacker had approached the HANL in search of investigative work, but was turned down—so Cantor said, "I know a guy you should meet." And he introduced Bockhacker to Lewis.

"What's your ethnicity?" Lewis asked.

"I was born in Colorado in 1902, Swiss dad, German mom."

"What did you speak at home?"

"German."

Lewis nodded his approval. "Were you in the war?"

"Too young. I spent the war years, and a few more after that, in Germany. Came to Denver in the late twenties, was out of work, so I moved to L.A."

Lewis hired Bockhacker at a rate of thirty dollars a month and designated him Agent W2.

Bockhacker started right away. He boldly approached Hermann Schwinn and asked if he could help with the *German Radio Hour*, a Bund program that aired in L.A. on KRKD on Friday evenings. The men got along famously and Bockhacker quickly became a trusted confidant of and chauffeur for the Nazi leader. Things couldn't have gone better. Bockhacker became the host of the *German Radio Hour* on nights when Hermann Schwinn, the usual host, was otherwise occupied.

W2 kept his ears open and got the idea that Schwinn was a new man with a keener mindset and improved leadership skills since his dressing down for loose-cannon behavior. Despite the easy rapport he felt with Bockhacker, Schwinn insisted the neophyte supply paperwork verifying his bona fides.

"Give Your Blood or Your Life"

One of the first key pieces of information W2 learned was that every official written communication that Schwinn issued was copied, sent overseas, and was in a thick file in Berlin.

In July 1936, W2 reported on a speech Schwinn gave at a Bund meeting, which included this quote: "We expect all of you to give all that you can for the cause, morally and financially. But there may come a time when you must aid physically as well in a new and greater struggle. We expect you to give your blood or your life, whichever may be necessary." The speech ended with what Schwinn referred to as an "All-American Hitler salute."

"Free America!" the crowd chanted, arms thrust forward, palms down, stiff fingers pointed upward.

W2 reported that Schwinn had been ordered by Berlin to form a front group for the Bund to hide behind if necessary. It was the Militant Organization of Patriotic Americans (MOPA), a phrase once used by Fritz Kuhn to describe the Bund. On paper it appeared to be unrelated to the Bund—that is, unless you looked at the address, 634 Fifteenth Street, the Deutsches Haus.

Lewis wouldn't have to worry about MOPA doing anything in secret. Schwinn named William Bockhacker (W2) to head the front organization, a task that largely consisted of creating a paper trail.

Let the Summer Games Begin

The wars in Europe and Africa expanded during the summer of 1936. German soldiers invaded the Rhineland. Italian soldiers trampled on Ethiopia. Fascists made progress in the Spanish Civil War.

L.A. was cruelly hot that summer, so hot that the air itself seemed to have died, settling into the basin of Los Angeles in a foul brown blanket. The movie people got to play in the hills, where the air was fresher, or out in the desert making Westerns, while others performed on sound stages, every bit as air-conditioned as a Loew's Palace.

For a fervent fortnight, L.A. folks focused on Berlin, where the Summer Olympics became a showcase for Nazism, one rudely interrupted by Jesse Owens.

National Bund leader Fritz Kuhn made the most of the Berlin Olympics, traveling to Berlin for the games and wrangling a handshake and a photo op with Hitler himself. By the time Kuhn was back stateside, he had the photo blown up and framed and was telling people he was Hitler's best buddy.

Truth was, Kuhn was in Hitler's doghouse. He'd been ordered to Americanize his organization, yet was still allowing German citizens to remain in and join the Bund.

Kuhn's peculiar leadership style guaranteed that in the Bund, the right hand was never going to know what the left was doing. His outposts were three thousand miles apart, and he visited them all, alone in a car, drinking and sometimes sleeping behind the wheel.

Flag Furor at the Coliseum

In L.A., the opening of the Olympic games was celebrated in the L.A. Coliseum, the mega-arena built for the 1932 Summer Olympics just off the campus of the University of Southern California. The Bund was there en masse and threw a hissy fit when, during the parade of nations, the German contingent entered the stadium carrying the *old* German flag.

The year 1936 had been, the Nazis hoped, the year that FDR would finally be booted by ballot from the White House. It was a bitter disappointment when Roosevelt won reelection by a landslide.

Pelley in L.A.

In November 1936, Hermann Schwinn wanted to consolidate, to merge the Bund and Silver Lodge, and toward that end invited Lodge leader William Dudley Pelley—who was also "running for President"—and head Bundist Fritz Kuhn to meet and then speak at the Deutches Haus.

While Pelley's arrival went unobserved, Kuhn arrived out front in a Ford Sedan with Michigan plates. As he stepped out of the car, a row of Schwinn's storm troopers clicked their heels and gave a full Nazi salute.

"*Heil Hitler! Heil Kuhn!*" they said.

Schwinn had rehearsed them well. A small band burst into a noisy fanfare. Kuhn returned the Nazi salute, stuck his formidable jaw into the air, and climbed the steps into the Deutsches Haus.

After a brief forehead to forehead discussion between Pelley and Kuhn, each spoke to a packed house in the meeting hall. Both Bundists and Silver Shirts were there in great numbers. There was barely room for air in the meeting hall where eight hundred smoking fascists were packed in.

Pelley spoke first, wearing leather boots and an empty revolver holster. Pelley wore a gray beard under a weak mouth and looked like a guy who wanted to sell you a used car. When introduced by Schwinn, Pelley paraded down the center aisle into the arena behind a color guard carrying the Silver Lodge flag, which was white with a large *L* on it. Pelley strutted at the front of the meeting hall, chest puffed out like Mussolini. Pelley was flanked on either side by four man-mountain bodyguards, ready to snap bones over anything less than worship for their leader. Pelley soaked it in. He strutted for a full two minutes like a vain peacock before beginning his speech.

"I have always loved Germany," Pelley said. "That it why I am proud to claim to be the Adolf Hitler of America."

There were Nazis in the audience that didn't appreciate this outsider, this non-German making a statement like that. But they warmed up once Pelley started talking about hating Jews. He was not euphemistic when discussing the enemy. The speech was ninety minutes of unadulterated antisemitism.

"The Jews in this country are facing the direst event of their lives!" Pelley proclaimed. "They are on the eve of a pogrom. Do you know what pogrom means? It means 'open season on Jews.' In this country there is evil and to defeat that evil we much *finish* the Jew."

Pelley's speech hit the high points of his philosophy. America was controlled by Russia, by Jews, by gentiles who were controlled by Jews. Alf Landon, Republican candidate for president, controlled by Jews. Franklin *Rosen*velt, controlled by Jews. Only one candidate was free of Jewish control, and that was Pelley himself.

Pelley concluded, "By the grace of God I will march up the steps at Washington and show them this is still a Christian nation!"

(Pelley's presidential campaign didn't go well. Washington State was the only state that put him on the ballot, and nationwide he garnered about two thousand votes.)

Between speakers, all stood as a string combo and a trio of sturdy women vocalists performed "Deutschland über Alles." Then Schwinn introduced the main act.

Kuhn, drunk, spoke of his new friendship with Pelley, of the many things the Bund and Silver Shirts had in common, including a common enemy, Communist Jews.

Kuhn said, "We must be prepared to fight for the right kind of government. There will be bloodshed and fighting. There will be a time to wipe out our enemies." Chillingly, Kuhn ended his speech with: "Until the nation is purged, the Bund and the Silver Lodge must forever stick!"

Thunderous applause. The Bund Choir came out and belted out German tunes.

Also speaking at the meeting was Agent C19, Charles Slocombe, whose infiltration of the Silver Shirts was so thorough that he'd been chosen to give the warm-up speech for William Pelley. "The liberal press will never tell you. We will all be better off under fascism than under democracy," Slocombe said.

Henry Allen's Briefcase

During L.A.'s plastic holiday season, Jingle Bells in the desert, 1936, Slocombe uncovered a plot to overthrow the U.S. government. The evidence was discovered by C19 in a briefcase belonging to Henry Allen, a Bundist and two-time felon who'd done prison time. Documents inside the case incriminated George Deatherage, a Minnesota fascist, whose KKK-like group was called Knights of the White Camellia, and a coconspirator, an iron-jawed woman named Mrs. Leslie Fry, who, it was said, had been sent only weeks earlier by Hitler to psychologically pollute America.

Fry was a mature, sober, and dangerous adversary, an instigator of coup d'état. Her top propaganda tool was a startup rag called the *Christian Free Press*. The first to realize that Nazis were losing American recruits because Hitler hadn't been saved by their Lord, Jesus Christ, she devised a Nazi message for Christians. Mrs. Fry was the publisher, editor, and head writer, but her name never appeared.

Slocombe set out to befriend Deatherage and Fry. He had better luck with Deatherage; Fry was not befriendable. Interestingly, she only gave orders—and expected them to be obeyed. Slocombe tried to get inside Fry's brain trust but quickly learned there wasn't one. Her orders came only from an unidentified source in Berlin, an inner circle Slocombe was not going to penetrate.

Fry never spoke in public and Leon Lewis might not have known she existed if it weren't for Slocombe. The briefcase documents were photocopied, and included blueprints and descriptions of military and civil organizations crucial to the U.S. government. The coup was scheduled for after the 1940 elections. Documents identified Fry as a paid Nazi agent, a.k.a. Jane Doe Shishmereff, a.k.a. Jane DeSchishmaress, a recent member of the American League of Christian Women and the Militant Christian Patriots.

Lewis's investigation into Fry's bio revealed a version of her past very different from any she'd claimed over the years. She was the daughter of American parents, born in 1882, in Paris, as Louise Chandor. As a young girl, she wed a well-to-do Russian naval officer but was quickly widowed when Bolsheviks killed her husband in the Russian Revolution. Next seen, she was known as Paquita Louise de Shishmareff. She floated around North America for years (a period about which Lewis could learn nothing) and had surfaced only recently in L.A., now known as Mrs. Leslie Fry. There was a chance that all of those bios were fiction. No one knew who she was, only that she needed to be obeyed.

Leon Lewis notified the FBI of the Henry Allen suitcase, and it was seized. Allen thought Fry had betrayed him. Fry, a smart one, suspected Slocombe.

Battle of Hollywood

Hitler found conquering Hollywood fraught with difficulties he hadn't anticipated. The Nazis' weak point was creativity. The Hitler stiffs had none, and you could get nowhere in Hollywood without it. You had to have that spark, and those with that spark almost never liked Hitler. Plus, the studios were set up so that the real power, the entity that needed to be conquered, was nowhere near a sound stage.

The Nazis and Silver Shirters were not clever enough to worm their way into the Hollywood fabric quietly. There was more shouting than doing. The goal was to "purge the Jews from Hollywood." This picked up a predictable amount of support from blue-collar studio workers, gentiles who felt underpaid during the Depression and were resentful of the Jewish immigrants who ran the industry.

It was common back then for antisemites to assume that Jews ruled all industries, but it was almost always a delusion. FDR was as WASP as they come. Power in America was overwhelmingly Protestant. But Jews really did control Hollywood.

At first, the Silver Shirts were so successful at recruiting in the studios that they formed a "secret Hollywood post." Lewis's operatives listened as Nazis bragged about the situation at the studios.

"One man is fired for his anti-Jew proclivities and another Nazi is hired to take his place," they bragged. The Silver Shirt newspaper, *Liberation*, ran a series of shouting articles on the menace of the Jew-run movie industry, befouling America with un-Christian entertainment.

But with the efforts of Leon Lewis, the tide turned. Nazibusters received regular reports of new Bund/Lodge/KKK recruits who worked at the studios—in particular Twentieth Century-Fox, MGM, Paramount, and Universal—so they could be weeded out.

Picnic in the Park

During Summer 1937, Bockhacker attended a celebration at Hindenburg Park, which had been the proposed site of Ingram Hughes's "necktie party." This was a picnic, a Bund event, but with many Silver Shirts in attendance. There were folks on blankets with food, cold beer, a bandshell and a band, and lots of stuff for the kids. It was a typical American picnic, that is, if you ignored the four-foot wooden swastika and the antisemitic materials for sale, some written by Pelley himself, some by the mysterious Leslie Fry.

At the picnic, W2 observed members of the Bund and Silver Shirt leaders Henry Allen and Kenneth Alexander quaffing lager from pewter steins, artistically glazed and fired. Earwitnesses said they were discussing the many hateful things they had in common. (Alexander ceased to be Leon Lewis's problem soon thereafter when he moved to North Carolina to work closer to Pelley.) The speeches that day, W2 noted, toned down the antisemitism.

One W2 report read that actor Henry Fonda and his wife, perhaps working as spies themselves, came to the Deutsches Haus to eat, after which they visited the Aryan Bookstore. The memo said that the Fondas had to have been blind if they didn't realize the complex's Nazi connections. Shortly thereafter, W2 reported that the Fondas had invited the Bund's Male Choir to sing at their home in the Hollywood Hills.

Exposé in the Sunday Worker

In March 1937, a journalist named John L. Spivak published an exposé about the Nazis in L.A. in a Communist newspaper called the *Sunday Worker*. The piece was written with the cooperation of Leon Lewis and Mendel Silberberg, and told of "international intrigue, espionage, and activities designed to undermine a democratic government." Designed to incite a strong public reaction, the article was a disappointment in that sense, but it also exposed to the Bund how much was known about them.

At about this time, there came to L.A. the most dangerous antisemitic fascist infiltrator yet—and the kick was, he wasn't an American, and he wasn't a German. He was Irish!

CHAPTER 15

Leopold McLaglen, Terrorist

As someday it may happen that a victim must be found
I've got a little list—I've got a little list
Of society offenders who might well be underground
And who never would be missed—who never would be missed!

—Gilbert and Sullivan, *The Mikado*, 1885

Irish fascist Leopold McLaglen arrived in L.A. in 1937 and joined both the Bund and the Silver Shirts. He was a catalyst for violence, and his plots had the Nazi leaders drooling for blood. He bragged that he was teaching martial arts classes so that Nazis would be able to "kill Jews with *Jiu Jitsu*." He continued: "I have made a list of Jew celebrities in Hollywood. My plan is to firebomb their homes."

In addition to being a vicious antisemite, McLaglen was also the brother of Victor McLaglen, the only man in history to fight a world heavyweight boxing champion, whupped by Jack Johnson, March 10, 1909, and also win an Academy Award, Best Actor in a Leading Role for *The Informer* (1935).

McLaglen's plan was immediately picked up by Slocombe. McLaglen's death list included Jack Benny, James Cagney, Eddie Cantor, Charlie Chaplin, Al Jolson, Sam Goldwyn, Louis B. Mayer, Paul Muni, Joe Schenck, B. P. Schulberg (Budd's dad, a silent movie era producer), Walter Winchell, and William Wyler.

He promised that when the time came, *der Tag*, he'd provide two dozen experienced assassins, both Nazis and Russians. He bragged of frequent strategic discussions with Hermann Schwinn, who in turn consulted with San Francisco's German consul, Manfred von Killinger. He said he knew that there would be criticism, killing that many powerful Jews and Jewish celebrities all on the same night—Charlie Chaplin was beloved, after all—but the benefits would outweigh the negatives.

"We will no longer have to deal with the Hollywood Anti-Nazi League," McLaglen said, eyes on fire. "We will kill the whole damn bunch for all time."

McLaglen's plan ran deep. It included both genocide and coup d'état.

Checklist of Terror

Leon Lewis, reading C19's reports on McLaglen, took the threats very seriously. There were pieces in motion. It wasn't "just talk."

And it got worse: There were plans to use gas grenade launchers to put cyanide into Jewish homes, to throw a beer hall *putsch* just like Hitler's that would coincide with the mass robbery of war materiel from a National Guard armory, and to blow up a munitions plant in San Diego.

McLaglen spoke of bringing in professional killers. "I know White Russians and Nazi boys who will kill Jews happily."

McLaglen demanded to be taken seriously by his enemies. He himself had the skills to execute complex operations and the stomach to commit mass murder.

The Military Plot

McLaglen's military plot was complex. He believed America would leave Germany alone if preoccupied with a potential war in the Pacific: "I will convince the U.S. military that the Japanese are spying on America from submarines off the California coast."

It was McLaglen's military plan that did him in. Slocombe monitored McLaglen as he faked photos and tried to sell them to an officer from the Office of Naval Intelligence (ONI). McLaglen's office was bugged and L.A. County sheriff's deputies listened in as McLaglen incriminated himself. He was arrested and charged with extortion and preparing false evidence.

C19 had a long discussion with McLaglen's prosecutor. He admitted he was an inside man and promised cooperation as long as his name, and Lewis's operation, were kept secret.

As was now his routine when evidence was discovered, Lewis had Slocombe swear out an affidavit describing McLaglen's "terrorist plot," just in case something happened to him before he could get in court.

With McLaglen behind bars, the plans to kill powerful Jews and deceive the Navy slowly fell apart. Nobody knew how much the enemy knew. Suddenly, it was like the government was listening in on their conversations. Paranoia set in. A newspaper article described the case against McLaglen and made it clear that the government knew the contents of their most private discussions.

Now the L.A. Nazis were preoccupied with security.

There was a mole somewhere.

"Poland and War"

The June 1937 edition of the RKO newsreel *The March of Time* was entitled "Poland and War." It gave Americans information regarding antisemitic atrocities.

The narrator said things like "In [Jewish] ghettos, for the first time in many years, pogroms are breaking out" and "In the repeated attacks on Jews are seen the workings of the Hitler machine."

There was no footage of violence being enacted upon Jews, so American politicians were filmed condemning the atrocities.

A Party for Vittorio

Interestingly, Benito Mussolini, who ran Fascist Italy, one of the Axis Powers, was not overtly antisemitic and saw no reason to round up Jews in his country, no reason to restrict Jews socially or professionally.

Even Harry Warner didn't criticize Italy, where Hollywood movies continued to be shown dubbed into Italian. The only restrictions Mussolini put on Hollywood films came not because they were produced by Jews, but because Mussolini wanted Italy's filmmaking business to flourish—and because his young son dreamed of becoming a filmmaker.

In 1937, Mussolini sent his son Vittorio to Hollywood to learn about film production and finalize a coproduction deal with Hal Roach, the comedy genius behind the Our Gang shorts and Laurel and Hardy.

On September 28, Roach threw a party at his estate to celebrate Vittorio's twenty-first birthday, a lavish white-tie affair under the stars, with champagne, two orchestras, and bright with stars—Fred Astaire, Constance Bennett, Cary Grant, Bette Davis.

Roach had the nets taken down and held the shindig on the tennis courts. Vittorio wore a red carnation and spent the evening dancing close to Roach's daughter Margaret.

Outside the grounds, things were tense. Fearing attack, the LAPD had the building surrounded. And for good reason. Anti-fascist activists were plotting to ruin Vittorio's birthday party. The damage came the next day, however, when they took out ads in the papers, listing the war crimes of Vittorio's father, and listing the celebrities who came to the party.

The protests grew larger when Vittorio's father went to Munich with Hitler. FDR gave an anti-Axis speech in which he railed against Germany, Japan, *and* Italy. The backlash became such that Roach scratched the deal with Vittorio.

Benito Mussolini's hands-off policy toward Jews didn't mean he was a nice guy. He'd sent the Italian army down to Africa to slaughter Ethiopians, for example. And his *lassista* attitude toward Jews lasted only until 1938 when Hitler demanded the

Italian leader enact antisemitic laws. In 1943, Hitler took complete control of Italy and the roundup of approximately forty thousand Jews commenced.

Herald-Express Exposé

On November 15, 1937, the *Los Angeles Herald-Express* published a story called "Plot to Massacre L.A. Jews Probed." The story did not connect the plot with the arrest of McLaglen but reported the info as coming from "multiple sources" within local Nazi organizations. It said that an "execution list" of powerful and famous Jews had been drawn up: targets for murder. No names. The article explained that no arrests were made because the plot was "just talk."

Credit for nipping the plot in the bud went to the Los Angeles County Sheriff's Office.

McLaglen on Trial

Wearing a very un-Irish monocle and a finely tailored suit, McLaglen pleaded not guilty to all charges. A trial was held in the bright light of a public courtroom and McLaglen was convicted of attempted extortion. The judge sentenced McLaglen to five years, *but* he would change that to five years' probation if McLaglen agreed to return to England and not come back. McLaglen did just that and became an officer in the Royal Air Force.

For Lewis, it wasn't always that easy. He sought to find a way to jail Henry Allen, the man with the pilfered suitcase, but managed to come up only with evidence of small white-collar crimes. It was just as well, because Allen, had he seen the evidence Lewis had against him, would have known Slocombe was the source.

Lewis and Slocombe feared that the prosecution of McLaglen might threaten C19's secrecy. Slocombe laid low until McLaglen was out of the country, a hiatus from undercover work, then returned to his duties inside the Silver Shirts.

Battle Fatigue

The year 1937 was a tough slog for the undercover Nazibusters, who were beginning to feel the fatigue of living a double life. The thing that kept everyone's nose to the grindstone was yet another congressional investigation into Un-American Activities, a committee to be chaired by Martin Dies, a Texas Democrat.

Dies was an unlikely hero in the fight against antisemitism. He'd once referred to the U.S. as "great, white, and homogenous." When Lewis learned that Dies would chair the committee, he feared that the investigation might target him rather than the Nazis he wanted to expose.

Lewis took an aggressive approach. He contacted Dies, told him of the Nazibusters' work, framed the Nazis as "un-American," and promised to give him not just the names and the evidence, but carefully prepared questions to ask when those men appeared before the committee for a good grilling. In essence, if Dies did things Lewis's way, Lewis would do much of the work for him and the congressman could take credit.

"Too Many Jews"

For the most part, this system worked. Dies's team made a showy investigation while the top secret Nazibusters supplied all the info. The government people still managed to sometimes be pains in the asses. Lewis heard Dies's new guy, Edward Sullivan (no relation to the newspaper columnist and future king of Sunday night TV) was in town. Lewis sought him out without identifying himself. Sullivan, sans filter, immediately showed his true colors.

"There are too many Jews in this lousy city," the investigator said.

"But I read in the papers that you were after Communists," Lewis said.

"Communists. Jews. It is the same thing," Sullivan said.

At which point Lewis introduced himself, grinning as the bigot almost choked on his Juicy Fruit-and-chaw. Sullivan was called back East and a new stooge took his place, this one capable of keeping his mouth shut as he went through the motions.

Return to Hindenburg Park

Late fall 1937, the Bund returned to Hindenburg Park. Guests paid a hefty thirty-five cents apiece to picnic and drink and listen to the speakers, who were L.A. consul Georg Gyssling and Manfred von Killinger, the new San Francisco consul who was better known as a Nazi death squad leader recently in town from Europe.

The audience was kept back from the stage by a formation of storm troopers standing at attention. As Killinger was addressing the crowd, the sound of a single prop plane was heard droning in the distance. It came closer. And closer.

The plane was approaching low, and there was a moment when the Germans feared they were to be bombed or strafed. But in reality, the plane had been chartered by the HANL for the purpose of dropping hundreds of leaflets on the Nazi gathering.

WANTED

Adolf Hitler • For Kidnapping

INDICTED BY WORLD OPINION FOR MURDER, AND KIDNAPPING WITH INTENT TO KILL

In the crowd there was much anger and fist waving at the plane, but Killinger took it well, smiling, shrugging, and getting on with his speech.

"Politically Aware and Socially Responsible"

On December 15, 1937, a Harry Warner pep talk recruited eighty WB employees into the HANL.

"It is time for you all to become politically aware and socially responsible," Harry said, "My father came to this country to escape the same kind of pogrom that Hitler has imposed in Germany."

That same week an agent of the Department of Immigration and Naturalization convinced fed officials to start an investigation into Hermann Schwinn, with the goal of deporting him back to Germany. The evidence? Reports written by N2.

In Hollywood, RKO had a movie camera inside Nazi Germany, and the resulting footage, still a few months away from American screens, would be quite an eye-opener.

CHAPTER 16

On the Rhine with *The March of Time*

Threefold is the march of time, while the future slowly advances, like a dart the present glances, silent stands the past sublime.

—Confucius, 500 B.C.

The January 1938 edition of the RKO-produced newsreel *The March of Time* was entitled "Inside Nazi Germany," using footage by a "roaming cameraman" by the name of Julien Bryan.

When Bryan wasn't allowed in Germany because American newsreels were too anti-Nazi, Bryan wisely said, "That is because we are not allowed to photograph Germany's many 'marvels.'" The Nazis went for the line and let Bryan in to shoot—but only under strict Nazi supervision. Despite the limitations put on the cameraman, his eleven minutes of footage "inside Nazi Germany" was promoted by RKO as cloak-and-dagger stuff, the first footage out of Germany without Nazi censorship.

The newsreel opened with "Beautiful Berlin," shots of the Zoological Gardens and the Brandenburg Gate. People appeared happy, well-clothed. The narrator then reminded the audience that it was an illusion, that the sixty-five million Germans had been whipped into "a nation with one mind. One objective: Expansion."

The film then turned to the mistreatment of Jews: guillotines, Stars of David painted on storefronts, signposts reading, in

German, "Jews Keep Out." The prerequisite "Nazi propaganda" section—Hitler speaking, military parades, *fräuleins* waving hankies at erect Nazi soldiers, pristine everything—didn't play at all the way the Germans wanted it to. Americans saw the propaganda for what it was: fiction, an attempt to whitewash a very dirty business, this Nazi business.

The newsreel then switched gears and included Nazi activity inside the United States: scenes of Fritz Kuhn, Hitler's "loudest mouthpiece" in the U.S. The newsreel ended with the German army, "the greatest war machine in history." If it behaved as war machines of the past have behaved, peace on Earth would be destroyed, along with many people and entire governments. On that note, the narrator ended the newsreel in the standard fashion: "Time . . . marches on!"

In Chicago, "Inside Nazi Germany" was banned because it criticized a nation officially friendly with the U.S. In response, some politicians sang the film's praises. Senator Key Pittman of Nevada said, "I think it is highly desirable that the picture be seen by every American." Others agreed, and the pressure was enough to get the Chicago Film Board to change its mind.

Fritz Kuhn addressed Bund meetings, slamming the film largely because he thought it made him look silly.

In America and abroad, pro-Hitler voices complained that some scenes in the film were "fake." By this, they meant re-creations, a technique that was used regularly and almost always without controversy.

"Roaming" cameraman Bryan added to the controversy by complaining about the film's publicity campaign, which claimed it had been smuggled out of Germany. Still, the controversy served him well, and he went on a lecture tour talking about how he got "inside" Nazi Germany.

In an odd touch to the scene, Warner Bros. dismissed the movie as German propaganda, and banned it from its theaters, claiming that the pro-Hitler images outweighed the anti-Hitler narration. That brought Time-Life Corporation president Henry Luce into the controversy, saying Harry Warner was being "ridiculous" when he failed to see the anti-Hitler nature of the film. Harry's ban earned him slams in the press over censorship, and he eventually relented when his daughter told him she'd watched the footage and didn't find it at all pro-Nazi.

Keep It Nice

There were a surprising number of cinema operators who didn't like anti-anything films, because they caused the audience discomfort, and movie houses were supposed to be places where folks could go to relax.

In L.A., "Inside Nazi Germany" played at the Carthay Circle Theatre and by all accounts was positively received, with audiences seeing it as strongly anti-Hitler and loving it, hissing at images of Hitler and Goebbels and Fritz Kuhn, while cheering scenes from Southbury, Connecticut, where local citizens kicked the Nazis out of town when they tried to build a "Youth Camp" there. (In 2023, your author had the honor of giving the keynote speech at a fiftieth anniversary celebration of the time "When Southbury Said NO to the Nazis.")

In most theaters, The March of Time newsreel was followed by a short film starring Eddie Cantor and Shirley Temple, asking for money for the "March of Dimes"—a play on words—and the name of the new anti-polio charity inspired by President Roosevelt, who'd been disabled by the disease.

New Agents

Late in 1938, Leon Lewis recruited six new Nazibusters. The length and breadth of Lewis's efforts were indicated by the new recruits' eclectic nature. Each would fill a niche to help paint a complete picture of Nazi activity. They were:

Charles Young (Agent Y2), a German-born U.S. citizen who loved Germany but hated Hitler. He had investigative experience, with an expertise in following the money. Lewis paid him fifty dollars a month. (Young remained imbedded in the Bund until Pearl Harbor was attacked in December 1941.)

Roy Arnold (R3), born in the U.S. (Maine), sold life insurance for a living. He refused to be paid as he hated the Nazis' guts and anything he could do to slow them down was a labor of love.

Mrs. Anna Friedman (Agent F, or sometimes written "Mrs. F"). When undercover, she played herself, a society lady. She went to Bund parties and gleaned info from talking to the Nazis' wives.

Harwood E. Park (P8) was an anti-sabotage agent. He was an American-born mechanic, an old-fashioned grease-monkey who could hold a biplane together with chewing gum if that was what you needed. He made the rounds at southern California aircraft factories in search of Nazi infiltration.

Inside the movie studios, the Nazibusters acquired a sleuth with experience investigating cases of antisemitism. He didn't get a spy number but he was Walter Hadel, and his job was to keep Nazis out of the studios, although it was difficult to do a background check on every grip, chef, and cable-puller. It was easier with the technical jobs—sound, camera, art direction, et cetera—as those people came with experience and were known. Hadel wrote that he was most concerned with the casting-couch sex style of some studio executives. It would be easy to get a Nazi into a bigwig's inner circle, if she were a pouty-mouthed starlet.

And lastly, the operation picked up an agent inside local government, capable of keeping tabs on police activity on the city, county, state, and federal levels. He was government insider Jimmy Frost (again, no number), and his mission turned into a courier job, relaying secret messages from the Nazibusters to the LAPD.

In the meantime, the agents still working at Deutsches Haus reported that the Nazis were increasingly paranoid about "Jew spies." For years their plans had fallen through. Something always went wrong, and there was only one possible explanation: moles inside the Bund and the Silver Shirts. Jew spies! Schwinn now regularly called for Bundists in good standing to be shadowed.

"Tell me where they go and to whom they talk," Schwinn said, his upper lip extra twitchy. One time, W2 was called upon to tail a Bund member. He didn't, just reported back that the subject went "straight home."

The reports of Nazi paranoia caused the Nazibusters to arrange new meeting spots. For a time, they got together at a sleazy downtown hotel on Main Street, where guests slept on the bloodstains of those who came before. The place was disgusting, but it had multiple exits in case of emergency.

Speaking of Pouty-Mouthed Starlets

In 1938, a diminutive Australian actress named Mary Maguire had just completed a brief and tepid run at Warner Bros. and, now a free agent, jumped into Twentieth Century-Fox head Joe Schenck's lap.

Schenck never suspected there was anything sinister about the starlet. He was single, a famous swinger, and drew starlets like deer to a salt lick. They wanted a break in showbiz. He gave them a fur and the minimum studio contract. Everybody was happy.

She told Schenck, a habitué of the track, that she was the daughter of a man who, after playing Australian football and boxing, struck it rich breeding Thoroughbreds. She left out the part where she was engaged to a Nazi.

Joe made a couple of public statements to the effect of "I believe in Miss Maguire's career," which indicated carnality, but once Joe heard of her Nazi fella, she was gone.

Was she a spy trying to get inside the Hollywood machine from the top? If so, it didn't work.

"My fiancé and I never talk politics," Maguire said. "How could I work in Hollywood if I were a Nazi?" she asked.

Moot point. Hollywood never hired her again.

Dies Committee Summary

The Dies committee made good use of Lewis's inside dope and published their conclusions as *Report on Activities of Nazi Groups and Their Allies in Southern California*. It was a summary of written reports filed by Lewis's agents: Neil Ness, Charles Slocombe, William Bockhacker, and Charles Young.

The conclusion read: "The Bund was an organization set up by the German government and functioned under the control and supervision of the Nazi Ministry for Public Enlightenment and Propaganda." That is, Dr. Joseph Goebbels.

The document accomplished a great deal for the historical record. It exposed the Bund as part of Berlin's international fascist propaganda network and documented the secret meetings between Bund leaders and suspected German espionage agents, and that the Bund was joined at the hip with other right-wing groups active on the West Coast, most notably the Silver Lodge and the Ku Klux Klan. The briefcase evidence from Henry Allen was presented. The report even called out the elusive Mrs. Leslie Fry as an agent of Hitler's propaganda machine.

It looked briefly like Dies was firmly on the moguls' side when he came to the Warner Brothers Studios for a luncheon with moguls Louis B. Mayer, Hal Wallis, Joe Schenck, Harry Cohn, Walt Disney, and Samuel Goldwyn. Trouble was, Dies was being equally friendly with the other side, as evidenced by his investigators going to the Deutsches Haus to have drinks with Hermann Schwinn. The investigators offered to sell Schwinn details of the investigation on him.

"Do you know how they are getting their information?" Schwinn asked.

"I don't know," the guy said, with a shrug.

The publication of the *Report* was historic but hardly timely. Ten months slogged by after the Nazi portion of the Dies investigation was finished before the report was issued, a time during which the stooge government investigators tilted at communistic windmills.

(Dies, the congressman, would burn Lewis in 1940, authoring a seven-part story in *Liberty* magazine called "Communists in America." Part Five targeted Hollywood, claiming the studios were infested with Commies, writers a lot of them, who were sneaking subtle little Commie messages into Hollywood movies. Shockingly, the article then, without mentioning his name, outed Lewis: "The studio heads for many years maintained an elaborate 'detective agency' whose professed purpose is to keep the producers informed regarding Nazi activities in the United States and particularly in California.")

Annexing Austria

In 1938, a portion of old Chinatown—seedy and dilapidated, seemingly oblivious to European culture, so dense with corruption and violence and multiple layers of inscrutable mystery that the LAPD wouldn't go there—was razed, and the Spanish clock tower of the new Union Station rose in its place.

In Europe, on March 12, 1938, Hitler's army crossed the border into Austria and in two days were marching victoriously through Vienna. Immediately, Austrian Jews were rounded up, beaten, humiliated, and taken away. Seventy thousand Jews disappeared in a fortnight.

In Hollywood, studio personnel directors watched sadly as one by one, every Jewish person they employed in Austria dropped off the grid. One employee who was lucky enough to survive the purge was the nephew of Universal Studios chief Carl Laemmle, Max Friedland, who reported that Nazis rousted him out of bed and dragged him to Gestapo headquarters for interrogation. (Following this incident, the retired Laemmle spent, in his estimation, eighty percent of his time trying to get Jews out of Nazi Germany. Laemmle, by his own count, managed to save about two hundred Jews. Others say the number is actually much higher. He used his own Beverly Hills mansion as a muster point for newly stateside Jews to go through the visa process.)

During the first week of Austria's annexation, every Jewish theater owner had been arrested and charged with tax evasion.

On March 30, 1938, Warner Bros. discontinued all film operation in Austria. On March 31, Jack Warner sponsored a dinner in honor of Thomas Mann, the Nobel laureate novelist, whose books had been burned in Germany. Mann spoke of the impending holocaust and begged Americans to wake up and stop the unthinkable tragedy.

"Conquest—No. 1"

A month later, RKO's *The March of Time* issued their follow-up to "Inside Nazi Germany," this one entitled "Conquest—No. 1." It called Vienna "a new outpost in the ruthless Nazi realm." (Again, Harry Warner, for reasons hard to fathom, refused to show the film in WB theaters, calling it propaganda.)

Proof that Harry Warner was wrong came from audience reactions to the newsreel. Americans watched the demonstrations of military might, and the smug dictators who controlled them, and saw forces of evil, forces that one day would need to be stopped.

Back at Nazibuster HQ, Leon Lewis was a visibly tired man, the hardcopy quasi-encoded records of his spy ops overwhelming his corner office. He alone knew where things were, and even then, only sometimes. He needed help . . .

CHAPTER 17

Lewis Gets a Partner

Organization is something you do before you do something, so that when you do it, it's not all mixed up.
—A. A. Milne

By 1938, Lewis's Nazi-busting activities had him exhausted and disorganized. He found the help he needed in one Joseph Roos, an Austrian by birth but raised in Berlin. Roos was thirty years old and was already working part-time for Lewis in an advisory capacity, but the German invasion of Austria forced him to quit his day job as a script doctor at Universal and become a full-time spymaster. Once he understood what Nazism was all about, he found it difficult to concentrate on boy-meets-girl, boy-loses-girl plots. Lewis sensed Roos's organizational genius and delegated tremendous responsibility upon him.

Although Roos's ancestors were rabbis, Joseph maintained an informal relationship with his religion. He moved to Chicago in 1927, tired of ducking the growing number of Brown Shirts in Berlin. In America he became a reporter for Chicago's German-language paper. One assignment involved a return to Berlin to cover the tenth anniversary of the Weimar Constitution, and he was horrified to see the trickle of Brown Shirts he remembered swollen into a mud-colored sea.

Roos moved on to English newspapers, reporting for the *Chicago Daily News* and the *Chicago Herald-Examiner*, "keeping tabs" on Nazis of the Windy City. He first spied for his country when he was recruited by Colonel George C. Marshall, who would later go on to be U.S. Army Chief of Staff. But in 1933, Marshall was ahead of the curve in understanding the menace that Nazis in America represented. Over the next year, Roos filed a hundred written reports to Marshall on Nazi activity in Chicago.

Lewis–Roos was a match made in Heaven. Lewis was zealous about what he was doing but had no practical experience in running a spy mission. His agents had been very productive but easily burned. He needed a creator of scenarios, a writer of plots, three-dimensional schemes—and that was Joseph Roos.

"They [the pro-Nazi groups] made a lot of talk about what they were going to do to the Jews and so forth, but they always knew we were there," Roos wrote years later. "They never knew who among them was the informer, so they were scared to try anything."

The Roos Decimal System

The first thing that Roos did for Lewis's spy op was to implement a detailed yet efficient filing system. Working long hours, Roos created drawers of index cards, like the Dewey Decimal System card catalog in the library, only with each card bearing the known info for one L.A. Nazi: appearance, address, cohorts, family details, license-plate number, and so on.

The new filing system came in particular handy when Jewish gangsters in L.A.—Mickey Cohen and "Bugsy" Siegel, the most famous—received a phone call from top Jewish hood Meyer Lansky. The boss was in cahoots with New York City Judge Nathan Perlman and Rabbi Stephen S. Wise to use Jewish tough guys in a violent but nonlethal campaign, to let Nazis know Jews intended to fight back. A lot of casual Nazis got their noses bloodied and didn't come to the next meeting. By late 1938, due to violent interruptions, fascist meetings across the country found it increasingly difficult to meet. The Jewish Minutemen were busting up Nazi meetings and heads in Newark, New Jersey. Meyer Lansky and Murder, Inc. were giving the Nazis what-for in New York City. Chicago Nazis were getting beat up by the boxers and tough guys of Kedzie Avenue. In Sharon, Pennsylvania, a Silver Lodge meeting run by William Pelley's second-in-command Roy Zachary, was busted up by World War I veterans and Newark Minutemen. Zachary was forced to flee.

Roos's new filing system allowed Lewis's operation to supply the ONI with a close-to-comprehensive rundown of the names and addresses of the very people who were plotting to attack U.S. ships—should *der Tag* one day come.

(After Pearl Harbor these same lists of Nazis, now more valuable than ever, would be given to U.S. counterespionage forces to keep enemy agents off the piers and out of the ship-building plants.)

Strategy

After instituting his new filing system, Roos concentrated on strategy.

"We should stifle them by causing them legal difficulties," Roos said. "Nickel and dime stuff. Whatever it takes. Annoy them, but from afar."

Roos managed to get Silver Lodge L.A. leader Henry Allen arrested for receiving relief funds through fraud.

Allen was only in jail in San Diego for a matter of hours, but when he walked out and got into a car, Leon Lewis and Charles Slocombe were in a car following him.

Joe Roos had managed to get Allen arrested but failed to do it anonymously. Soon thereafter, Roos was mugged on the sidewalk in front of his house. He was badly beaten and the beating would have gone on and on except a car approached and broke up the party. Joe told his wife that he got the bruises from a fall.

"How many times did you fall?" she asked.

"Jews! Jews! Everywhere"

Berlin was displeased with the in-fighting between California Bund leaders and sent a Gestapo agent to fix it. He was Hans Diebel, who at first just observed. He noticed Hermann Schwinn's inability to maintain an even strain.

Diebel moved right in, became the new manager of the Aryan Bookstore, and regularly received large shipments, ostensibly materials to sell in the store, but suspiciously big. Was something else being smuggled in—with the bookstore as a front? Probably.

Schwinn may not have gotten along with Gyssling, but he did have friends, one of them being Henry Allen. On April 11, Schwinn, Allen, and Slocombe (C19), packed duffel bags full of vile leaflets and went from the Deutsches Haus to Hollywood to cause a fuss.

The leaflets in those bags read:

JEWS! JEWS!

Jews Everywhere!

OUT WITH THE JEWS!!

LET WHITE PEOPLE RUN THIS COUNTRY AS THEY DID BEFORE THE JEWISH INVASION.

Schwinn climbed to the roof of the Broadway Department Store at the corner of Hollywood and Vine. Allen went onto the roof of a bank on the opposite corner, while Slocombe climbed to the roof of Club Cosmo. Schwinn and Allen emptied their duffels over their roof's edge and allowed them to rain down onto the busy intersection. They stood tall and laughed at their leafy bombardment.

Slocombe dumped his leaflets on the roof of the Club Cosmo, so that his duffel bag would be empty when the three men reconnected at Deutsches Haus.

"Leon Lewis Will Be Hearing About This!"

Slocombe joined in the gloating and listened as Schwinn said something that caught his attention.

"Leon Lewis will be hearing about this!" Schwinn said with delight. "His phone will be ringing off the hook!" This was when the Nazibusters learned that the Nazis knew their leader by name.

Slocombe thought for a moment he was about to be outed, but

instead Henry Allen sidled up to him and said, "I just want to tell you how impressed I am with your style."

Schwinn said in front of Slocombe that they'd "known for years" that Lewis was "responsible for all that goes wrong for us." Trouble was, you couldn't believe anything Schwinn said. He was apt to claim anything at any time.

Allen had nothing further to say about Lewis at that time. He returned his attention to Slocombe. (Lewis later thought this through and concluded that "Red" Hynes of the LAPD Red Squad had informed the Friends that he existed. Or perhaps Roos's outing led to his association with Lewis. Whatever, they now knew who the enemy was.)

"You were with the KKK, no?" Allen asked.

"Yes," Slocombe said, "but we never pulled off anything like *this*." Slocombe allowed his eyes to go wild, feigning euphoria over the storm of leaflets.

They spoke in hyperbole: This was "history-making." Lines straight out of T. S. Eliot, "This was disturbing the universe!"

Slocombe's excitement precisely mimicked that of a newly subversive man/boy, serious for the cause but giddy with breaking the rules and getting away with it. Allen was smitten.

"Schwinn says you have been very effective as his right-hand man."

"I am flattered," Slocombe said.

"I think it is time you become a Silver Shirt," Allen said.

"I think that is a wonderful idea! Wunderbar!" Slocombe said, and the men shook hands heartily.

A Kidnapping Plot

As Slocombe was being outfitted into a blue-and-red Silver Shirt uniform, Henry Allen again brought up the name Leon Lewis.

"When the day comes, Lewis will wish he'd never heard of us," Allen said, pounding a palm with a fist.

"What are you going to do?" Slocombe asked.

"Kidnap his daughters," Allen said. "They are seven . . . and *fourteen*." Allen's eyes danced. "We went to his house, you know."

"Who?"

"Mrs. Fry and I."

"To Lewis's home?"

"Yes, but he wasn't there. No one was home."

"What did you do?"

"We broke in. Wore rubber gloves. Wrapped our shoes with oilcloth. We wandered the rooms, taking notes on the layout, plotting escape routes for different contingencies. In the long run, Mrs. Fry decided that breaking and entering wasn't the way to go."

"What did she say to do?"

"She said, 'Write a message threatening his family—his daughters will be kidnapped if he doesn't stop his investigation—and tie it to a brick.' She told me, 'Switch the license plate on your car, drive by the house, throw the brick through a window. Make the note on a printing press so there's no handwriting to trace.'"

Spy vs. Spy

Slocombe, of course, warned Lewis of the threats and evasive moves were made. What happened next is lost in the mists of time. Perhaps "Bugsy" Siegel intervened. This was around the time that L.A. gangsters like Siegel and Mickey Cohen were beating up Nazis on behalf of their Jewish brothers who suffered overseas. The gangsters knew who to brace because they were supplied a list of local Nazis with home addresses.

What we know is that Fry had trouble finding a volunteer to throw the brick. The men were afraid of being caught by cops. Threatening to kidnap was a major crime.

Fry now had enough evidence to call out Slocombe as the spy who always saw to it that Bund plans went wrong, but she still couldn't get Henry Allen to agree. Slocombe countered by saying he suspected Fry herself of being a Russian agent.

Last Act

Fry's last act in L.A., as it turned out, was putting together the second annual Anti-Communist Federation conference.

Her efforts were well infiltrated, and Lewis knew every detail of the plans. He put four additional operatives inside the conference. There were three hundred guests, maybe a dozen reporters, and three thousand protesters in the street, completely overwhelming the event.

Joe Roos, still sore from his beating, had a team working the site, taking photos of everyone coming and going. From the roof of the Chevrolet Building, a Lewis operative was reading license plate numbers through a binoculars while a scribe jotted them down. When the Nazis realized, soon enough, that they were under surveillance and being photographed, they staged a loosely organized retaliation, throwing rocks at the rooftop paparazzi. But they couldn't throw like American men and their rocks fell woefully short.

Inside the event, William Bockhacker (W2) was given the task of "checking the credentials" of all the delegates and pressmen, to make sure "no Jews try to sneak in."

Cops were called and, somewhat surprisingly, they came. The LAPD broke up the protest, and Hermann Schwinn ordered free beer at the bar for all the heroic policemen.

In the entranceway at the Deutsches Haus, the Bundists had hung a banner. It read:

> Track down the head and sponsors of their
> Jew agents in your locality, Los Angeles, Calif.

Then a list of names:

> Leon L. Lewis, 660 Roosevelt Building
> Mendel Silberberg, Roosevelt Building
> Ernst Lubitsch
> Judge Isaac Pacht
> Eddie Cantor

Mrs. Fry gave a speech: "We must attack *big* Jews." She said these Jew men were pigs and had committed gross acts. The "Judeo-Bolshevism" should be investigated and ruined by secrets revealed.

Another speaker was Joseph Ferri, an agent of the pro-Mussolini group the Black Shirts. He said fascists from around the globe needed to fight "shoulder to shoulder." He then went on an antisemitic rant, which caught everyone's attention. Mussolini had been slow to call out Jews as the enemy, so it was interesting that his agent had come aboard with effortless gusto.

The theme of the evening's speeches became familiar. Thumbs-up to Germany and Japan. Thumbs-down to England and Russia. After the talk was over, the conference passed several resolutions unanimously, including one "demanding" that the U.S. Congress make a law prohibiting non-Christians from holding political office.

Following the conference, Mrs. Fry left Southern California, her propaganda mission either complete or aborted. We'd like to think "Bugsy" Siegel gave her the business—slapping around women was a specialty of his—but we don't know. She took a powder, and no threats, tied to a brick or otherwise, ever made it to Lewis's wife and daughters. No kidnapping was attempted.

Schwinn's Ambition

Hermann Schwinn was no longer content with being just the L.A. *Führer.* He wanted to run the national show, which meant taking on Fritz Kuhn. Schwinn said it out loud when in his cups: "The Bund will never Americanize with that clown Kuhn in charge."

Schwinn took a train to New York for a national Bund convention and declared his candidacy. He spoke before the delegates and told them that he had recently returned from Berlin where it had been decided to completely Americanize the Bund, thus making it easier to recruit new members.

What Schwinn didn't say was that while in Berlin, he was shown a document that listed every order he'd ever given in Los Angeles. Not only was he asked to explain the reasons for some of those orders, but he realized, to his horror, that someone in the Deutsches Haus was spying on him and sending reports to Berlin.

Kuhn didn't like the idea of Americanization, didn't trust that it came from Berlin, and refused to acknowledge it. And he was beloved, so he got his way. Schwinn came off like a shrill and sweaty agitator.

Kuhn was reelected *unanimously*. As the convention was going on, Hitler was busy taking more land. Hitler annexed portions of Czechoslovakia. Days later, Nazis marched into the Sudetenland. The Bund, nowhere near Americanized, was delirious with joy.

With increasing frequency, Bund and Lodge plans were disrupted or prevented. W2 wrote to Lewis that the Bund was planning to attack a Communist rally in a Glendale park in a few days. Lewis called the Glendale police, tipped them off, and when the Bundists arrived at the park ready for trouble they were turned away by the cops.

Spies Exposed

W2 reported that working as a Bund driver, he'd chauffeured one Erich Bruening to San Pedro to meet the German ship *Donau*, docking that morning. Bruening photographed American ships in the harbor, met quietly with the captain of the *Donau*, and later showed William Bockhacker his Nazi credentials.

"You see this? This means I outrank everyone in the puny Bund," Bruening said.

Days later, W2 investigated an "economic envoy" from Germany named Helmuth Bollert, and discovered he was under direct orders from Goebbels to attack anti-Nazi forces. W2 figured Bollert to be a formidable foe until he discovered him to be a bad drunk. In his cups, he bragged loudly and boorishly of being a Nazi. He wasn't the sort of guy you'd trust with a secret.

On the other hand, some Nazibuster operations were sophisticated. They teamed up Charles Slocombe (C19) with a new recruit, Harwood Park (P8), and had them on a water taxi, observing and documenting suspicious activities off San Pedro and Long Beach.

The anti-Nazi spies were much better at counterespionage than the Nazis proved to be. Pilot Hans Schiller, they revealed, was flying arms to Mexican fascists. Prince Kurt zur Lippe was revealed as a paid Nazi agent.

C19 picked up a conversation in which Schwinn admitted there were orders from Berlin to urge all Bund members with U.S. citizenship to apply for jobs with defense contractors, in particular Lockheed Corporation and the Douglas Aircraft Company.

Slocombe was a busy guy. From inside the KKK, he picked up intelligence on a dangerous new group called the Civilian Army of American Bluecoats, antisemites who were actively recruiting a Christian army for when the purge came.

Mrs. F attended a party at which drunken Nazis bragged that, when the time came, all the U.S. aircraft would have been tinkered with so that they'd come apart in midair.

Christian Vigilantes Arise!

On September 1, 1938, the Bund and the Silver Lodge got together and distributed a new handbill, which was entitled "Boycott the Movies." The illustration at the top of the flyer showed a man with a disturbingly large nose, a cartoon Jew, standing beside a beautiful and naked woman, teeny-tiny nose, both inside a Star of David.

It read:

Christian Vigilantes Arise!

Buy Gentile. Employ Gentile. Vote Gentile.

BOYCOTT THE MOVIES!

Hollywood is the Sodom and Gomorrah

WHERE INTERNATIONAL JEWRY CONTROLS

VICE—DOPE—GAMBLING

Where Young Gentile Girls Are Raped

By Jewish Producers, Directors, Casting Directors

Who Go Unpunished

THE JEWISH HOLLYWOOD ANTI-NAZI LEAGUE

Controls Communism in The Motion Picture Industry
Stars, Writers and Artists are Compelled to Pay for

COMMUNISTIC ACTIVITIES

The new leaflet made its debut on September 8, when bundles rained down onto downtown L.A. from the rooftops of May Co department store, the Fifth Street Store, and the Spring Street Arcade. Bockhacker was supposed to be one of the men throwing the propaganda off the rooftops. He chose not to, later claimed he had, and was caught.

A leader of the Bund storm troopers, thirty-one-year-old Mike Drey, was watching Bockhacker, saw no rain of leaflets from his rooftop post. He did not confront Bockhacker, however. The issue was delicate. He decided to put Bockhacker to a test, one that would force him to show his hand.

"Bockhacker, I have an assignment for you," Drey said.

"Yes, sir."

"Do you know where the German consulate is?"

"I do. It is Downtown. I pass it all the time, Herr Drey."

"You know, it is the site of constant demonstrations. Jews on the picket line."

"Yes, sir."

"I want you to take a bundle of the new flyers and take them there, make it rain from the roof. Make it rain on the heads of the enemy."

"Yes, sir."

"And take my lieutenant, Werner Stumpf, with you, Bockhacker. Show him how it is done. Stumpf, grab a bundle and go with Bockhacker. He will brief you."

Oddly, Stumpf didn't stick like glue to Bockhacker, perhaps unaware of his assignment's purpose. Instead, Stumpf suggested they get on two roofs, one on either side of the consulate (not within eyesight of each other). Stumpf dumped his bundle. Bockhacker left his still tied closed on a fire escape.

Bockhacker's Adventure

Stumpf reported back to Drey, who slapped a tail on Bockhacker. On foot in downtown L.A., Bockhacker spotted two men, making all the same turns he did. He thought he recognized one of them. When he stopped and looked back, they looked away. If he stared in their direction, they leaned on a wall and lit cigarettes. He got the impression that they didn't want to catch him. They just wanted to watch him. But they made W2 nervous, and he picked up his pace. He was taking long strides as he approached Bunker Hill, once the picturesque perch of oil millionaires' homes but now razed and built up into just more Downtown.

As Bockhacker scrambled for an idea, he looked across Hill Street where it meets Third. There was the touristy funicular, Angels Flight, a narrow-gauge trolley that ran up the steep hillside. Riders passed under an ornate archway painted a golden yellow. It was used a lot when new, back in the day of horses. But now, next to the steep railway, it was for visitors and photo ops. Next to Angels Flight was a tunnel allowing drivers to go through, that is, under Bunker Hill. W2 was saved, much as Alyce Schmidt had been a few years earlier, by a taxi. Bockhacker hailed a cab, not always easy in L.A., and went through the tunnel, leaving his pursuers behind.

Free of his shadows, W2 must've told Lewis the jig was up, because that's where the W2 file ends. In November 1938, Lewis wrote that Bockhacker's cover had been blown, and he was being dismissed as an operative.

That autumn, discord between L.A.'s Jewish organizations threatened a splintered front against the Nazis—that is, until Germany erupted into an antisemitic frenzy, a campaign so outrageous that it solidified Jewish resistance in southern California.

CHAPTER 18

Kristallnacht

There were many ways of not burdening one's conscience, of shunning responsibility, looking away, keeping mum. All too many of us claimed to have known nothing, or even suspected.
—RICHARD VON WEIZSAECKER

In August 1938, representatives of the Anti-Defamation League attended a meeting at Harry Warner's house, where they sought to replace the Nazibusters as suppliers of info to the Dies committee. Many members of the Hollywood Branch were there, but neither Leon Lewis nor Mendel Silberberg were invited. The ADL promised that they would do things "the way they were done in Chicago." The ADL boys tried to trash Lewis's efforts, which resulted in a shouting match, with Louis B. Mayer and Eddie Cantor being strongly on Lewis's side. At the end of the night, the ADL men were told to take a hike.

On August 15, 1938, the HANL held a "political cabaret" event called *Sticks and Stones* to raise money for its anti-Nazi efforts. A series of skits were performed, all of which trashed Nazism (and sometimes the Dies committee) in raucous ways. The cast included Milton Berle, Gale Sondergaard, and John Garfield.

On September 16, 1938, a magazine called *Ken* published information regarding the Deatherage–Fry–Allen plot to kill "big Jews," info that came out of Allen's briefcase. The ADL leaked files to the press. This was the last straw, ending all cooperation between the ADL and the Nazibusters. For years, Lewis had regularly briefed Chicago on Nazi events uncovered in L.A. Those briefings stopped.

On the other hand, Fry and Allen were both out of L.A.'s hair for a while. She was in Europe for a few months, then arrested as an alien risk, trying to reenter the U.S. at Ellis Island, and held captive until the end of World War II.

Hollywood was safe, for the moment anyway. The war went back to one of words. Hermann Schwinn published an article in the L.A. German-language newspaper called "Objectionable Motion Picture People." The article included the real names and origins of Hollywood personalities whose Jewishness was not well known. Edward G. Robinson was originally Emanuel Goldenberg. Who knew?

"Pelly"

The Dies committee had to overcome a potential scandal when letters surfaced, written to Martin Dies from someone who signed his name "Pelly," a misspelling of William Pelley's name. The letter claimed that "Pelly" and the committee were in cahoots.

So, when Pelley was called to testify, the questioning involved him denying that he wrote the letters and no one bothered to ask him whether or not he was plotting to overthrow the government. (When Pelley left the Silver Lodge, he used the anti-Communist work being done by the Dies committee as the reason why the lodge was "no longer necessary.")

The Whispers of Bigots

On September 19, Harry Warner addressed an American Legion convention, destroying the antisemitic myths being spread by bigots, and—in case there were isolationists in the crowd—rallying the troops for the war they knew was coming.

Warner said, "Certain bigots whisper that Hollywood is run by 'isms.' They lie! Drive them out from their insidious propaganda machines, drive out their bunds, their clans, their Black Legions,

Silver Shirts, and Brown Shirts. Help keep America for those who believe in America."

The speech went so well, he had it transcribed, 150,000 copies made, and distributed it to movie houses, media outlets, and American Legion posts.

Night of Broken Glass

November 8, 1938. Strictly translated, *Kristallnacht* means "Crystal Night," but over time has been accepted as meaning "Night of Broken Glass." A Nazi diplomat, third secretary of the German embassy in Paris, had been assassinated in Paris by a seventeen-year-old Polish Jew. The Nazis used this as an excuse to go to war against the Jews. Openly. Ninety-one Jews died in the streets. Seven thousand Jewish businesses were destroyed. From this point on, Jews arrived at the concentration camps by the trainload.

In response to the horror, the HANL held a huge rally entitled "Quarantine Hitler" at L.A.'s Philharmonic Auditorium. Attendance: thirty-five hundred plus. SRO. Director Frank Capra spoke. Donald Ogden Stewart, voice of the organization's radio show, gave a speech.

Actor John Garfield delivered a call to action: "We must fight a militant campaign, ladies and gentlemen, against the rising wave of intolerance both in this country and abroad." He received a standing ovation.

The event was kind of a big deal, dripping with celebrities, and yet none—zero—of L.A.'s daily papers gave it an inch. *Variety* did mention it, but only to criticize it as the sort of event that was bound to hurt the industry's bottom line.

Party at Eddie Robinson's

After the "Quarantine Hitler" event, there was a star-studded party back at Edward G. Robinson's house. Stars: Fred Astaire and Ginger Rogers, Bette Davis, Robert Montgomery. Moguls: Jack Warner, Carl Laemmle; independent producer Walter Wanger. The great director John Ford. All were members of the HANL, and a meeting was held, during which they proposed to lobby for an embargo of German goods. Out of the meeting at Eddie's came the idea to call their new group the "Committee of 56" after the number of men who signed the Declaration of Independence.

In December 1938, with WB financial assistance, the Committee of 56 published a manifesto in a periodical called *Hollywood Now*. They accused the leaders of Nazi Germany of wantonly persecuting defenseless minorities, imprisoning ministers of all religions, enslaving labor, and victimizing their own citizenry.

"They send their agents to spy on us. They exalt Error above Truth, Superstition above Science, Oppression above Justice, and War above Peace," they wrote.

Committee of 56 was the name of the group, but they were smaller in number than that. The manifesto bore only thirteen signatures, but they all represented Hollywood Power: Carl Laemmle, Groucho Marx, Bryan Foy, Henry Fonda (who'd also attended pro-Nazi meetings, perhaps as a spy himself), Claude Rains, Philip Dunne, Bette Davis, James Cagney, Melvyn Douglas, Edward G. Robinson, and Harry and Jack Warner.

Groucho made a toast, "To Warner Brothers. The only studio with any guts."

Not that anyone cared about the numbers. The signing was very photogenic, and a great cluster of photographers were on hand, including all the newsreels.

A Song by Irving Berlin

Two days after *Kristallnacht*, America took a long step toward a unified anti-Nazi effort when Kate Smith asked her friend Irving Berlin (born Izzy Baline) for a song that would be appropriate to celebrate the twentieth anniversary of the end of World War I. Berlin gave her a song that he'd written back then for a musical, but ended up not using as he considered it too somber for a comedy. The song was called "God Bless America," and Kate Smith blasted it out over the radio on the evening of November 10. "Stand beside her, and guide her . . ." And America listened—and stood.

Boom!—patriotism took a quantum leap, and the song has been one of America's favorites ever since.

Leni's Visit

In November 1938, acclaimed Nazi filmmaker Helene Bertha Amalie "Leni" Riefenstahl came to Hollywood to publicize her new film, *Olympia*, which documented the Berlin Olympics two years earlier. She came ashore at New York Harbor, disembarking the *Europa* on November 4, and toured America by rail, stopping in major cities carrying cannisters of her film, looking for distribution deals. No takers.

Notable in her new film were the scenes of the Hitler-centric Opening Ceremonies with fifteen seconds of the Führer himself overwatching synchronized goose-stepping, a sport chilly enough for a winter Olympics and sharp as razor wire.

The rest of the film was pure beauty, a celebration of the athletic form and the ballet of athletic competition. *Variety* called it "convincing, exciting, and dramatic." She even gave Black American Jesse Owens his due, begrudgingly perhaps.

Hitler's Honey

Riefenstahl was born in 1902 in the outskirts of Berlin and entered show business as a beautiful teenager doing sexy dances in German silent films. She became an actress, starring mostly in German pictures, sometimes topless, but also in *S.O.S. Iceberg* (1933), a Universal picture filmed in Greenland.

Her charisma attracted Hitler's attention. Her great beauty and fine long bones approached his Aryan ideal. Upon meeting, he kissed her hands until she had to respectfully pull them away.

When Leni told the Führer that she wanted to be a filmmaker, he made her his personal filmmaker, tasked with capturing the beauty of his Nazi machine on film. She took the assignment and ran with it. Her first film, *Triumph of the Will* (1935), turned her into a superstar, transforming the rhythmic machinations of his war machine into a ballet, reminiscent for some, of the rhythmic march through the woods in *All Quiet on the Western Front.*

In 1936, *Time* magazine put her on the cover, pictured skiing in a bathing suit.

In Hollywood two years later, Leni received the iciest of all shoulders. It was practically unanimous that her political stance, as a friend of the devil, outweighed any beauty or talent she might have, and it rendered moot how good her goddamned film was.

A lone voice in Leni's behalf came from gossip columnist Hedda Hopper, who said the filmmaker had "charm to burn."

Hopper's fellow columnist Walter Winchell spoke for the majority: "She's pretty as a swastika," he wrote.

The moguls said as one that their theaters wouldn't show her film.

"We should give her money so she can spend it on Hitler?" they asked, leaning into their kosher Bowery Boy roots.

At L.A.'s new Union Station, Leni was met by German consul Georg Gyssling, who presented her with a bouquet of flowers and escorted her to a car. They were alone. Leni had hoped for an impromptu press conference as happened when celebrities arrived. She got crickets.

The HANL went after Leni hard, calling her "Hitler's Honey," and the "Führer's fräulein." It took out ads in *Variety* and the *Hollywood Reporter*: "There is no room in Hollywood for Leni Riefenstahl. In this moment when hundreds of thousands of our brethren await certain death..."

Her visit to L.A. became humiliatingly awkward for her. She tried to go to a nightclub but was turned away at the door.

Gyssling gave her a party with two hundred of his best friends at his estate on North Curson Avenue. Riefenstahl later complained that there was not a single celebrity there. She wouldn't have thought it possible. She accomplished zero networking.

She stayed in L.A. until mid-January 1939, still schlepping her cannisters of film, and headed east on the Santa Fe *Chief.* In New York she boarded the *Hansa* and sailed back to Germany.

"How was America?" asked the German press.

"I was welcomed everywhere, except in Hollywood which is controlled by Jews," she said. "Of all the studio heads in Hollywood, only Walt Disney treated me nicely."

A Plea to the Jews Who Control Our Films

That same month the *Hollywood Spectator* hit the newsstands with a banner headline that read: A PLEA TO THE JEWS WHO CONTROL OUR FILMS TO USE THE MIGHTY VOICE OF THE SCREEN ON BEHALF OF THE JEWS WHO ARE VICTIMS OF MANIAC OF GERMANY.

The same issue that called for anti-Nazi films on the front cover contained an article inside that condemned Warner Bros. preproduction of a feature called *Concentration Camp*, calling it an attempt to "capitalize on the tragedy."

This is one of the first usages of the phrase "concentration camp" in the U.S. There had been talk of work camps where conditions were horrible, but still no mention of gas chambers. This film, had it been made, would've been a consciousness-raiser. But it wasn't to be. The Production Code forbade it.

How America was kept in the dark for so long regarding the Holocaust is a subject too complex to explore here. We'll chalk it up to a naive and insensitive American society, slow to think the unthinkable, and slow to sympathize with anything perceived as "foreign," anything happening so far away. Throw in some antisemitism and you've cooked a stew of ignorance.

Schwinn's Perjury

In December 1938, Joe Roos investigated Hermann Schwinn's 1932 Immigration and Naturalization papers. He found that Schwinn had been in L.A. for less than five years, the required minimum for residency in a single city, when he started the citizenship process. *And* he'd lied about it under oath. Schwinn had committed perjury in order to become an American.

Roos took the info to the U.S. Immigration Service and the U.S. Attorney General, and deportation hearings began. During those hearings, Schwinn learned that there were two reasons the government wanted to take his citizenship away. One, he'd lied about his residency. And two, he was not a man "of good character." The first charge was easily proved. It was in writing. To demonstrate the second charge was true, witnesses—armed with info from the Nazibusters—testified that Schwinn threatened violence against Jews daily.

Defending himself, Schwinn called the first charge "an honest mistake." As for the second, he offered up a sob story about being a "hard-working immigrant in search of the American dream." Schwinn screamed that he was being railroaded, that he'd made a simple mistake, writing 1926 when he meant 1927 on a form he'd filled out years before.

Some might have felt sympathy, but Judge Ralph Jenney was not one of them. He revoked Schwinn's citizenship.

While Schwinn's citizenship was being stripped away, Bund members who were seeking U.S. citizenship found that their statuses were being held up. The Nazibusters had given the INS a list of Germans whose American citizenship should be denied because they were agents of the German government.

Same Ol' Same Ol'

As 1938 came to a close, Harry Warner's health went south. Stomach ulcers. He had to be hospitalized for a time. On January 1, 1939, Italy's fascist government banned Hollywood pictures.

All in all, 1938 had been a good one for Lewis's troops. A wedge had been driven between Allen and Fry, Allen was arrested, Fry was gone, and Schwinn was spending more time planning a defense for future court dates than he was plotting to kill Jews. The situation in the world had grown much worse, but Hitler's L.A. clowns continued to in-fight, taking their eye off the ball.

The Nazibusters were still in the same old position: If they didn't battle the Nazis no one would. The FBI was stronger than it had been when Lewis's efforts began in 1933—having gone from five hundred to nine hundred special agents—but remained woefully inadequate to investigate a national problem. The government still seemed far more interested in outing Commies than in combatting Nazis.

And there was more Nazism than ever to combat. Hitler was injecting a steady flow of agents into L.A. and other major U.S. cities, their assignment to gauge public opinion regarding the war in Europe and America's readiness for war, as well as to plan sabotage and devastation should war come. Roos's master list of Nazis grew longer.

News Research Service

At a January 1939 meeting of the Hollywood Branch, Lewis let it drop that he was thinking about writing a tell-all book about the Nazis. Independent movie producer Walter Wanger told Lewis he had a better idea.

"Not a book, a newsletter," Wanger said.

Lewis's eyes lit up. The Nazibusters formed their own press agency, the News Research Service, and went into the newsletter business, an all-out counterpropaganda machine. Generically called the *News Letter*, between early 1939 and Pearl Harbor, the periodical went out to an ever-growing mailing list. Subscribers grew in numbers and in influence.

The editor and principal writer was Joe Roos, who—as a former reporter and Hollywood screenwriter—was perfect for the job. Under Roos's leadership, they went to press once a week, to the minute. The newsletter came out fifty-two times a year for three years.

Roos's power grew. He not only provided content that would efficiently make its way into American hearts and minds, he cultivated power relationships with the U.S. Navy, and members of Congress. FBI director J. Edgar Hoover became an avid subscriber.

The newsletter's influence is best demonstrated by the publication on March 6, 1939, in *Life* magazine, of "Fascism in America," based on Nazibusters evidence. "Star-Spangled Fascists" followed in the May 27, 1939, issue of the *Saturday Evening Post*, written by Stanley High and also based on information culled from editions of the *News Letter*.

One startling *News Letter* article told of Bundists and Silver Shirts sneaking across the Mexican border to meet with Nazi *banditos*. They needed no stinkin' badges.

One notable subscriber was columnist and radio host Walter Winchell, who held a loyal audience estimated at fifty million people per week. On April 17, 1939, Winchell culled info from the *News Letter* to report how the Bund was trying to physically push around anti-Nazi broadcasters. (Roos's counterpropaganda machine continued to break stories even after Pearl Harbor changed everything. For much of 1942, the News Research Service offices were host to an alphabet soup of federal agents. And the movie moguls paid for it all.)

Numbers Up

Bund numbers were up. Schwinn's Americanization efforts had helped recruiting, just as Berlin had hoped. To accommodate the new recruits, Schwinn created the American Patriots, which was affiliated with but not technically part of the Bund, so American men could join without automatically associating themselves with Nazis.

The American Patriots was just one of the new fascist American organizations cropping up, sometimes on their own, sometimes with a nudge from Hitler's agents. There were the Actioners, the American Rangers, the American Vigilantes, the Vindicators, and others—all in recruiting mode, so Lewis and Roos found them easy to infiltrate.

Costume Ball Busted

The Bund distributed a leaflet that claimed L.A. County District Attorney Buron Fitts was a secret member of the German American Bund. Why is hard to say—mischievous disinformation, perhaps. They even faked a photo to show Fitts and Schwinn standing side by side. The lie regarding the D.A. turned out to be a mistake. Fitts was running for reelection and couldn't allow a rumor like that to take root, so he retaliated to demonstrate he was American as apple pie.

Fitts waited until the night of a costume ball at the Deutsches Haus. A band played. Lights were low. Candles burned at each table, which had been pushed to the sides of the room to open up the dance floor. Reflecting the Bund's new demographic, there were many in attendance who wholeheartedly believed in Nazism but spoke no German.

Bursting in was John A. Klein, chief of the D.A.'s Bureau of Investigation.

"What is this?" Schwinn barked.

"D.A.'s office. This is a raid," Klein replied.

"Fitts! He is with the Jews," Schwinn said, and spat on the floor.

Seized in the raid were ten thousand Nazi pamphlets, which weren't in the hall at all but rather packed in bundles in several cars parked outside.

Five Nazis, including Hermann Schwinn, were detained. Schwinn would later gripe that the cops "personally manhandled me, including handcuffing and beating."

"Life's tough" was the response. His arresting officers, Jess E. Winn and Everett P. Davis, shot back that Schwinn had been abusive during the raid, swearing at them in German. They might've smacked him a couple of times.

Schwinn and the others were hauled downtown, held overnight, and released with a warning. Print any more hateful leaflets and they'd be jailed in violation of the California State Syndicalism Act, which prohibited literature that taught, aided, or abetted the commission of a crime.

In the wake of the raid, chief of investigations Klein said that this should be a lesson to anyone else out there who might consider spreading the propaganda of hate against any American citizens, regardless of their religion. "It is the determination of District Attorney Fitts to wipe out such un-American practices. We are determined to nip such practices in the bud," Klein concluded.

Considering that Nazi agents had been working in L.A. County at this point for going on seven years, it seemed odd that Klein would refer to "the bud."

Deputy D.A. William E. Simpson noted an irony. The Bund members were complaining about mistreatment, without once thinking what would have happened to them if they were subversive in their home country.

"They would have been sent to concentration camps," Fitts added. "Bund propaganda is an abuse of their freedom of speech rights. I shall do everything in my power to see to it that professional haters who seek to undermine the morale of our citizenry are strenuously and vigorously fought at every turn."

Nobody thought Fitts was a secret member of the Bund anymore.

International Fascist Federation

Despite spending increasing time in court defending his right to stay in America, Schwinn still had time to bring international fascist groups working inside the U.S. together under the Bund umbrella. Most of the groups were American, but there were also Italian, Japanese, and Mexican fascists, now as one under Schwinn and prepared for violence should Hitler give the word. *Der Tag.*

There was another group that Schwinn recruited into the fold: so-called White Russians, who were so anti-Communist that they would side with Hitler over their own homeland. These were the guys Leopold McLaglen had hoped to use in his aborted kill plan. Now Schwinn was in regular consultation with the top White Russian operative in the U.S., Anastasy Vonsiatsky.

KKK/MGM

In February 1939, Charles Young (Y2), the spy inside the Los Angeles Ku Klux Klan, reported that there was a new plan to assassinate top Jews in Hollywood, with Louis B. Mayer being at the top of the hit list.

Y2 further reported that the plan had gotten past the talking stage and that sniper rifles and ammunition had been purchased.

"Unfortunately, we don't know who the assassin is, or the time and location of the attempted attack on Mayer," Young reported.

The threat was short-lived and demanded no action. The designated shooter, who was never identified, had apparently developed a yellow streak.

Garden Party

On February 20, 1939, Fritz Kuhn held a national Nazi rally in New York's Madison Square Garden, with American flags flying beside swastika flags, photos of George Washington next to photos of Adolf Hitler, and the place packed with goose-steppers and their wives.

Things didn't go as Kuhn had planned. An unemployed plumber from Brooklyn named Izzy Greenbaum disrupted Kuhn's speech by running onto the stage and unplugging his microphone. He was beaten and dragged away, but Greenbaum stole the show. The "rally" in the Garden also drew mass protests outside and brought the ire of Mayor Fiorello La Guardia, who ordered that the German American Bund's books be thoroughly vetted. It was Fritz Kuhn's biggest nightmare: an audit.

Kuhn's Plummet

Aware that forensic accountants were after him, Kuhn drank even more than usual. One night he swervingly followed influential radio broadcaster Walter Winchell—a staunch anti-fascist and close friend of J. Edgar Hoover—into New York's Stork Club, took a seat facing Winchell and stared at him menacingly for about an hour before leaving, long enough for Winchell to mention him unpleasantly in his next day's column.

The vetting of Kuhn's books led to tax evasion arrest warrants for Kuhn as well as the Bund's national secretary, the treasurer and secretary of the German American Business League, the manufacturer of Bund uniforms, a vice president of a company that imported swastika emblems, and the company that printed the Bund's propaganda.

The law caught up with Kuhn in Krumsville, Pennsylvania, speeding westward in a Mercedes-Benz. Kuhn was taken in handcuffs to the nearest justice of the peace, who happened to be twenty miles away in West Reading.

"I'm ready to face the charges, and I'm confident I'll be exonerated," Kuhn said—and his sorry ass was dragged back to New York, where, in addition to tax evasion, he was charged with embezzling almost fifteen thousand dollars from his Bund, most of which he spent on girlfriends.

Kuhn made bail easily enough, but trouble followed him.

Fritz Kuhn visited the L.A. Bund for the final time in 1939. He said, "I am a man on the run. My home has been machine-gunned. I cannot stay in one place. I have three bodyguards with me at all times now."

Kuhn, pushed his head in the direction of three Aryan gorillas standing along one wall. Despite their man-mountain measurements, a big-and-tall store had jury-rigged brown shirts for them.

Schwinn, no fan of Kuhn's, was still certain that Kuhn was being framed by a corrupt government, but most of the L.A. Nazis felt Kuhn was a shmuck who probably was stealing from them.

Back East, Kuhn was in Webster, Massachusetts, one weekend, accompanied by Count Anastasy Vonsiatsky, White Russian leader and husband to a fifty-million-dollar heiress. The men had been drinking in a Webster bar and were entering the Count's large luxury car when policeman Henry Plasse noticed their inebriated gait and decided neither was in any condition to drive.

The officer recognized the men as visitors to Webster and wanted to give them a break. After a short conversation with the men, Plasse decided Kuhn was the more sober of the two and he should drive. The men got into the car, and as Kuhn pulled away he stuck his head out the window and yelled, "Fick you, *mutterficker*."

Officer Plasse recognized his error and leaped into action—literally—landing on the running board of the car. He reached in the driver's side window, grabbed a handful of Kuhn and forced him to stop the car. The men were held at the police station until a court clerk could arrive and fix bail at fifty-nine dollars for the pair, which they scraped together from what they had in their pockets.

Kuhn and Vonsiatsky were given a date to come back for their trial. Sober by now, they didn't look like they intended to come back. As soon as they were gone, Webster Police Chief John G. Templeman couldn't hide his distaste for Kuhn.

"He was just another wise guy who thought this was a hick town and he could stage one of them beer hall *putsch* things and be the dictator in it. We don't let people go swearing at police in this town, drunk or sober."

Kuhn's embezzlement trial was humiliating for him. His main mistress, who'd received much of the embezzled funds, testified against him. The headline read: DER ROMANCE IS OVER.

The jury found Kuhn guilty. He served forty-three months in prison. During that stretch, his U.S. citizenship was revoked.

Report from Deutschland

A few months earlier, the German American Bund's third in command, Arno Risse, had gone to Germany to observe for himself what was going on there. Now, in March 1939, he was back in America and going from Bund outpost to outpost giving everyone the good news.

In L.A., Risse spoke for two and a half hours at the Deutsches Haus. The good news was that World War was inevitable. Germany, he said, looked like "one great armament factory." Everyone in the country was consumed with war preparation. War, he said, would be "all out."

When it came time for Q&A after the speech, someone asked, "What about the Jews?"

Risse's face took on a mischievous look. "They are no longer a problem in Germany," he said.

The question came with a follow-up: "What was done with them?"

"They have all been taken to concentration camps. What has been done in Germany must be repeated here in America," he concluded.

The new blunt rhetoric amped up anti-Nazi anger in L.A., an anger that grew until it came to the Bund's doorstep and exploded into violence.

CHAPTER 19

Deutsches Haus Riot

We will show them that Jews can be tough, and that Nazis too can have problems.

—Meyer Lansky, 1938

By 1939, the German American Bund had suffered a series of unfortunate and painful incidents, in which Bund meetings and rallies were busted up by tough Jewish men—some gangsters, some boxers—breaking a few teeth and smashing things in general. The largest Nazi riot in L.A. came on February 22, 1939. On that date Mickey Cohen, Benjamin "Bugsy" Siegel, and a hundred of their best friends surrounded the Deutsches Haus as a Bund meeting took place inside.

The meeting had been advertised as a celebration of George Washington's birthday—the Bund loved birthdays—and the surprise guest speaker was Hermann Schwinn, who'd been laying low since deportation proceedings began against him.

Schwinn was bitter. *The American Legion had demanded he be deported by resolution, and the damned government was taking it seriously.*

As Schwinn spoke, a bloodthirsty mob assembled out on Fifteenth Street. Along with the gangsters, there were demonstrators, from the Socialist Workers Party and the Young People's Socialist League, carrying signs that read Smash Hitler and Fight Against Antisemitism.

There were a surprising number of women among the protesters, pipingly singing the "Internationale" in clear, untrained voices. A box truck rolled slowly around the block with a loudspeaker mounted on it. Inside, a man broadcasted a relentless mantra, "Down with Hitler! Down with fascism!"

Along with protest signs, it seemed as if every protester had brought a bushelful of rotten vegetables, eggs, and rocks. When a Nazi wearing a brown shirt tried to enter the Deutsches Haus, objects both disgusting and harmful rained down. The most serious injuries at the riot were Nazis who'd been hit by thrown rocks.

Before long, the front steps to the building were slick with rotten vegetable slime. The protesters kept attendance down, as many potential attendees chose safer activities.

The Nazis inside the hall were still not safe, either. Two rocks smashed through front windows. For those that did make it inside, slime dripping from their uniforms, there was a second problem: how to get out.

After an hour delay, there was an attempt to start the rally, and David Hall Jr. got off a couple of remarks—"Washington was a leader of a revolution who was like Hitler today"—before more breaking glass interrupted him.

Police were called from a telephone inside the building, but when they arrived, seven radio cars strong, they only made a half-assed attempt to disperse the crowd, which barely budged.

With Hall keeping his head covered, Schwinn took the podium and managed to insult FDR and several members of his cabinet before realizing no one was listening because of the chaos outside.

Eventually, the police decided against direct confrontation with the angry mob. They cleared the area surrounding a side door and led the Nazis to safety one patrol carload at a time.

After the Deutsches Haus riot, Mickey Cohen felt his job was through, the public had picked up where the gangsters left off.

Santa Monica Mountains Mansion

Even though his message in America was gathering momentum at an agonizingly slow rate, Hitler remained so confident that he would one day be America's president that he ordered his "West Coast White House" to be constructed in the Santa Monica Mountains.

As Nazi troops marched into Czechoslovakia, ground was broken on a fifty-acre compound above the Pacific Palisades. The engineer was Norman Stephens, who had free reign to spend his heiress wife's money. He eventually spent four million dollars to build a four-story mansion surrounded on all sides by a high wall with barbed wire on top.

Details on the construction and the intended use of the property came to the Nazibusters via their inside-government agent, Jimmy Frost.

Frisco's Hunky New Consul

In March 1939, Hitler fired San Francisco German consul Manfred von Killinger and replaced him with a handsome and square-jawed charmer named Fritz Wiedemann. *Life* magazine published photos of his smile and called him "immaculate."

The new consul's message was that Germany and America should get along and combine forces against the real enemy, the you-know-whos. Hitler gave Wiedemann a five-million-dollar budget. A small portion of that went toward propaganda, the rest to plan and execute acts of espionage along the West Coast.

Wiedemann was so good-looking that L.A.'s libidinous gossip columnists followed his every move, his name in bold type. The Nazibusters quickly learned that he was publicly charming but a son of a bitch in private. In fact, investigation revealed a troubling biography for Wiedemann. For one thing, he'd been Hitler's commanding officer during the Great War. After the war, Wiedemann lived privately until Hitler took power. He then joined the Nazi Party and became Hitler's personal secretary. Now he was in San Francisco helping Americans and Germans "to just get along."

Wiedemann's smile was phony, the reasons for his new assignment sinister. He was a spymaster, a veteran of pulling the string on private intelligence ops. His actual task was to join forces with prominent American industrialists—Henry Ford being one of them, fascist to the bone, builder of a hundred fifty thousand trucks to be used by the Nazi army—and campaign for American neutrality in Europe.

One of Wiedemann's first reports back to Berlin was highly critical of the Bund: "Clownish. Needs to be muzzled."

He was an expert organizer. When he set out to build a boycott of Jewish businesses, he successfully recruited more than a thousand German-owned businesses to join his German American Business League.

The glamorous reception he received upon arrival in San Francisco didn't help him do his job. While gossip columnists continued to be enamored by his immaculateness, Wiedemann was a magnet for protesters.

Just when press coverage eased to a simmer, Wiedemann's mistress showed up and the new consul was again in the news. She was Princess Stephanie von Hohenlohe of Austria, who was rumored to be Jewish and had been married to Prince Friedrich Franz of Austria. She once warranted a memo from the Office of Strategic Services—the OSS, the American overseas intelligence agency and precursor for the CIA—as she'd thrown herself into the middle of negotiations between Germany and England. The OSS decided she was "a gold digger." (After the war, Stephanie resurfaced as a chum of columnist Drew Pearson and a writer of German-language newspaper and magazine articles covering the Washington scene.)

A New Enemy

The Nazibusters became so familiar with the inner workings of fascist networks, that they learned there was a new category of enemy infiltrating Southern California: The Japanese. Lewis and Roos took it upon themselves to spy on Japanese agents.

It was Agent F, Mrs. Friedman, who gathered the key intelligence. One evening, she observed the man suspected of being Japan's top agent in L.A., Hajachi, having a meeting with Hermann

Schwinn in the secret-meeting room on the second floor of the Deutsches Haus.

The suspicious activity being monitored by C19 and P8 on their water taxi increasingly involved Japanese vessels. These reports were sent to Commander Ellis Zacharius of the Office of Naval Intelligence (ONI).

HUAC Comes to Town

In May 1939, the Dies committee (HUAC) came to L.A. to hold hearings. An FBI agent, sent in advance to investigate the Silver Lodge, admitted to the Shirts that he thought it was a waste of time.

"I shouldn't have to investigate loyal Americans like you," the special agent said.

Henry Allen told Charles Slocombe that the Bund had "three friends" on the HUAC, so there was nothing to fret about.

Hermann Schwinn testified before the committee on May 18, 1939. His subpoena had required him to come to the hearing with a membership list for the Bund. Schwinn, however, arrived empty handed.

"Isn't it true that there is a list, that the membership files are contained in five wooden boxes kept in a wooden cabinet on the second floor of the Deutsches Haus?" Schwinn was asked.

Schwinn denied it, but the question had stung. For the question to be asked with such specificity, someone with inside knowledge of the Bund's inner workings had briefed the HUAC. Schwinn didn't know who supplied the information, but he was certain that he (or she) worked for Leon Lewis.

Schwinn did eventually turn over a list to the HUAC, but it was the Bund's mailing list, for people to be advised of upcoming social events, and not a Bund membership list.

Neither Schwinn, nor the Nazis who later testified for the committee, revealed a damn thing during their testimony. They repeated the same mantra. They were an American organization.

An anti-Communist organization. Germany sought nothing but good will with the U.S.

"We sing and discuss politics," one Nazi told the committee cheerfully.

Returning to the Deutsches Haus after testifying, Schwinn told his colleagues that he had "bamboozled" the stupid politicians. But he was still nervous about the insider info HUAC had used to ask questions. That, and the recent riot, had resulted in a change in Bund policy: No more leaflets announcing upcoming meetings or social functions.

"From now on, we tell our friends where and when we will meet by word of mouth only," Schwinn said. With that, Schwinn split for Las Vegas, where he eloped with his longtime fiancée.

The couple made their first public appearance together in June, in federal court as the new bride sat behind her husband for an INS hearing regarding Schwinn's deportation. (The deportation process was lackluster compared to the rapid way Schwinn's citizenship had been stripped. The government had other things on its mind and never did get around to deporting him.)

Dies vs. HANL

The Dies committee did nothing to impede Nazi activity in Hollywood, but they did try to put a hurt on the Hollywood Anti-Nazi League, which they proclaimed to be proof that Hollywood and Moscow were in bed together.

The HANL responded loudly themselves, railing against the Dies habit of making accusations without evidence, reiterating that the HANL mission was solely to fight Nazism, and proclaiming none of their members belonged to the Communist Party.

Twentieth Century-Fox production chief Darryl F. Zanuck publicly acknowledged that there were Communists in Hollywood, just about all of them writers, and that they "no more represented Hollywood than a droplet of water represents a lake."

Camp Sutter

On July 3, 1939, L.A.'s first Nazi youth camp opened in Hindenburg Park. It was called Camp Sutter, and it taught German American boys and girls to swim, play baseball, hate Jews, and love Hitler. Boys and girls were trained at the site, at a cost to parents of four dollars a week.

The camp's appearance and the uniforms worn by the children greatly resembled those of the Hitler youth camps back in the *Vaterland.* As they laughed and played, the kids wore swastika armbands and Sam Brown belts, which were part belt, part suspenders, with a strap that went from the front of the belt to the rear diagonally across the chest and over the right shoulder.

The children rose in military fashion to a bugle at 6:30 A.M., spent the day both playing and engaging in military drills. In the evening, they were read bedtime stories taken from German history (and American history in which Germans played a part).

American children were receiving military training, and being brainwashed into believing that when the time came to fight, they should fight for Germany. There were other horrible things going on at the camp, but more about that later.

Spitfires for the RAF

In August 1939, Harry Warner, his health having rallied, traveled to England to consolidate WB distribution there, in case all his employees were drafted.

During the Battle of Britain, in which the RAF battled the Luftwaffe in the skies over England and the English Channel, July through September 1940, the Warner brothers raised money to buy two Spitfires for the RAF, warplanes that were named The President Roosevelt and The Cordell Hull (after the U.S. Secretary of State).

Subtle Forces

With the Nazi loudmouths falling by the wayside, the fascist menace in L.A. grew increasingly subtle. There was persistent talk from the Nazis under surveillance that Hitler was going about the infiltration of America just as he had Germany in the 1920s. There were Nazi cells across America, eighteen cells in L.A. alone, always less than a dozen strong, doing nothing to draw attention to themselves, but ready to work together when *der Tag* came.

Schwinn had a trusted lieutenant named Hans Diebel, who enacted a quiet way to work Nazi thinking into American stream-of-consciousness. Diebel recalled the days when there were only a handful of Nazis in L.A., and they addressed women's lunch groups, singing the praises of Hitler. Diebel organized a small troupe of charismatic Nazis to hold a series of "private discussion groups," small recruiting meetings, visiting the halls of other L.A. clubs, and—offering the friendliest version of Nazism they could come up with—they invited any interested parties to come to the next Bund meeting at the Deutsches Haus.

Many of the clubs of L.A., as you might imagine, were full of society ladies who had tea and finger sandwiches, and held charity events that were coveted in the daily newspapers. One valuable recruit was a socialite named Mrs. Fisher, who then recruited other gals in the L.A. Women's Club.

It was Mrs. Friedman (Agent F), who followed these activities and within a few weeks was able to report the location of several Nazi cells in L.A., one of them Downtown, on Flower Street, uncomfortably close to Lewis's office in the Roosevelt Building.

Invasion of Poland

On September 1, 1939, a million and a half Nazi soldiers marched into Poland and World War II in Europe was on. France and Great Britain declared war on Germany. The escalation of hostilities in Europe caused the FBI, still understaffed but now tenacious, to investigate threats of sabotage and espionage, especially in plants where warships and planes were being built.

After years of giving the Nazibusters a quick side glance, the FBI was now very interested in using Roos's evidence to stem the tide of Nazism in L.A.—if the FBI got the credit, of course.

And this was fine with Lewis, who was far more interested in safety than kudos.

Invocation of the Espionage Act

Three weeks after the invasion of Poland, the U.S. State Department invoked the Espionage Act from World War I, which required that everyone working in foreign embassies register as an agent of a foreign government or face a stiff fine. (This law would come in handy as top California Nazis never bothered to register and could be arrested at any time.)

The escalation of the war in Europe affected the messaging of the Bund as well, which now shifted to "Keep America Neutral." The new message, formulated in Berlin and sent to all Nazi leaders in America, was to influence Americans to believe the first World War was caused by England. The storyline that it was a war to save democracy was a joke. The Nazis spread the word that Great Britain was scum, sick folks who wanted to drag America into a war just to save their own asses. The new Nazi propaganda told Americans they couldn't believe anything they read in the newspapers, that it was fake news. And finally, to get folks to hate FDR, by accusing him of being a pawn of the Jews.

Nazis' recruiting methods relied less on euphemism than before. At a "German Day" celebration, a recruiting booth bore a sign reading:

People who have Jewish blood
Or Colored people do not apply.

At the Nazibusters' increasingly cramped office, a new urgency came with each terrifying story out of Europe.

CHAPTER 20

New Digs and Tragedy

The eternal conflict of good and the best with bad and the worst is on.

—MELVIL DEWEY, inventor of the Dewey Decimal System

The Nazibusters could feel the momentum they'd gained all but wiped out by the invasion of Poland, September 1, 1939, which energized the Nazi movement not just in L.A. but across the U.S. Despite a Nazi cell only a few blocks away, Lewis did not give up his private office in the Roosevelt Building, but all of Roos's files were moved to a new larger space on Hollywood Boulevard catty-corner from the Chinese Theater. The sign on the door read: News Research Service. With extra space, Roos expanded the scope of the *News Letter* to include items from the Europe war.

Ness Testifies

On October 5, 1939, Neil Ness, Agent N2, who'd been retired and laying low, resurfaced briefly to testify before the Dies committee. Wearing a tweed jacket and smoking a pipe, Ness testified behind closed doors for his safety.

"Could the witness identify himself for this hearing?"

"Yes, I am a former member of the German-American Bund."

"Members of the Bund have described that organization as 'American.' Have you found that to be so?"

"No, sir. In fact, Bund members have sworn allegiance to National Socialism and to Adolf Hitler."

"Do you, by your own knowledge, know of incidents involving an interaction between Bund members and foreign agents?"

"Yes, I do. Our leader, Hermann Schwinn, introduced me to a man named Schneeberger who told me he was plotting an attack on the United States military in Southern California."

"Did you know Schneeberger's given name?"

"I did not. I wasn't told and I didn't ask."

"What did Schneeberger say to you?"

"He said he'd been to New York and Chicago and was on his way to Japan."

"Did you pick up details regarding the plans to attack the U.S. military?"

"Only that they were very interested in U.S. Naval ships in San Diego. We drove up and down the coast and he was most interested in anything involving U.S. defense."

"What other Bund schemes were you privy to?"

Ness said he'd overheard top Bundists planning something they called "*der Tag*" or "the day," during which they had plans to black out L.A.'s electricity and contaminate its water supply.

"These plans were part of a scheme to start a war?"

"No. These plans were to be implemented if war comes," Ness said. "The men frequently spoke of espionage during wartime, blowing up power and munitions plants, attacking the docks, creating a siege on L.A."

"Do you feel the Bund could be characterized as a political organization?"

"No. There is nothing political about the Bund. They are part of the German government."

Schwinn "Handles" the Press

Ness's testimony (if not his name) made the papers and sent a flock of reporters to the Deutsches Haus with a thousand questions for Hermann Schwinn.

"No, I've never received funds or packages from German ship

captains . . . No, no one at the Bund has ever planned acts of sabotage or espionage . . . No, we never . . ."

It went on and on.

The rise in Nazi spirit after the invasion of Poland was squelched. Deutsches Haus became like a ghost housc. Whereas the restaurant and the bookstore had been doing steady business, they now felt tainted by the revelations of the HUAC hearings.

Night of the Jaeckel

Less than a week after N2's shocking testimony, Charles Young (Y2) had dinner with a German aviator named Karl Jaeckel who said he'd been given ten thousand dollars by Hitler to sabotage U.S. military airplanes. He felt the Bund was made up of clowns but wondered if Young might be willing to blow up some planes. The gig paid $350 per month.

Young said he'd think about it and reported the plot immediately to Lewis, who passed the tip along to ONI, which made sure neither Jaeckel nor his friends got within throwing distance of an aircraft.

The plot was foiled without Jaeckel ever suspecting Young of being his snitch. In fact, the men continued to dine together, and Y2 learned much more. Jaeckel said the top Nazi spy in southern California was H. A. Russell, a man who dealt in diamonds during the day and espionage at night.

"How many operatives does Herr Russell have?" Young asked.

"About twenty. They are busy forming 'Peace Groups,' convincing stupid Americans to stay out of the war if they know what is good for them."

As 1940 began, the Nazibusters refocused their efforts. The Bund had been weakened—and revealed to be a front for more serious Nazi efforts elsewhere. The spies financed by the Hollywood Branch would still hang out at Deutches Haus to see and hear what they could, but there would be a new emphasis on exposing L.A.'s Nazi cells of less than a dozen people who were plotting acts of sabotage.

Death of Julius Sicius, February 1940

Leon Lewis received new info regarding Camp Sutter, the Nazi youth camp. It was sick enough that kids were being indoctrinated to Nazism at a tender age, trained in infantry skills, but the reality of the camp was even worse than that. This camp, one of fifteen such camps in the U.S. run by the Bund, was less subtle than some others and even more sinister.

During the summer of 1939, ten boys and forty girls had attended the camp—a strange ratio, until you realize that the girls were the whole point. The Bund youth leader was a pervert named William Sellin and at his camps girls were taken one at a time into a basement of the camp's main building and taught how to sexually please adult German men.

"Wife School," they called it.

The info regarding the sex abuse came from the Nazibuster spy at the camp, a man named Julius Sicius, a smallish and balding bartender who had at one time been a charter member of the Friends of New Germany and Robert Pape's secretary.

Sicius was unlike other Lewis spies in that he had spent years being a true believer in the Nazi movement, with the Friends and then the Bund, but had had a change of heart. He worked as a bartender in the Deutsches Haus, which was an okay job until the Bund stopped paying him. He became frustrated and desperate for money. He and Joseph Roos found each other in a roundabout way. It was Sicius's idea to sell photographs of Bund members to a Yiddish newspaper called *The Forward.* The newspaper said thanks but no thanks and referred Sicius to Joseph Roos.

Roos listened patiently to what Sicius had to offer and didn't immediately like the idea. Sicius was not a man who understood the loathsomeness of antisemitism.

"I will hire you to inform on the Bund," Roos said, "But I do not want you to take the job out of bitterness."

Sicius nodded solemnly.

"I do not want you to inform on your former brethren out of a sense of revenge," Roos continued.

"I understand," Sicius said—but Roos was not convinced he did.

"You must do it out of a love and respect for the German American people, who have been tainted by the hatreds of the Bund."

"Yes, I will do it," Sicius said.

And so Sicius returned to his job behind the Nazi bar, his eyes and ears open, writing down what he saw and heard each night and mailing it to Joseph Roos. Sicius was given the code designation S4.

Although Lewis was at first worried that Sicius was a plant, he quickly learned the value of having a waiter on his staff, for waiters overhear a lot, approaching tables as they do during drunkenly candid conversations.

One of the key pieces of information Sicius provided was a link between Nazis and more benign isolationist organizations. Because of his unique perspective, S4 could report that the Bund was more dangerous than the Friends had ever been. The days of Captain Schmidt being "expelled" for spying were over. The Bundists made it clear: If they caught a spy reporting to the Jews, he or she would be killed.

As it turned out, that was S4's penultimate dispatch. In February 1940, Sicius was spotted by a Camp Sutter camper, a child, as he jotted down the license plate numbers of cars in the camp parking lot.

"You're a *dirty spy*," the Nazi kid said.

Startled, Sicius stammered, "N-n-no." He tried to regain his composure. "I wrote a memo to myself. I wasn't taking down numbers," S4 bluffed.

Sicius reported the incident to Roos, his last dispatch. He thought he'd gotten away with it. Apparently not.

Soon thereafter, Sicius was found dead on the Sunset Boulevard sidewalk, almost directly under the HOLLYWOODLAND sign. The coroner said he died of a basal skull fracture and softening of the parietal and occipital lobes—that is, clobbered over the head from behind.

This confirmed what Lewis had so feared. The Bund was now intent on rooting out and executing his spies.

The Gyssling Party

In 1940, Hitler sent Charles, Duke of Saxe-Coburg and Gotha, to L.A. to assess how much Hollywood juice Hitler had. The duke was both an SS general and a cousin of Britain's Duke of Windsor.

On April 5, 1940, German consul Georg Gyssling held a secret party for the duke in a bungalow of the Beverly Hills Hotel. We know about it because the guest list was seized by U.S. Army Intelligence. Notable attendees were Walt Disney, L.A. County Sheriff Eugene W. Biscailuz, Gary Cooper, Marion Davies, Mr. and Mrs. William Randolph Hearst (which meant Hearst was there with both his wife and his mistress), Will Hays of the PCA, and USC president Dr. Rufus von Kleinsmid.

Details of the meeting are unknown. (Scary stuff. Whatever went on was forgotten following Pearl Harbor. America at war was a unified thing. Fascists now kept their mouths shut. Even Walt Disney, a zealous isolationist, got with the program. Once America was drawn into the war, Donald Duck himself was teaching kids about the evil of Hitler and Nazism.)

America First Committee and Lucky Lindy

On September 4, 1940, the America First committee was formed, a group of influential Americans who believed the U.S. should, at all costs, stay out of World War II. The committee was chaired by retired General Robert E. Wood, now an exec with Sears Roebuck & Co. The group was immediately popular, as it had an air of respectability and cleverly disguised its pro-Nazi message behind Old Glory. One of America First's primary spokesmen was Charles Lindbergh, the globally famous aviator, first man to fly solo across the Atlantic, an American hero, "the most photographed man in the world."

The group's biggest event was a rally at the Hollywood Bowl, June 20, 1941, where Lindbergh said there were three forces drawing the U.S. into war: the British, the Jewish, and the Roosevelt administration. Of the three, he said, the Jews were the most dangerous.

"They present a unique danger as they control our motion pictures, our press, our radio, and our government," Lucky Lindy said.

FDR recognized that Lindbergh and the America Firsters presented a unique danger. They spoke plainly, were incorporated as a nonprofit, had a theme song that mentioned Yankee Doodle, and appealed to the conservative middle American.

"No more Gold Star mothers," was one of their slogans. It went straight to America's heart. No more American boys going overseas and coming home in a box.

Bottom line: England needed U.S. support just to keep the Nazis out of London, and because of America First's popularity, giving money and materiel to Winston Churchill was not a popular move in huge swaths of the country.

Some conservative Americans loved Lindbergh's take on the country's problems, while others—including Republicans Wendell Wilkie and Thomas Dewey—found it shocking, as if Lindbergh were taking a page from Hitler's playbook.

That was the point that needed to be made: Though wrapped in the Stars and Stripes, the America Firsters were, according to one government intelligence memo, "the raw material of American Fascism."

Modifying America First's Behavior

In October 1940, Japan signed the Tripartite Pact, making it—with Germany, Austria, and Italy—one of the Axis powers. (This turned out to be important, as it allowed FDR to declare war on Germany after the U.S. Navy was attacked by Japan.)

Leon Lewis and Joseph Roos sent spies into America First. Within weeks, the Nazibusters' *News Letter* published evidence that America First had been infiltrated in L.A. by Bundists. "Subversive Activities in America First in California," the article was called. The article was effective in an unexpected way. General Wood himself called for an investigation into his local chapters, ordering that they be purged of foreign influencers.

Fight For Freedom Committee

As a counter to America First, the Fight for Freedom Committee was formed in 1940 in New York City to push for American aid to England during the Blitz and to encourage Americans to be prepared when war inevitably came. The committee was chaired by Henry Hobson, an Episcopal bishop of southern Ohio, and Senator Carter Glass of Virginia.

They had their own manifesto, which began: "The American people have recognized that the war abroad involves our destiny just as it involves the destiny of the European nations and the other victims of totalitarian aggression. We have recognized that an Axis victory would be a threat to our nation and to all the principles of life in which we believe." Entering the war immediately, the manifesto read, was "the surest and swiftest road to peace."

"No One Asked You About Your Religious Affiliation . . ."

In June 1940, Harry Warner called an assembly, like in school. With all Warner Bros. employees in one room, he said, "I hold in my hand a Nazi publication called *Defilement of Race*," Harry said. "It says the Third Reich intends to rid the world of both Jews and Christians."

He paused for a moment and let that sink in.

"When you were interviewed for the job you hold here, no one asked you about your religious affiliation. That's because all faiths are respected at Warner Brothers. I, as you've probably heard, am a proud Jew." A titter of laughter. "I want you to think about one thing: If the Nazis take control of this country, they will come after the motion-picture industry first. I encourage everyone to join the studio's Rifle and Pistol Club and use our target range." He concluded with a plea for donations to the British Relief Fund. The employees responded by donating five hundred pieces of clothing and five thousand dollars.

The transcribed speech was copied and sent to all WB employees, all American Legion outposts, the White House, and to Martin Dies of the House Un-American Activities Committee.

WB's efforts to help the British and the French in their time of need continued. Harry donated twenty-five thousand dollars to the Red Cross for twenty new ambulances for England and France. Harry announced a new effort to rescue the children of WB employees affected by the Blitz.

Fascism Has No Sanity Clause

Some of the news was bizarre. Mussolini made a stink about no more Marx Brothers movies in Italy. The reason: Groucho, Chico, Harpo, and sometimes Zeppo and Gummo, were "exemplars of anti-fascist culture."

Such whiny complaints were nothing compared to the almost panicky reaction to Hollywood's first true anti-Nazi picture, a film that exposed forever that Goebbels's dream of a Hollywood takeover was a childish fantasy.

CHAPTER 21

The Mighty Voice

This is no "Beast of Berlin," but a statement of sober inevitable facts, so brilliantly realized that no one can hide from it.

—Otis Ferguson, *The New Republic*, in his review of *Confessions of a Nazi Spy*

Warner Bros. had been ahead of the other studios in its public anti-Nazi stance, so it is fitting and wholly predictable that WB would be the first major studio to use Hollywood's "mighty voice." The film was called *Confessions of a Nazi Spy.* Filming began on February 1, 1939.

From the start, threats poured into the studio: "If you persist in your plan to make this picture, you will regret it. We know the theaters and will prove it when and if you show this picture."

WB proceeded despite the threats, despite Consul Georg Gyssling's predictable objections, and regardless of Production Code queasiness. The reason: The film was based on a true story. In January 1938, working on a tip from British intelligence, the FBI had busted a Nazi spy ring working in the Greater New York City area. Among those arrested were card-carrying members of the German American Bund.

The FBI agent who received credit for the bust, Leon G. Turrou, turned the story into a book called *Nazi Spies in America*, which was published in 1938, and serialized in the *New York Post.* When the eighteen arrested Nazis went on trial, Warner Bros.

sent screenwriter Milton Krims to cover the spectacle—and the eventual screenplay was based on public testimony.

Casting became an issue. Although the main parts were cast easily—Edward G. Robinson, George Sanders, Francis Lederer, Paul Lukas, and Lya Lys, making her debut—below them, there were many German actors who didn't want to be in the movie, especially those with relatives in Europe. Others agreed to appear only under an assumed name. Some asked that their names not be in the credits.

There were so many threats upon the project, the usual bomb and death scares, that it became routine and, eventually, all but ignored. Fake signs were put up at the studio to misdirect potential saboteurs.

It's Raining Sabotage

There were two mishaps on set that were believed to be intentional. On one occasion, Edward G. Robinson and costars Paul Lukas and Dorothy Tree were sitting around a desk rehearsing a scene when the sound man, moving a heavy boom in preparation for the shot, lifted the arm of his device. With no warning, a seventy-five-pound piece of the boom fell, cracking the desk below and narrowly missing Robinson's skull.

Production was halted as studio officials came to the set. They found that the heavy arm of the boom had been "nearly sawed through" and the normal movement of the boom operator had caused it to fracture and fall.

On another occasion, a light fell from above and almost conked director Anatole Litvak. This, too, slowed filming down. Afterward, there was a thorough search of the mechanical equipment used on set before shooting began. The cast and crew spent the rest of the picture with one eye on the catwalks.

Authenticity

Robinson, an A+-lister, insisted on being in the picture, felt it was his duty as a Jew. He played the hero, FBI Special Agent Ed

Renard, who brings down the Nazi ring with courage and patriotic benevolence.

Director Litvak gave the film an authentic look, so that studio-shot scenes and newsreel footage could be—almost—seamlessly crosscut. As the technique was new, some called it cheating, as if they were trying to put over staged scenes as actual footage. (Today we can distinguish by mismatched textures and light sources in the images, but 1939 viewers were less sophisticated.)

The movie included evil Nazis, of course, but also made the point that you couldn't tell a Nazi by his or her appearance, casting innocent looking women in braids as Nazis to drive home the point. Happy playing children were shown wearing Nazi-in-training uniforms. German American Bundists was shown cheering as their leader told them that America was founded on German blood and that they all should believe in a "German destiny" for America.

The script demonstrated how the Bund sought to recruit by making fascism seem so doggone American: "National Socialism in the United States must cloak itself in the American flag," the movie's Bund leader says.

To be fair to German Americans, scenes were included of those who hated and feared the Nazis—although you couldn't tell the difference by looking at them. (And it was true. In real life, only a small percentage of German Americans bought into that Hitler crapola.)

The movie's denouement occurs in a courtroom—Nazis on trial.

"Some will say we are separated by vast oceans from the bacteria of aggressive dictatorships," says the prosecutor. "But we know these bacteria can slowly poison the organism of our civilized society. America is not simply one of the remaining democracies. America is democracy!"

Nazibuster on Set

Charles Slocombe, C19, reported that the Silver Lodge absolutely had people on the set of *Confessions*, and they knew when and where the cast and crew were leaving WB studios in Burbank for location shooting. Adjustments were made.

C19 also reported that the head of Warner Bros. security was a KKK "wizard." He was carefully watched during shooting.

Despite the obstacles, the film was completed, the first Hollywood movie to call the Nazi threat by name, and to attack it.

Opening Night

The April 27, 1939, premiere represented the moment that Dr. Goebbels's foolish plan to conquer Hollywood crashed and burned, stomped to dust by a rising eagle with arrows of freedom clutched in its talons. The venue was the opulent Warners Beverly Hills Theater on Wilshire. Police snipers manned rooftops across the street. Plainclothesmen watched the crowd inside. The cannister of film arrived via armored car, and an armed guard took it into the theater and transferred it to the projectionist behind closed doors.

Lobby cards breathlessly exclaimed: "The film that calls a swastika a swastika!"

The days of patting people down before they entered a theater were still decades away, but cops were posted at the entrance, scanning customers for suspicious bulges. No trouble came.

The Warner brothers, chests puffed out with pride, knew they'd done something important.

Producer Lou Edelman said, "It is like Hollywood's Bar Mitzvah, the movies have come of age."

Morton Thompson in the *Evening Citizen News* wrote, "Warner Brothers has stopped fooling around and has come forth."

James Francis Crow, in that same paper, wrote, "*Confessions* is a frontal attack on this era's most sinister menace to reason, justice, and humanity."

Harry Mines in the L.A. *Daily News* wrote of the movie, "It's bite is even more terrific than it's bark."

No picture had ever been viewed this way since *All Quiet on the Western Front*. It wasn't just good, it was important. It received rave reviews *and* made money.

It showed things never seen in a Hollywood feature: heel clicking, finely tailored uniforms, the "*Sieg Heils*," swastikas, armbands, goose-stepping, casual cruelty.

Some in L.A. noticed that the word "Jew" did not appear in the script or the signage on the sets. Most moviegoers did not.

Backlash

The Bund went after *Confessions*, viewing it only through its own Coke-bottle lens, "This sort of 'entertainment' disgusts true Americans," the Bund editorialized.

Georg Gyssling, whose primary directive in L.A. had been to avoid this sort of thing, tried his best to stifle *Confessions*. He appealed to the Production Code Administration and its antisemite chief Joseph Breen: "If you do not halt this film, Herr Breen, Germany will be forced to counter with official sanctions against the motion-picture industry." Gyssling said.

Breen, his Production Code, and WB had had it up to here with Gyssling. Instead of buckling to the pressure, as they had in the past, the studio refused to make the edits the consul "demanded."

When the movie came out, Gyssling engaged the aid of Franz Ferenz, the guy who ran the German-language theater in L.A., and distributed thousands of leaflets attacking the Warner Bros. picture.

"Just another product of the money-grabbing Jew industry!" the leaflet screamed.

Nazis vandalized theaters that screened *Confessions*. Seats were slashed. There were fights. Some screenings were delayed by bomb scares. The worst incident occurred at the Strand Theater in Milwaukee, Wisconsin, when a tear-gas cannister went off during a showing, and there were injuries in the resulting stampede. In most American cities, the reaction was mild.

Father Coughlin, the fascist priest, went on his syndicated radio show one Sunday afternoon and told America that *Confessions* was an "un-American abomination." What did you expect? Coughlin said, "Harry and Jack Warner, and Edward G. Robinson are all Jews."

In Germany, *Confessions* was greeted with anger: "If we let them get away with it, Hollywood will pepper us with anti-Nazi films," Joseph Goebbels said.

He had no idea. The propaganda machine, a weaponized Mighty Voice that Goebbels wanted to control so badly, had turned on him with all its cinematic guns blazing. Movies that fiercely criticized and lampooned Hitler almost immediately went into production. (For a rundown of Hollywood's pre–Pearl Harbor anti-Nazi pictures, see the Appendix.)

Theaters showing anti-Nazi fare continued to be routinely harassed—vandalism, bomb threats. Pro-Nazi Americans sometimes attended screenings and heckled relentlessly. They claimed the moguls were making anti-Nazi pictures just to push America into a war from which the studios would derive profits.

Some psychologically oriented film critics said that nerves over an impending "World War Number Two" sent audiences of the cinema to escape and seek out lightweight entertainment, not to have their anxieties further aggravated by films depicting the "slaughter abroad."

Blaming Hollywood

When Goebbels now spoke of Germany's relationship with the U.S., he expressed disappointment. He'd hoped he and the Americans could get along.

Hitler blamed Hollywood for the rift: "I believe the will of the American people remains with me despite the gigantic Jewish capitalistic propaganda through the press, radio, and films. There is not one word of truth in all these assertions," Hitler said.

Either you thought everyone was lying and Hitler was telling the truth, or the other way around. Everyone knew on which side of that fence they stood.

Death of Carl Laemmle

On August 24, 1939, Carl Laemmle, Hollywood's senior filmmaker, retired head of Universal, died in his Beverly Hills home at the age of seventy-two. When the other moguls were making flickering silents in Fort Lee, New Jersey; Midwood, Brooklyn; Astoria, Queens; and along Twenty-third Street in Manhattan—all locations in which the weather and changing light caused great aggravation—Laemmle set up shop, in 1909, in an abandoned brewery at Sunset and Gower, in a land where the light and weather were almost always the same.

Eventually, the others joined him. He became Hollywood's favorite mogul, a genuinely nice man. His funeral, at the Wilshire Temple B'nai B'rith, drew two thousand mourners. Every studio in town went silent for five minutes. Eulogies discussed *All Quiet on the Western Front*, one of the great films of all time, with the additional honor of being the first Hollywood product to truly piss off Adolf Hitler.

1941 Hollywood Branch Roster

On record is the roster of Hollywood Branch members who attended a 1941 meeting, chaired by independent producer Walter Wanger. Secretary that evening was Leon Lewis. Other members on hand were Mervyn LeRoy, of MGM; Herman Jacob Mankiewicz, also of MGM, but about to become immortal in Hollywood as the ballsy screenwriter of *Citizen Kane*; Dore Schary, an MGM studio exec with great ideas, often gritty and raw; Eugene Zukor, only son of Adolph, Paramount; Herbert Aller, representing the IATSE union; Maxwell Arnow of Walter Wanger Productions; Arthur Arthur, Columbia; Ralph Blum, talent agent; Jack Chertok, Jack Cummings, Jerry Hoffman, all of MGM; Lou Edelman, Warner Bros.; Matthew Fox, D.

S. Garber, Leonard Spigelgass, and Maurie Weiner, Universal; Henry Ginsberg, Jack Karp, Mark Sandrich, Paramount; and Harry Maizlish of KFWB, the Warner Bros. radio station.

America Marches On!

With an independent producer in charge, the Hollywood Branch, in conjunction with the American Legion and the Anti-Nazi League, became a prolific producer of anti-Nazi counterpropaganda.

Beginning in 1938, the Hollywood Branch produced a weekly radio program called *America Marches On!* that nationally broadcast the dangers of Nazism in America. Head writer was John Lechner, who closed each broadcast with "Americans are opposed to Nazism, Fascism, and Communism."

Despite that sign-off, Martin Dies of the congressional Dies committee accused *America Marches On!* of being a Communist program and forced it off the air.

In 1940, a thirteen-part radio serial called *Airing the Fifth Column*, also written by Lechner, was broadcast. Lechner used Nazi-buster evidence in his scripts.

Harry Warner, in conjunction with the American Legion, produced a series of short films exposing the Nazi menace. Titles included: *The Flag Speaks* (the flag itself was the narrator of the picture), *Give Me Liberty*, and *The Bill of Rights.*

The premiere of *The Flag Speaks* received the full Warner Bros. premiere to-do, with spotlights searching the skies and a parade on Hollywood Boulevard, ending at Grauman's Chinese Theatre, where the film was shown. Inside the theater, Boy Scouts led the audience in the Pledge of Allegiance, and an award ceremony was held and plaques given to an American Legion commander and Louis B. Mayer.

During the last months before Pearl Harbor, the Hollywood Branch was an efficient liaison between the U.S. government, the American Legion, and the Nazibusters' card catalog of anti-Nazi evidence. (Even after Pearl Harbor and America's entrance into World War II, the Hollywood Branch continued weekly meetings, staying vigilant in search of Nazi infiltration into the movie business.)

ADL on Board

Throughout the 1930s, the Nazibusters and the Anti-Defamation League were at odds, not wholly trusting one another, and in direct competition for funding. Lewis's distrust of the ADL was for good reason. Several times they'd published exposés that compromised his operation: Neil Ness had to retire, and Charles Slocombe was implicated, but had gotten himself into a position where he was beyond suspicion. Many Bundists thought it was Schwinn who'd blabbed, trusting new friends with secrets.

As the 1940s began, however, the Nazibusters and ADL joined forces against their common enemies. The ADL now routinely sent its national outposts alerts based on Nazibuster evidence.

Blitz

In May 1940, Germany attacked Great Britain by air, concentrating on London, an attack that came to be known as the Blitz. The King's wife, Elizabeth, climbed to the Buckingham Palace roof and fired at the Luftwaffe with her pearl-handled pistol. Fears were that the Luftwaffe would soften Great Britain up for a massive land invasion. Jack Warner, now wholly in Harry's anti-Nazi camp, became a bit hysterical when he learned of air-raid sirens in London and sent out a memo forbidding anyone to speak German on the Warner Bros. lot.

In July 1940, Harry Warner announced a new program, called the Warner Club, that worked to get European children out of war zones and into the U.S. where they'd be safe.

In the Roosevelt Building, it was again time for the Nazibusters to freshen up their undercover crew, this time with a decidedly feminine touch . . .

CHAPTER 22

Out of Their Comfort Zone

Women have always been spies.
—Harriet Rubin

On June 1, 1940, one month into the Blitz, Lewis received a phone call from an unidentified friend at Warner Bros.

"I've got a couple of women you need to meet. I think they have something to offer your efforts."

"Please, send them to me," Lewis said.

And presently, the women came to Lewis's office. There was a handsome older woman, fifty-something, and a beautiful blond and blue-eyed companion who was in her mid-twenties. Similar bone structure and coloring—he correctly assumed them to be a mother and daughter.

"Hello, ladies. I'm Leon Lewis." They shook hands. "Please, sit. What can I do for you?"

"We were hoping you could give us a job," the younger one said eagerly.

"As what? Wait, who are you?"

"Sorry," the older one said. "I'm Grace Comfort. This is my daughter Sylvia. I am a career Navy widow, my husband was twenty-six years on active duty, but his pension is not enough for us to live on."

"So, we need work," Sylvia said, using extremely direct eye contact.

Lewis felt like she was attempting mental telepathy, but he wasn't receiving.

"I see. What should I employ you as?" Lewis said.

"Spies!" Grace said, frustrated that he hadn't figured it out. "This place isn't *wired*, is it?"

"We just moved to L.A. from San Diego, looking for work, and we found some Nazis who definitely need spying on," Sylvia added.

"What are your skills?" Lewis asked.

Sylvia said, "I take shorthand. I'm tremendously literate. I went to San Diego College. My dream is to work in the movie business, reading scripts or something."

Lewis frowned. "How old are you?"

"Twenty-seven, not that that should make any difference," Sylvia said.

Lewis laughed lightly. "Tell me about the Nazis."

Again, it was Sylvia who spoke up. "I got a job soon after moving up from San Diego. I did secretarial work for my next-door neighbor's brother."

"It's a 'who you know' world," Grace said, and both women laughed.

"What was your employer's name?" Lewis asked, pulling out a long yellow pad to take notes.

"William Pierce Williams," Sylvia said. "He's a schoolteacher at North Hollywood High School. He also has a company called the Educational Service Bureau."

Lewis wrote that down, too. "Did you know anything about him before you took the job?"

"A little. He was just a guy who needed someone with secretarial skills. I knew he'd been in the army and that he grew up in Texas. But slowly I came to realize he was not what he seemed."

"Tell me," Lewis urged.

"My first clue came when I read a copy of this newsletter he puts out. I was stunned by the hatred of Jews. It was *gross*."

Grace jumped in, "Sylvia brought it home to me. We were aghast at the viciousness—and we agreed that something should be done about it."

"The leaflets are called 'Do you know . . . ?' I brought a sample. Here." Lewis looked and nodded. Sylvia added, "I think things are escalating. I think Williams isn't satisfied with just printing propaganda. I think he wants to do something really bad. He has plans to organize Nazi groups in L.A., Santa Barbara, and San Diego."

"We took our evidence to the FBI, and they couldn't have been less impressed. 'Come back when you have something on the Commies,' they told us," Grace said with a sour expression.

"Then," Sylvia concluded, "our mutual friend at Warner Brothers suggested we see you."

Lewis thought using the Comforts to bust up a North Hollywood nerve center of Nazi activity sounded pretty good. He questioned them some more, to see how they thought, how quickly they could think, and was impressed.

Lewis did some research, in particular on Sylvia, who seemed the more likely plant. What he learned was she was sincere. Dad was career Navy. Sylvia grew up in San Diego, California. She was noteworthy even when young, honor roll, adventures in student politics. They wrote about her in the *San Diego Sun* as early as 1928. She not only received citizenship awards while only a sophomore at San Diego College but awards that were published in the next day's newspaper under headlines such as SORORITY GIVES EVENING BRIDGE. The impression was of an exceptional lady—but very much a lady, a class act, not a hair out of place, perfect posture, maybe a pair of white gloves. Sylvia showed dogs at the Catalina Kennel Club Dog Show in 1935 and was winner that year for showing the Best Pekingese Bitch.

On a second visit, Lewis told Grace and Sylvia, "Ladies, I would like you to join Williams's subversive organization and report back to me what you learn."

"For pay?"

"Some."

They were thrilled.

As usual, Lewis went over the methods of communication between him and his operatives, the importance of not being followed, and keeping the exchange of information secret.

Grace was to identify herself as G2, when she reported. Sylvia was S3.

"I want you to be very careful. At the first indication that your cover is blown, flee. We lost an operative who was found out," Lewis said, in reference to Julius Sicius.

Sylvia was already doing secretarial work for Williams, so she had ample opportunity to explain to the boss that she and her mom really admired the strong political stance Williams was taking in that newsletter of his. Sylvia, a beautiful woman, asked if there was anything they could do to help the cause.

Williams's face lit up. "Please come to the next meeting, and bring your mother," he said.

Williams had designs on the women, not necessarily sexual. He knew that Sylvia's mother was a Navy widow and had friends in high places. Could she use those connections to help him recruit in the naval ranks, where there were bound to be many patriotic Christian men who would hear his message? Grace promised she'd look into it.

Sylvia's spying was immediately productive. She quickly learned that between Williams and Hitler, there was only one degree of separation, that being Eugene Messerschmidt, an agent of Hitler sent to America to organize. She reported that Messerschmidt ran the small cells of Nazis that were being developed, groups of eight to ten men.

"The belief is that the smaller the group, the less likely it will be infiltrated by us," Sylvia reported.

S3 reported that Williams, under Messerschmidt's orders, had organized a cell to attack U.S. military sites. The cell included a commercial pilot, and several airplane mechanics. Sylvia asked Williams how he knew these men, and he said he'd met them when in the National Guard. Williams, Sylvia reported, had a small boat of his own that he took out at night at San Pedro to chart the location of each docked U.S. warship.

Sylvia had gone about as deep undercover as she cared to go, but Lewis wanted her to go deeper still.

"Establish a relationship with Messerschmidt, Sylvia. He is a bigger fish, I think, and the key to this threat."

Grace and Sylvia worked their way up the ranks, became members of executive committees, and were assigned to check ID at the door of meetings to keep Jews out. They even listened in on Nazi phone calls that exposed plans for several hate crimes.

Sylvia would eventually expose Williams's plan to recruit men already working at aircraft- and ship-manufacturing plants into one of the Nazi sabotage cells. She documented a recruiting trip Williams made to March Airfield in Riverside, California.

Leon Lewis notified the army intelligence officer in charge of L.A.'s harbor defense, and from that point on, Williams wasn't allowed past the gate of any plant under defense contract.

The Lady Flyer

Sylvia reported that many fascist and Nazi groups were joining America First. Although they didn't change their loathsome beliefs, they changed their message. America First went easy on the hate talk. They simply didn't want the U.S. to go to war against Germany. All they wanted was peace.

It was while getting inside America First that Sylvia Comfort befriended a woman named Laura Ingalls, who was the speaker at a pro-Hitler fund-raiser. (She is not to be confused with Laura Ingalls Wilder, who wrote the *Little House on the Prairie* books. This Ingalls was an aviator—they called her an "aviatrix" at the time—second in accomplishment as a lady pilot only to Amelia Earhart.)

Ingalls remained the only woman to fly solo from New York to Santiago, Chile. She set the record for most consecutive loop-dee-loops with 980 in Oklahoma in 1930. She also held the record for most barrel rolls with 714. Trouble with being a daredevil pilot was, there was no money in it. In 1939, she wrote to J. Edgar Hoover asking if the FBI needed a "lady flyer."

Hoover said no. "Men only," he added.

And so, pockets turned inside out, Laura took a job with America First, flying over the White House in Washington and dropping isolationist pamphlets on FDR's front lawn.

Each leaflet read: "Never before in history have American women been so aroused and determined to keep their country out of war."

The incident was enough to put Ingalls on the isolationist/America First speaking circuit. Her speaking style was described as "sarcastic, flippant, fluent, and dramatic." In the audience at one of Ingalls's speeches was Sylvia Comfort. They became fast friends, and in July 1941, Sylvia and the pilot were having lunch at Carl's Viewpark restaurant at Crenshaw Boulevard and Vernon Avenue, overlooking Leimert Park. After dinner, the ladies were scheduled to attend a meeting of the Mothers of Los Angeles, their goal to raise $450 so that Ingalls could once again drop propaganda on FDR's lawn.

"You and I are friends, right?" Ingalls said over cocktails.

Sylvia noticed Ingalls's bracelet. There was a swastika on it. "Of course, Laura," Sylvia replied, leaning in.

"Good, I feel I can trust you. I have something to say, and I could get in trouble if I said it to the wrong people."

"What is it?"

"I wanted to do what's best for my peace mission, so, I've . . . I've decided to join the Nazi Party."

"But . . . how do you feel about Hitler?"

"I admire him."

"I noticed your bracelet."

"It is not new, the swastika. It was an Indian symbol for centuries."

"The salute, the outstretched arm thing, is striking."

"I think we should have an American salute, Sylvia. Maybe an outstretched *left* arm!" It was a joke. "No one could confuse us for Nazis then. They salute with their right arm."

"You have German heritage, no, Laura?"

"I do. My mother was German, and my nurse growing up was German. I am going to fly to Germany. I want you to come with me."

"I—I'll have to think about it."

"Of course."

Sylvia later reported that she felt it was best to play along. After checking in with Nazibusters HQ, Sylvia agreed to fly to Germany with Laura Ingalls. In the meantime, Joseph Roos shared Sylvia's intelligence with the FBI.

Sylvia and Laura had long conversations about the pilot's frustrations trying to sell her L.A. home. Ingalls urged her friend to hurry up and get her passport for the trip.

Laura warned Sylvia: "If you go with me, there are going to be people who think you're a Nazi."

"Would you mind being called a Nazi, Laura?" Sylvia asked.

"I am convinced that the Nazis are doing the right thing. I have no reservations whatsoever about them. I wouldn't mind being called a Nazi."

Despite Laura's plans to fly to Germany, there was no indication that Germany wanted her any more than the FBI did. Sylvia reported that her subject was growing "increasingly frustrated" by Germany, from which she was getting no encouragement. Ingalls liked to brag that she was in "constant communication" with the German embassy using code names (Ellen, Sagitarius), but admitted that as of late, they hadn't been getting back to her.

"I can't stay in America," Ingalls said. "I have been rejected by everyone who might help my cause. Even the others in the isolationist movement grow hesitant and weak when I offer my services."

One of the problems was that the $450 the America First ladies' auxiliary raised for Ingalls's second leafleting of the White House lawn had gone to waste when Ingalls took off from L.A., crash landed in New Mexico, went the rest of the way to Washington, D.C. as a passenger on a commercial plane, and never got anywhere near the White House.

Landing Strip Climax

Sylvia continued to gather information on Laura Ingalls right up until the moment of their planned departure for Germany, which unfortunately for Ingalls was a week and a half after Pearl Harbor. Sylvia headed to Lockheed Air Terminal in Burbank with Laura, knowing the FBI was aware of the plan, but unsure of when they'd intervene. So, there was tension as Laura and Sylvia idled in Ingalls's plane on the runway. With timing suitable for Hollywood, the feds waited until the last instant before raiding the runway with sirens wailing, halting the takeoff, and arresting Ingalls.

Sylvia quickly got an FBI agent to vouch for her and was released.

Ingalls was booked for failing to register as a Nazi. After a quick trial, a jury took an hour and a half to convict her, and the judge sentenced her to eight months to two years in prison. She served twenty months. She was arrested again in 1944 trying to sneak into Mexico while carrying seditious materials. She avoided prosecution. We lose track of her at that point until her death in 1967 in Burbank, California, at the age of seventy-three.

Sylvia's adventure on the airstrip might've been her most nerve-racking moment as a Nazibuster, but there were many others, as we'll see.

Escape from Paris

By June 10, 1940, when the Nazis marched into Paris, Hollywood employees had escaped, leaving nothing behind to sack. It was a close scrape. Movie people from MGM, Paramount, RKO, and

Twentieth Century-Fox forged documents, snuck out of France, and hired a boat to Dover, a tense journey, Nazis around every corner.

After Hollywood abandoned Paris, the only film unit left in Europe was WB's crew at Teddington Studios in England, an operation that continued gamely into the war, until 1944 when it was blown up by a Nazi V-2 rocket, killing one of Jack Warner's good friends, Doc Salomon.

Shorthand

While the Nazis in L.A. tended to scoff at the feds, they feared Leon Lewis more than any other man. He had managed to learn their innermost secrets for years now, and they still didn't know how to stop the leaks.

In 1940, the talk became increasingly violent. The only way to eliminate Lewis's threat was to eliminate Lewis. But as usual, this time because of a Sylvia Comfort report marked URGENT, Lewis learned of the plans immediately, and things for the Nazis, as usual, went wrong.

Sylvia was privy to many secrets because of her superior secretarial skills. "I'm the only stenographer that they have," she explained.

Her job was to transcribe Nazi meetings in shorthand, which worked out perfectly: When she wrote out her notes for the Nazis, she simply carbon-copied a second set for Lewis.

Although it wasn't part of the plan, Sylvia Comfort achieved inside status with the Nazis for another reason: Nazis liked her. They *like* liked her. Sylvia knew how to handle wolves, regardless of politics, and parried crude Nazi advances like a shapely fencer.

Sylvia was asked at one point to be the private secretary for a Nazi named Andrae Nordskog who had a cell called the United Party Movement, but the job didn't last long, as the FBI shut the group down in days. Nazis were again befuddled at their inability to keep a secret.

Her next suitor was a man we know, the guy who ran the

German cinema in L.A., Franz Ferenz. She learned from him that screening Nazi movies was getting more and more difficult.

"Every time we find a theater to show our films, the landlord decides he doesn't want to rent to us. The Jews are keeping us out of L.A. cinemas," Ferenz said.

Sylvia received a private screening of pro-Nazi newsreels, and she reported that it was a good thing that their screenings were being hindered.

"They are powerful pieces of propaganda," Sylvia reported.

Being a Nazibuster became all-consuming for Sylvia. Each night, it seemed, she was out attending a meeting of this subversive group or that, taking copious notes, providing transcripts of meetings for the group's leaders—and of course, for her spymasters.

Mock Trial

Ferenz staged a mock impeachment trial of FDR at the Deutsches Haus in 1941. It went on for weeks and was well attended. A cardboard effigy of FDR was put in place to represent the defendant. (Irony of ironies, the "verdict," scheduled for December 8, 1941, never happened because hundreds of Japanese warplanes intervened.)

The Comforts reported to Leon Lewis that Ferenz was trying to stop an adult education teacher named Sam Evans from identifying Nazi propaganda to his students. Ferenz tried to stifle Evans by heckling his classes. When that didn't work, seventy-five Nazis went to the next Board of Education meeting and demanded that Evans be fired. Evans was so frightened by the experience that he requested a police escort home from the meeting.

Ferenz told Sylvia that he was assembling a brigade of well-armed Nazi soldiers on motorcycles that could "respond to any emergency." In October 1941, he told an audience that the biggest enemy of true Americans was a Jew named Leon Lewis. He then gave the audience the address of Lewis's office and invited them to take care of the problem.

The Memorial Day Plot

On May 7, 1941, Sylvia Comfort reported that Hermann Schwinn, who was still awaiting deportation orders that would never come, was telling his men that there were plans to sabotage aircraft factories along the West Coast on Memorial Day. Bombs were to be planted by men working inside those plants, and pilots in private planes would drop bombs on military sites, starting at the Mexican border and moving northward along the coast. Lewis and Roos sent the report immediately to the ONI and FBI, and all plants along the coast were ordered to close over the Memorial Day holiday.

Schwinn waited with wild eyes for the Earth-shattering kabooms, but they never came.

"Someone in Deutsches Haus has betrayed Hitler!" he screamed at the silence.

As spring turned to summer, Lewis, Roos, and their team turned to the East and saw another cause for concern. The Nazi-busters' enemies within the U.S. government were coming to town—with subpoena power.

CHAPTER 23

"A Raging Volcano of War Fever"

There has never been such an evil force on earth, so aware of itself, and impervious to the restraints of civilization.
—Senator Sheridan Downey

During the summer of 1941, there was born a subcommittee of the Interstate Commerce Committee that was tasked with determining if Hollywood was making anti-Nazi propaganda films to "excite war hysteria." The subcommittee was helmed by Senators D. Worth Clark of Idaho and Gerald P. Nye of North Dakota. Nye was the better known in L.A. because he'd addressed America First rallies there.

On the eve of the first hearing in Washington, D.C., Nye went before an audience and gave an address that was broadcast on radio. During his speech he slowly read the names of the Hollywood moguls—Zukor, Cohn, Warner, Schenck, Mayer. After each name, the live audience called out angrily, "Jew!"

The subcommittee maintained that Hollywood was "dedicated to warmongering" and "a Jewish-controlled monopoly," and that these handful of Jewish men were having clandestine meetings with FDR, conspiring to violate the official neutrality of the United States regarding the "situation in Europe."

In his opening statement, Nye said, "Go to Hollywood! It is a raging volcano of war fever. The place swarms with refugees and British actors. Hollywood Jews, the modern-day equivalent of Typhoid Mary, spread their deadly contagions among a defenseless public. . . . They talk of their freedom of speech, but the First Amendment protects speech, not entertainment. And Harry Warner is the worst of all the Jewish propagandists. He wants to see Ireland bombed into oblivion, just to prove his point [that Nazis are bad]."

Hollywood, of course, moved to defend itself, predictably, with Harry Warner taking the lead. He'd personally finance a series of radio broadcasts lauding Hollywood's patriotism. He called for the moguls to get together and hire a top lawyer to defend their interests against Clark and Nye's obviously antisemitic attacks.

The high-priced lawyer turned out to be Wendell Wilkie, the Republican who lost the 1940 presidential election to FDR. The committee voted to deny Wilkie the right to cross-examine witnesses, causing another huge wave of criticism. (The fix, it seemed, was in.)

Walter Winchell wrote in his nationally syndicated column, "Hollywood stands solidly against everything Hitler represents out of moral outrage, not because of some imaginary pact with the Roosevelt administration."

The subcommittee listened to witnesses who said Jews were the real threat to America. Why? Because it was the Jews who were producing propaganda and getting the American public riled for war.

Luckily for Hollywood, whose lawyer had been gagged, not all members of the subcommittee were sympatico with the creepy love some U.S. senators had for Adolf Hitler. One dissenter was Senator Ernest McFarland, who took it upon himself to ask a few tough questions.

"Senator Nye, you have condemned during these proceedings eight Hollywood films. How many have you personally seen?"

Nye said "about two" and when pressed failed to come up with a single title. McFarland asked Senator Bennett Champ Clark of

Missouri (not to be confused with Senator Clark of Idaho) the same question. Clark didn't go to movies. They were "distasteful."

Clark then brought a hysterical grandiose touch to his ingrained antisemitism: "The Jews at the present time operate seventeen thousand theaters. They have turned them into seventeen thousand mass meetings for war! They use their cunning to infect the minds of Americans with hatred. They inflame them! They arouse the emotions as they clamor for war."

Later, Clark added, "I shall do everything in my power to bring about once and for all the utter destruction of the monopolistic grasp of this little handful of men."

Nick Schenck on the Stand

On Tuesday, September 23, 1941, Joe's brother Nick Schenck—who ran Loews, Inc., which ran MGM, the man known in Hollywood as "The General"—testified before the subcommittee. Having come to Washington from his Gatsby-like mansion on the north shore of Long Island, Nick took the oath to tell the whole truth, looking distinguished in a powder-blue suit, matching shirt and tie, with a deep tan and gray hair.

"You are the top man at Loew's Inc., isn't that correct? You are it, in charge, correct?" asked one senator.

Nick answered, "Yes, I am responsible for it all."

"Wouldn't you characterize your warmongering movies as propaganda?" asked Senator D. Worth Clark.

"Oh, don't use that word. I certainly do not."

Clark asked if a specific film was propaganda. Nick said no. Clark asked about another.

"I am always going to say no. None of my films are propaganda. We present accurate portrayals of the plight of Great Britain and the menace of Nazi Germany. Pictures do not mold the public. The public molds us. I would not produce pictures that would make one race of people hate another. But I would produce pictures of this sort when something is happening on the other side, in the balance of the world that is occupied by Nazis. You can correctly charge me with being anti-Nazi, but no one can charge me with being anti-American."

One senator thought it suspicious that Hollywood functioned outside the American investment mainstream. How had Nick managed to get so rich and powerful without involving Wall Street?

"As I understand it," Nick testified, "a few years ago the bankers came to Hollywood and went through the business and said we were all crazy—that they would do this and that. But those suggestions were made because they did not understand us. After all, it is just a business where you deal with brains and imagination and creative ability, and you cannot buy that from us." MGM was a mystery, a creator of miracles. MGM was magic. You couldn't measure it in money. Bankers didn't get it.

At one point, Nick's taxes came up. Nick's voice firmed, and he didn't want anyone to think he wasn't paying his fair share. "The last two years I have had to borrow money to pay my taxes," he exclaimed.

The subcommittee wanted to know why all domestic motion pictures were supervised by a small group of men.

Nick explained that executives of the major film companies never "got together" to prevent independents from producing or marketing pictures. Such action would be "the worst kind of a crime." What Clark saw as collusion was actually just good business. "Independents have trouble borrowing stars from the major companies because the majors want to protect the stars' box-office appeal. For that reason, independents who prove themselves wind up eventually with the major companies."

Senator Charles William Tobey asked, "Loews, Inc., supervised the making of a picture called *Escape*, isn't that right, an anti-Nazi picture?"

"That's right."

"Were you personally involved in the acquisition of rights to make that film, Mr. Schenck?"

"Well, I read the book on a train and urged the studio to produce it."

"And why did you find that particular subject so appealing?"

"Well, Hitler has been in the news a lot. I figured the public would be interested."

Senator Nye took up the questioning: "Your company recently released a picture called *The Mortal Storm*, is that correct?"

"Yes."

"Do you think that picture has contributed to harmony and national unity?"

"I don't think you want unity with Hitler. We made this picture because these are the times we live in. Under normal circumstances, with the world at peace, a picture like *The Mortal Storm* wouldn't be one we would want to make."

"We are at peace," Senator D. Worth Clark interjected.

"Not exactly," Nick Schenck sharply replied.

Clark had a question: "Don't you think the atrocities committed in Germany are actually committed by a handful of very mean men?"

"I think MGM's depiction of Nazis has been not nearly as bad as what actually happens. I believe we only know about one percent of what is going on in Europe."

Nick endured a full day of questioning and did it without a break in composure or the slightest mist of sweat.

"Not Tough Enough"

The next witness in defense of Hollywood was Senator Sheridan Downey of California. He spoke of *The Great Dictator*, in which Chaplin portrayed Hitler tossing an inflatable globe around like a play object.

"I'll tell you what's wrong with that picture. It's too lighthearted, not tough enough the way it treated the Nazis. Chaplin gave the Nazis poetry and grace. They should be portrayed as the evil they represent."

"Evil. Senator, really!" Senator D. Worth Clark said.

"Yes, evil. There has never been such an evil force on earth, so aware of itself, and impervious to the restraints of civilization." Downey seemed to put an end to the antisemitic fun when he read a statement saying that he'd made a review of Hollywood films distributed over the past couple of years and had found no "insidious propaganda for war as has been alleged."

"Business with Butchers"

Next to speak in Hollywood's defense was Harry Warner, who was allowed to read a written statement without interruption. He had made a checklist of things that had been said about him that weren't true. Regarding his anti-Nazi stance, he would apologize for nothing.

"The Nazis are a totalitarian global revolution intent on undoing all democratic principles," Harry said. "When we stopped working with the Nazis what seems like an eternity ago, our company took a large financial hit, but we never considered a compromise. We could not justify doing business with butchers. Warner Brothers pictures are carefully prepared on the basis of factual happenings and they are not twisted to serve any ulterior purpose.

"Speaking of ulterior motives, let me point out that every form of mass communication known to man has been used to disseminate the truth about the Nazi menace: radio, newspapers, magazines, novels—and yes, movies. But only the movies have been accused of creating propaganda. Only the movies have been charged with being Communist and un-American. Gentlemen, I'd like you to consider why that is."

The last Hollywood witness was Darryl F. Zanuck, who ran Twentieth Century-Fox for Nick Schenck's brother Joe. Zanuck said that the committee itself should be investigated. Their attempts at censorship were troubling, that they would want to render Hollywood's product as "worthless and sterile as those made in Germany and Italy."

The subcommittee took a break near the end of September 1941 and might've reconvened had world events not gotten in the way. In the long run, the subcommittee's "investigation" did nothing to change the power structure of, not output of the Hollywood studios, largely because Pearl Harbor happened, after which all those anti-Nazi movies were considered by the public as Patriotic with a capital P. America, as one, went to war, and Hollywood went to work "boosting morale."

The Hollywood monopoly—that the same men who owned the studios owned the talent and the theaters, to the point where independents couldn't function—was busted up by legislation after the war. And that was the beginning of the end for the old studio system.

CHAPTER 24

War Comes to America

Victory at all costs, victory in spite of all terror, victory however long and hard that road may be; for without victory, there is no survival.

—Winston Churchill

By 1940, security-minded Americans were beginning to doubt if the American Nazi menace had teeth. So many threats, so many plans, not that many acts of sabotage. Then, during the late summer and autumn of that year, things started exploding.

Years earlier, Neil Ness (N2) had filed a report in which he listed sites being considered for Nazi sabotage. On that list was the Hercules Powder Plant in Kenvil, New Jersey.

The list had been given to the FBI. Who knows what they did with it—but on September 12, 1940, the Hercules Powder Plant exploded with a flash that lit up the nighttime sky for miles around and caused a mushroom cloud to rise five thousand feet in the air. More than fifty workers were killed, hundreds of others injured. An estimated sixteen thousand pounds of "smokeless gunpowder" had gone up at once. The explosion blew to smithereens the sprinkler system and the resulting fire burned unchecked. They never figured out who did it.

Two months later, three defense plants in New Jersey and Pennsylvania suffered explosions within twenty minutes of each other. Sixteen people died; many more were wounded.

Significantly, there were no explosions in California. Our

heroes were not gloating, however. Vigilance was needed. There were still unknown saboteurs working in West Coast manufacturing plants.

The *News Letter* named the leader of the potential saboteurs as Hermann Schwinn. The item was picked up by newspaper columnists, who in turn called out J. Edgar Hoover for Commie-hunting while the real enemy crept into the American fabric. When the FBI did take action, they were clumsy. Agents bugged Georg Gyssling's phone, but all they picked up was Gyssling and his staff laughing at the lousy job the FBI mechanics had done.

"Look, you can see a wire going from my desk and out the window. Look, it goes to that car down there. Hello, FBI fools," someone, perhaps Gyssling himself, said before the listening device went silent.

FDR Boots Gyssling

As spring turned to summer in 1941, the German army invaded Russia, forming the Eastern Front, where millions of soldiers would die. The U.S. was already acting like a country prepping for war. Ships and planes were being built as fast as possible. And FDR was ordering all German diplomats out of the country, including Georg Gyssling.

In preparation for his departure, Gyssling started shoving damning documents into his fireplace, until his entire block was covered with charred bits of paper. On June 29, the German Consulate was emptied and locked, once again becoming American property.

The press surrounded Gyssling as he headed to the train station with his young daughter. He was sad. "I have so many friends here. It has been fourteen years. My Angelica was born here." The pair trained to Washington, D.C., and caught a plane for Germany.

On July 23, 1941, Harry Warner used his celebrity as a Hollywood mogul to lobby FDR, urging the President to send troops to Great Britain, to shore up defenses for what seemed the inevitable invasion of the British Isles by the advancing German army.

Silver Lodge leader William Dudley Pelley was a man on the run, wanted for parole violation in connection with his 1934 stock fraud conviction and growing weary. So, he pulled the plug. He dissolved his lodge, claiming that it was no longer needed as the government (Dies committee) was fighting communism for him. Then he surrendered to authorities in North Carolina.

Codes Discovered

With war imminent, everyone could feel it, the victories earned by the Nazibusters became more important. In October 1941, now less than two months before Pearl Harbor, Charles Young (Y2), found himself alone in the office of a suspected German spy.

So, Young went through the desk drawers and trash can, and pocketed as many pieces of paper as his pockets would hold. Later, he realized he'd stolen ten pages of secret German naval codes. Nice! These were immediately sent to the War Department in Washington, D.C.

Acts of War

War with Germany came closer to being an inevitability when the U.S. freighter, the *Montana*, was sunk by Germans between Iceland and Greenland on September 16, 1941.

On October 17, 1941, the *Kearney* was torpedoed but not sunk by a German sub, and on October 31, German subs for the first time attacked a U.S. warship, sinking the destroyer USS *Reuben James*.

By this time, the Nazibusters of Hollywood were concentrating almost all of their attention on sabotage cells in California, with only a minor effort to keep track of what was left of the Bund. Schwinn was under intense FBI scrutiny. Mrs. Fry had fled. Hans Diebel was in the process of being deported.

The FBI's investigation of Schwinn found evidence of criminality scarce. The best they could do was portray Schwinn as a guy who encouraged draft dodging.

American Kristallnacht

In November 1941, there was an attempt at an "American *Kristallnacht*," organized by a man named Larry Griffith, whose crew of thugs was called the National Minutemen—not to be confused with the Minutemen of Newark, New Jersey, who used their pugilistic skills to bust up Friends and Bund meetings.

Griffith's brigade of haters went out one night and, using glass-cutters, carved the word "JEW" into Jewish-owned storefronts. (Even after Pearl Harbor, Griffith's group continued to commit troubling acts of vandalism, often featuring blades. Sylvia Comfort wondered in one of her reports when Griffith's vandals would stop cutting up personal property and start cutting people.)

Griffith's final published propaganda before Pearl Harbor accused "rich Jews" of owning machine guns that they would use to "mow down" gentiles. He claimed that he and a couple of mad scientists were working on a way of poisoning needles and shooting them into Jews using blowguns or rubber bands.

Pearl Harbor

On December 7, 1941, a Sunday morning, the Japanese air force attacked the U.S. Naval Base in Pearl Harbor, Hawaii, sank many ships, and killed thousands of American sailors. FDR declared war on Japan, Germany, and Italy. As soon as war was declared, the First Amendment rights that the Nazis in America hid behind evaporated. Now they were committing sedition.

Der Tag Comes—and Goes

For the California Nazis, *der Tag* had finally come. The day. But there were no explosions in aircraft construction plants. No "big Jews" were offed. No ships sunk in the harbor. No merging of trained troops wearing brown and silver shirts. America geared for war unimpeded.

The Nazis were not just quiet; they were in hiding. Using lists provided them by the Nazibusters—and based on almost no information gathered by the FBI itself—the FBI raided multiple Bund cells across the country in the first days after Pearl Harbor. There were seventy-six arrests in all.

Hermann Schwinn was arrested at the Deutsches Haus, thrown in the county jail, and booked on suspicion of breaking federal laws. Hans Diebel, already facing deportation, was busted only minutes later as he tried to sneak into the Deutsches Haus through the back door.

According to records, only Franz Ferenz and Sylvia Comfort came to visit Schwinn and Diebel. Those visits ended when Schwinn and Diebel were transferred to Camp McCoy in Wisconsin. The Nazi leaders were first indicted by a New York grand jury in July 1942. They were indicted a second time in August by a Washington, D.C., grand jury. The charges were sedition and, yes, conspiracy to dodge the draft. In September, Schwinn and Diebel were convicted on the conspiracy charge and sentenced to five years in the fed pen.

Schwinn had hidden sensitive materials in the Deutches Haus, in a place where he'd hoped the FBI would never find them. But the Nazibusters told the FBI the location of Schwinn's hiding place. The FBI hauled away two trunks full of maps, cameras, crystal radio sets, photographs, propaganda, and wads and wads of cash.

Franz Ferenz was arrested on December 9, woken from a sound sleep in his bed, handcuffed, and thrown roughly into the back of a cop car. By December 11, the number of subversives arrested in the L.A. area ballooned to 418.

The Deutsches Haus in L.A. was abandoned, dark, and after a few weeks wearing a FOR SALE sign.

By the time "*der Tag*" arrived, the German American Bund was through. It was eight years in the trying, but the organization never caught on as its founders had hoped. Truth was, only a small percentage of German Americans were behind Hitler. The rest were lovers, not haters.

The debate of intervention versus isolationism was over. Even those who had favored isolationism now leaped into the fray. Nothing unites a people like a common enemy.

Dirty Little Secret

Sadly, after Pearl Harbor, antisemitism in America grew worse, not better. In 1940 about half of Americans thought "Jews should leave the U.S." In 1945, after four long years of war, that number increased to sixty-seven percent. It wasn't until the revelation of the Holocaust—Anne Frank, hollow eyes, living skeletons, gas-houses, and crematoriums—that some Christians in America developed empathy for the oppressed people.

The Comforts reported that people normally apolitical were now spouting antisemitism, because they blamed the Jews for dragging the U.S. into World War II. You'd think they'd blame the Japanese, but who knows how people think?

On January 24, 1942, the FBI "hired" Joe Roos as an unofficial agent, his job to acquire evidence on Nazis in L.A.

The FBI was dismantling the Nazi machine in California. But, with antisemitism on the rise, Lewis and Roos stayed vigilant, now working to protect L.A.'s Jewish citizens, rich and poor.

Charles Lindbergh, a Nazi sympathizer who'd considered a run against FDR in 1940, now kept his opinions private. Even before America's entry into the war, Lindbergh had been backing away from his pro-Nazi stance, saying he was concerned that the Nazis were handling their "Jew problem" in an "unreasonable" way.

The great majority of American Nazis went so far underground that they disappeared entirely. Some of them, of course, were drafted, but an effort was made to send young German American men to fight in the Pacific, where their allegiance would not be questioned.

Luckily for those who remained stateside, their whiteness allowed them to blend back into the crowd, unlike the tens of thousands of Japanese Americans who were plucked from their peaceful lives and interned.

Some German Americans changed their names and claimed to

be of Swedish descent. The Germania Club, scene of Gangsters vs. Nazis fighting in Chicago, changed its name to the Lincoln Club.

A Meeting of the Minds

Tough Jews continued to take a poke at smug Aryans whenever they had a chance. Take L.A. gangster Mickey Cohen. He'd boxed as a kid and could dish out world-class hurt. During the spring of 1942, four months after Pearl Harbor, now twenty-eight years old, Cohen was busted and spent some time in a downtown L.A. holding cell awaiting a court appearance to discuss ownership of a filed-off gun that had been found in his illegal Santa Monica Boulevard bookie joint. Cohen's first thought was, "Who'd I forget to grease?"

At the same time, two men were arrested for sedition, on evidence secretly supplied by their secretary Sylvia Comfort, and tossed into the same cell with Cohen to await questioning. Ellis Jones, a Yale graduate, was leader of the National Copperheads, Robert Noble, leader of the Friends of Progress, both groups Sylvia had infiltrated effortlessly with her charisma and secretarial skills.

Jones once told an audience that all true Americans should be ready to "turn the ghettos of New York, Chicago, and other cities into a slaughterhouse."

The pair, it was alleged, had published propaganda stating that the Japanese bombing of Pearl Harbor was "justified," that General Douglas MacArthur had abandoned his troops in Bataan, and that he was a "phony."

The propaganda was offensive enough to attract the attention of California Attorney General (and future Chief Justice of the Supreme Court) Earl Warren, who said, "These are loudspeakers for a group of Nazi sympathizers. If MacArthur and his boys can protect our nation at their posts of duty across the Pacific at Bataan, the State of California can and will at least protect their good name back home."

Cohen later claimed that he wasn't initially in the same jail cell with "those assholes," but after a talk with the guards, Noble and Jones were moved. Cohen had heard of Noble. He was a "real rabble-rousing anti-Jew Nazi bastard." He didn't know Jones but later wrote, he was just another "weasel bastard."

Now he could hear the two men talking, bad-mouthing Douglas MacArthur.

Cohen took exception. "That's a hell of a way to talk about the hero of our country," he said.

Noble looked at Cohen and smirked. "Oh, you must be one of those Jews, huh?" Noble said.

That did it. Cohen took a quick look around to make sure no one was watching and charged the men. In a flash Cohen grabbed both by the head and knocked their skulls together as hard as he could. Noble turned his back to Cohen, his hands on his head. Cohen kicked him in the seat of his pants so hard that his face hit the wall, breaking his glasses.

Cohen went to work with his fists, as his victims bellowed bloody murder. Guards came running.

"Why'd you put us in here with him," they screamed. "The guy's an animal."

Cohen had returned to his seat and was calmly scanning a newspaper. He told the guards that the two men had gotten into a fight with each other.

"I stayed out of it. I don't know what happened. I didn't want to mix with them," Cohen said, the wide-eyed picture of innocence.

"You're a lying bastard," they screamed, but no one paid attention.

Sylvia Comfort Under Suspicion

Sylvia Comfort stayed close to her original subject William Pierce Williams, and also to Franz Ferenz, and Ellis Jones, but had stopped seeing Robert Noble, who'd ghosted her. In and out of jail, Noble had had plenty of time to think—when he wasn't getting his head bonked by Jewish gangsters. Who knew what when? Where did Nazi secrets go to die?

When friends and colleagues came to visit Noble, he issued a warning they didn't expect: "Do not trust the Comforts," Noble said.

Most of the men he spoke to *loved* Grace and Sylvia, and thought Noble paranoid. Noble was out of jail the next time Sylvia tried to attend a meeting of his Friends of Progress. Noble himself blocked her path and told her that she was not welcome.

One fellow came to Sylvia's defense. He was Larry Griffith, the terrorist wannabe who ran the National Minutemen.

Griffith yelled at Noble: "You're the one who cannot be trusted. You work for the FBI!"

When Sylvia reported the incident to Leon Lewis, he told her to be extremely careful, that Noble was a "psycho."

"If you would like to discontinue the mission, I would certainly understand," Lewis said.

"No, no, I want to continue. Seems we can use this fuss I caused to our advantage," she replied.

"Yes, use the hostility between Noble and Griffith. Kindle the flame," Lewis said.

"Right, Chief," she said.

But it didn't pan out. Noble's legal predicament took him off the board before his rift with Griffith could be exploited.

Sylvia Under Arrest

The Comforts, Grace and Sylvia, continued their spy work during the war. The Nazibusters had known for some time that small cells of Nazis, prepared to commit acts of terrorism, were said to be plentiful in and around L.A. But it was Sylvia's undercover work that revealed the key details.

One of Sylvia's most valuable post–Pearl Harbor reports concerned the founder of the American Rangers, Jack Payton, who was plotting a "campaign of terror." Sylvia learned that Payton had formed three hundred small cells. Around this time, the U.S. Secret Service interviewed Sylvia's original subject William Pierce

Williams. After the interview, Williams showed up at the Comforts' house.

"Sylvia, I must talk to you. I think we are in trouble. I was just braced by the Secret Service. They will be questioning you next."

"Thank you for the warning, William," Sylvia said. "Stay safe."

The next day, Sylvia and Grace were arrested together while waiting in line at the post office, accused of writing threatening letters to the president. Leon Lewis surreptitiously showed a judge evidence that the Comforts were undercover and secured their release.

It was during that process that Sylvia learned, her "good buddy" Williams had betrayed her during his interview by the Secret Service, offering her as a sacrificial lamb in hopes that he and the rest of his operation would be left alone. It didn't work.

Despite that knowledge, Sylvia, like any good spy, maintained her cover, didn't let on that she knew Williams had betrayed her.

"You'd've been proud of me, William," Sylvia said. "They tried to make me talk, but I kept my yap zipped."

Sylvia Ends Her Mission

Sylvia Comfort stayed on the job, attending many fascist meetings, right up until the moment, in December 1943, when a fascist radio commentator named G. Allison Phelps reported on the air that the lovely secretary Sylvia Comfort, the scribe for many local organizations, had been spotted going in and out of the office of Jew lawyer Leon Lewis.

That ended her Nazibuster mission. At Lewis's suggestion, she moved to Washington, D.C.

Ferenz Goes Down

Noble and Jones weren't the only creeps the Comforts got busted. In 1942, seven other L.A. Nazis went down on sedition charges. They would be tried in a Sacramento court. At the trial for all nine Nazis, Jones testified that the FBI had been infiltrated by Nazi spies of the Friends of Progress, but refused to name names. "I don't believe that there are any spies in the FBI now," Jones said.

On February 23, 1942, Ferenz was attacked during a break by a woman wearing slacks, very unusual at that time. She stomped on his foot and kicked him in the shins. Ferenz complained: "She stuck a burning cigarette in my face. Look here! See that, she burned me. She tried to put my eye out!"

After the session reporters huddled around the skirtless woman, who refused to identify herself.

"Just call me Molly Pitcher," she said, a nickname for revolutionary women.

When order was restored, an elderly man named D. H. Rathbone took the witness stand and admitted that he was a printer, with a press in his home on Telegraph Road, and that he had printed pamphlets for Noble.

"Do you have a sample with you?"

"Yes, sir."

"Could you read from it, please?"

"Sure. Ahem: 'The meanest joke the Germans ever played on the U.S.A. was when they saved FDR from dying of infantile paralysis, enabling him to double-cross the American people into slavery to the British and Jewish criminals.'"

When Noble himself was called to the witness stand, he refused to answer questions until Chairman Jack Tenney threatened him with a contempt charge. Noble was asked his opinion on the attack on Pearl Harbor and replied, "I believe the Japanese did the right thing." He added that the U.S. should just withdraw its troops, as the war was basically over. Germany had won the war in Europe, and the Japanese had won the war in the Pacific.

Noble was asked if it was true that he'd made the following statement: "I say I am for Germany and for Hitler. *Heil Hitler!* I do not know why people are shocked when we say we are for Germany and for Hitler. You know as I told you Germany has won this war and we might as well recognize the new order and the United States of Europe."

Noble replied that he did say that. He didn't remember saying "*Heil Hitler!*" but admitted that he "was perfectly willing to."

At least one of the defendants used the "I'm not a Nazi, I'm a pacifist" defense. This was a Mrs. McBride, charged with failure to register as a subversive. She was asked if she hadn't been a regular at meetings of the German American Bund during the late 1930s, and she admitted that she had.

"The only reason I attended those meetings was because they were trying to keep us out of the war. I am more American than a lot of those news columnists. I consider them propagandists. I have never belonged to any subversive organization."

"And how do you feel about the government in Germany today?" she was asked.

"I prefer the German form of government to any other form of government now in Europe," she replied.

The Nazis were all convicted, with the leaders getting the harshest sentences: Noble five years in jail, Jones four.

Bockhacker Gets the Last Word

The courts weren't done with the men and women who, for years, had been on the Nazibusters' radar. On January 4, 1943, Schwinn, Diebel, Noble, Jones, Mrs. Fry, Franz Ferenz, George Deatherage, and twenty-four others were indicted by a Washington, D.C., federal grand jury, charging them with conspiring to impair the U.S. military and to promote insubordination and mutiny.

William A. Bockhacker, formerly Agent W2, testified regarding his infiltration of the Bund. He told the court that Bundists were "ready to fight at any time with arms if necessary." The Bund's storm troopers believed that they should obey any order from the Bund leaders, without question.

Bockhacker testified: "At one point one of the leaders, Herman [sic] Schwinn, told me that the Bund was making a fight here in the United States. He said to me, 'The fact that you are an

American is fine. We are trying to educate the American public about the National Socialist movement.'"

Victory Lap

You could forgive Lewis and Roos for taking a victory lap. All of their greatest enemies were in jail, Hollywood had remained true-blue American, and not a single airplane or shipbuilding plant on the West Coast had blown up on their watch.

The Nazibuster list of suspicious individuals employed in defense plants bore fruit repeatedly. Several bad eggs were given the boot from the Douglas Aircraft Company plant in Santa Monica and the Lockheed Corporation facility in Glendale. Among those fired for being a security risk was a KKK Grand Dragon.

EPILOGUE

As Paul Harvey used to say, here's the rest of the story.

Paul Joseph Goebbels

Dr. Goebbels stuck to his Führer till the very end, which came on April 30, 1945. As the Russians approached Berlin from the east and the Americans and their allies approached from the west, Hitler shot himself in his bunker. Goebbels, also in the bunker, was out of his mind with grief, tears streaming down his face as his leader and his dream crumbled around him. He lasted about a day, then arranged with his dentist to inject his children first with morphine and then with cyanide. He left the bunker, explosions from Russian artillery all around him, and walked—his club foot causing him to struggle more than ever—to the chancellery garden, where he, too, killed himself.

Boyle Heights

L.A.'s Jewish neighborhood of the 1930s stopped being heavily Jewish during the mid-twentieth century when several freeways were built through it, including the East L.A. Interchange, which is at one point twenty-seven lanes wide. The construction helped cars get around but changed Boyle Heights for the worse, tearing down houses, obliterating main drags, and vivisecting what was left.

R.I.P. Old Studio System

During WWII, the U.S. Government and the Hollywood studios became strange bedfellows, working hand in hand to boost morale, both among the troops overseas and back home. Sadly, however, the war wasn't over for long before conservative politicians in America again went to war against Hollywood and its "un-Christian and Communist ways."

In 1947, the House Un-American Activities Committee turned on Hollywood.

In 1948, in the case known as United States v. Paramount, Inc. et al., a federal court prohibited the studios that made the films to be owned by the same people as the theaters that showed those films. The ruling effectively ended the old way of making motion pictures.

Leon Lewis

Leon L. Lewis remained the executive secretary of the LAJCC (Nazibusters) until 1946, only months after the end of World War II and the near complete destruction of the Nazis. He returned to his private law practice after thirteen years away.

Asked about his fight, Lewis said, "It was the non-Jews in my employ that made the difference in the fight, for they realized that attacks on American Jews impinged directly upon the self-interest of all strata of American life."

With both daughters married and one grandson, Lewis lived out the last years of his life with his wife, Ruth, at a home on El Cerco Place in Pacific Palisades, California. He died of a heart attack while driving on the Pacific Coast Highway near his home, at age sixty-five, on May 21, 1954. His funeral services were held in the chapel of Malinow and Simon Mortuary on Venice Boulevard.

His obituary ran in many newspapers, because he was the first executive director of the ADL and a former national director of B'nai B'rith. It also mentioned that he was active in the American Legion and the Disabled American War Veterans, serving as head of the DAV's Americanism Committee, which investigated "subversive activity." The wrap-up of his career said that he was the director of the Community Relations Committee of the Los Angeles Jewish Community Council. There was no mention of Nazis, or that time he saved the city.

Unfortunately for Los Angeles's Jews, antisemitism did not end on V-E Day, or with the slow reveal of the horrors of the Holocaust, so Lewis's coleader of the LAJCC, Mendel Silberberg, stayed on with the LAJCC until his death in 1965.

Neil Ness

Neil Ness, Leon Lewis's prolific Agent N2, was so determined to maintain his cover that he was blackballed as a Nazi and was unable to return to his career as an engineer. He was waiting to be called as a witness in an anti-Nazi trial, a reprieve from his false public persona, but he didn't make it that far.

On January 9, 1943, the story goes, the LAPD hauled in a very drunk Neil Ness, who fell and hit his head on the concrete floor of the drunk tank and was found dead the next morning. An L.A. county coroner's physician performed the autopsy. Cause of death: a basal skull fracture. Official manner of death: falling down.

But many would never believe it. The same wound could have been caused by a blow to the back of the head. Five months after Ness's death, Lewis revealed who Ness really was and cleared his name.

John Schmidt

Like Ness, Leon Lewis's first spy, John H. Schmidt, did not survive the end of the war and died under what had to be called suspicious circumstances. And like Ness, Schmidt had a date to testify in court when he died. Schmidt was scheduled to testify at the big sedition trial in Washington, D.C., but on April 3, 1944, Schmidt's wife, Alyce, called police.

"My husband John is dead. I believe he has been poisoned."

A cop asked, "Address?"

"235 South Coronado."

And so, they came and got him. He was fifty-nine years old.

"He's supposed to testify. He's received so many death threats," Alyce cried.

Dr. Stanley McCool, who had been treating Schmidt for "pernicious anemia" told authorities that he believed Schmidt had died of natural causes. But after hearing Alyce's claims that he'd been murdered, Dr. McCool refused to sign the death certificate.

Alyce said that John dined out on Friday evening and returned home feeling extremely ill. He remained in bed for two days and died. The FBI, to its credit, ordered a chemical analysis of Schmidt's vital organs to be conducted by Coroner Frank Nance. Nope, no poison, the coroner said, natural causes—but many, including the widow, would never believe him. Schmidt's obituary, with information supplied by Alyce, noted that he had testified several times in "Bund investigations" and against the organizers of other Nazi-inspired groups.

Charles Slocombe

The agent who spent the most time undercover was Charles Slocombe, Agent C2, but he was never called upon to testify in court, a fact that may have saved his life. That hardly negates any of his accomplishments, however, as it was material from his reports that fed the *News Letter* and taught America of the Nazi threat.

Slocombe had been so good at his job that he'd been named *Kreis Führer*, regional leader, of the Bund, so good that one of Lewis and Roos's new spies, a fellow named John Barr (J2) filed a report saying that Slocombe was one of the worst of the Nazis. Barr had gotten inside the Nazi organization by working for a newspaper called *The American Gentile*.

"A bad egg, plotting sabotage," Barr reported. Again, proof that the spies Lewis and Roos sent into the fray didn't always know about one another.

At the same time, Slocombe was reporting to Lewis and Roos that he'd heard talk of German submarines patrolling off the coast of Mexico, just south of the California border, poised and ready to strike at San Diego or San Pedro. The submarine commanders would tender ashore late at night and meet with Nazi spies in Tijuana.

Slocombe was so respected by the Nazis that he was asked to spy on the U.S. military, to find out, for example, if the harbors outside America's West Coast docks, were being mined to hinder invasion.

And he'd done it at-risk in two ways. The Nazi threat was well-known. But Slocombe had heart disease and was being treated by a cardiologist, with Lewis paying the bills.

Slocombe, bum ticker and all, was the fellow who stayed a spy once Leon Lewis's op was concluded. After WWII, Slocombe rooted out subversives for the Long Beach Police Department. One of his last Nazibuster jobs had been looking for harbor spies while running a water taxi, an occupation he continued after the Nazis were gone. He worked as a tugboat captain in Long Beach Harbor. He dedicated his later years to the development of the harbor and, in 1985, received an award from the harbor community. He was eighty-five when he died in his Long Beach home in 1992. At the time of his death, only a handful of people knew the heroic work he'd done for America.

Joe Roos

After Pearl Harbor, Roos made sure the War Department in Washington, D.C., had a copy of his files, information used to screen enemies from defense jobs. Over the following years, Roos wrote hundreds of radio scripts about human and community relations, work that earned him a Peabody Award.

In 1997, he was presented the University of Southern California's Lifetime Achievement Award. At that presentation, USC President Steven B. Sample said, "Joe Roos is the model for a servant in the community. Few have done so much to make southern California a better place for all people."

Joe Roos lived to be ninety-four, dying in L.A., December 11, 1999. He left his Nazibuster files to USC's Doheny Library.

Sylvia Comfort

Sylvia Comfort, after her move to Washington, D.C., in December 1943, became secretary for a California congressman, Rep. Gordon McDonough, a Republican. She decided who got in to see him and protected the secrets of his lair. She held the position until 1963, and died at age ninety, in Washington, on December 3, 2003.

William "Red" Hynes

Hynes, who gathered information for—and squealed on—a myriad of persons and organizations, ended up spending twenty-two years in the LAPD. He retired in 1943 and died in 1952 in Good Samaritan Hospital in L.A. at the age of fifty-five.

Harry Warner

After World War II, Harry founded Hollywood Park Racetrack and maintained a stable of Thoroughbreds. The 1950s were marked by tumult for the Warner brothers, aging siblings who no longer could see eye to eye on anything—Harry was not a womanizer, married to the same woman since 1907, but brother Jack was, and the contrast led to estrangements. But Harry did a smart thing at the beginning of the decade and turned to television production. He also made the most of the 1950s 3-D craze, an early attempt to pull people from the boob tube. Harry died on July 25, 1958, in Hollywood, at age seventy-six.

Georg Gyssling

Georg Gyssling, the former German consul in L.A., booted out of the country in 1941 by FDR, sent one last damning memo to the German Foreign Office after his return to Germany, which described in detail the aircraft and warplane manufacturing going on in California.

Gyssling maybe thought his days of intrigue were through, and that was when the Gestapo pounded on his door and dragged him in to be interrogated. Apparently, he passed muster, but he worked for them now, and he was assigned to partake in a counterfeit scheme, forging exquisite pound notes, designed to wreck the British economy.

At the end of the war he served in northern Italy, working with notable superspies like Allen Dulles of the OSS, brokering the peace at the Italian front. Then the Americans arrested Gyssling, charged him with war crimes, and tried him at Nuremburg. He was eventually acquitted, because he'd worked for "the resistance" during World War II. A free man, Gyssling moved to the south of Spain and died in 1965.

Hermann Schwinn and Hans Diebel

In November 1947, Schwinn was transferred to Ellis Island. In July 1948, he was put aboard the SS *Uruguay* and sent to Buenos Aires, which is where all the hip Nazis were going if they survived the war. Presumably he died there.

Transferred to Ellis Island with Schwinn was Hans Diebel, who returned to Germany after the war and lived in Frankfurt for the rest of his life, which ended in 1984.

Franz Ferenz

The Nazi who plotted the most and executed the least, Franz Ferenz—whose greatest contribution to his cause was as theater manager—spent the war inside San Quentin State Penitentiary. On April 24, 1945, an appeals court reversed Ferenz's conviction, a judge ruling he never plotted to violently overthrow the government, and boom!—he was out. They let Noble and Jones out as well. Ferenz came back to live in L.A. and died in 1956.

William Dudley Pelley

Far more than any of the other bad guys, William Dudley Pelley landed on his feet after World War II. He was in prison in North Carolina until 1950. Once released, he began his newest confidence game—this one involving flying saucers, alien abductions, and the looming threat of an invasion from outer space.

Same guy, different paranoia.

Now he was in spiritual contact with the Babe Ruth of prognosticators, Nostradamus himself, who'd introduced Pelley to the spirits of George Washington and Mark Twain. That all became the basis for his new religion, which he called Soulcraft. He died in Indiana in 1965.

Fritz Kuhn

Following Bund leader Fritz Kuhn's jail term for embezzlement, he was rearrested in 1943 as an "enemy agent" and interned by the feds. On September 15, 1945, the war over, Kuhn was deported to Germany. He sailed across the Atlantic aboard the SS *Winchester Victory* and worked as a free man for a small chemical factory in Munich before being arrested yet again as a potential war criminal under Germany's de-Nazification laws. He was sent to the repurposed Dachau concentration camp and released only shortly before his death on December 15, 1951.

Heinz Spanknöbel

The original leader of the Friends of New Germany returned to Germany in the early 1930s. Maybe he wished he'd stayed in California. In Germany he was thrown into the army, given a modicum of training, and sent to the Eastern Front, where he had the misfortune to be captured by the Soviets. When the war ended, he was not released. He died of starvation in 1947.

William Pierce Williams

Sylvia Comfort's boss, the North Hollywood High School teacher who was also a Nazi organizer, went off the deep end after World War II. Taking a note from his heroes, Hitler, Goebbels, and others, Williams shot his wife, Hannah, as she slept and then turned the gun on himself. Williams left a note: "Collapsed nerves. Returning to the Creator."

Walter Wanger Shoots a Guy in the Balls

Walter Wanger, producer of so much of Hollywood's first anti-Nazi content, was embroiled in a scandal in 1951. Married at the time to actress Joan Bennett, he shot her agent, Jennings Lang, with whom she was having an affair. The agent's wounds were in the scrotum and thigh.

Wanger learned that Lang and Bennett were having frequent afternoon trysts in the apartment of one of Lang's lowly office workers, a situation that percolated through director Billy Wilder's incredible mind and turned into the 1960 Oscar-winning movie *The Apartment.*

The Wanger case resulted in a spectacular trial. He was convicted, served four months, and returned to work immediately.

His last movie was *Cleopatra* (1963) with Elizabeth Taylor and Richard Burton. It went severely behind schedule and overbudget due to the relentless fornication of its stars. Despite all of that waiting for the trailer to stop rocking, the film earned Wanger an Oscar nomination for Best Picture.

He died in 1966, of a heart attack, at age seventy-four.

The Führer's Fräulein

Filmmaker Leni Riefenstahl was arrested after the war and used to identify war criminals in seized German film footage. The arrest was made by Hollywood's Budd Schulberg—later to win an Oscar for writing *On the Waterfront* (1954)—in his wartime capacity as an OSS agent. During her lengthy interrogation, she gave Schulberg, as he put it, "the song and dance. She knew nothing about the concentration camps or what went on there." She claimed to be apolitical, and she more or less got away with it, continuously celebrated as a great artist, her association with Hitler at least partially forgiven. She lived until the age of 101, dying in 2003, in a hotel room in Bavaria. She's buried in Munich.

APPENDIX

Anti-Fascist Hollywood Movies Before Pearl Harbor:

A REPRESENTATIVE FILMOGRAPHY

Bosko's Picture Show (1933), Warner Bros. cartoon. 6 minutes.

Includes a scene in which a caricature of Hitler chases a caricature of a Jewish man with a caricature of a hatchet. Back then, it got a laugh.

The President Vanishes (1934), Independent producer Walter Wagner. 80 minutes.

Wagner, who would make a career out of being anti-Nazi, was first to release an anti-fascist movie.

The villains here are "The Grey Shirts," a takeoff on Silver Shirts. The William Pelley–like leader is called "Lincoln Lee," a reference to the American Civil War. Members imitated the Hitler "*Sieg Heil!*" salute while saying, "Union!" The enemies that the Grey Shirts rant against are never specified, just "enemies of America with no power unless elected to office."

The film's villain is bigotry, and today that comes through loud and clear, but in 1934 there were audiences that missed the point and saw it as a Silver Shirt recruiting picture.

Hitler's Reign of Terror (1934). Independently produced by Samuel Cummins and Joseph Seiden. Director: Michael Mindlin. Writer: Joseph Seiden. Docudrama, combining real footage shot by Cornelius Vanderbilt, Jr., with re-creations. 65 minutes.

The most directly anti-Hitler movie of the first half of the

1930s. Predicts Hitler's threat to World Peace. Managed to be released unhampered, largely because it stuck to the truth without hyperbole and beat the birth of the Production Code by a few months. Still, distribution was chipped away by censors, review boards, and German consuls. *Hitler's Reign of Terror* was considered lost for years until a copy was found in cold storage at the Royal Belgium Film Archive in Brussels in 2013.

Old Glory (1936–40), Warner Bros. series of three-reelers.

At first, depicted great moments in American history—how *The Star-Spangled Banner* became the National Anthem, the signing of the Declaration of Independence, the Monroe Doctrine, the Bill of Rights, etc.—but as the European war grew, the focus shifted to preparation for war overseas and exposing the Nazis among us on the home front. Some editions are available on YouTube.

I Was a Captive of Nazi Germany (1936). Independently produced by Alfred Mannon. 72 minutes.

After *Hitler's Reign of Terror*, it was two years before another English-language film was made that was boldly critical of the Nazis. Another docudrama, mixing newsreel footage—boycott, book burning—with re-creations, telling the true story of Isobel Lillian Steele, a pretty, twenty-three-year-old American music student, born in Canada and raised in Hollywood, who was arrested in Berlin on suspicion of espionage and jailed in Alexanderplatz for four months. She was released when an Idaho senator intervened.

In the movie, Steele plays herself. The film opened on Broadway in New York, without PCA approval. Other than Steele, the film was shown without credits. The evil Gestapo agents who menace Steele in this picture were prototypical movie Nazis.

The movie made it to L.A. in 1937 but only for a brief run at a small theater. The poster out front read, "The story of a Hollywood girl in Naziland, always in the shadow of the beheading ax."

Black Legion (1937), Warner Bros. 83 minutes.

The real-life Black Legion had been an offshoot of the KKK, formed in the 1920s by a Dr. William Jacob Shepard. The organization was known for its anxiety-inducing initiation rites, which included Black Mass–type ceremonies out in the woods, with blindfolds and loaded guns. Any initiate who turned on the legion or betrayed its secrets would be killed—slowly. . . .

The Black Legion's primary object was to lynch Blacks, Jews, Catholics, and any weirdos they might find alone. The legion's numbers grew exponentially in 1931 when Shepard gave the reins to Bert Effinger of Ohio, whose rabble-rousing speeches, like those of William Pelley, featured antisemitic visions from the beyond.

Effinger couldn't keep a secret. He frequently spoke in a loud voice of his desire to storm Washington and take control of the government by force.

"This is my plan to wipe out the Jews," he stage-whispered. "We will infiltrate a kosher dairy and inject typhus into the milk and cheese delivered to Jewish customers."

In the long run it was Effinger's paranoia that did in the Black Legion. He envisioned his organization riddled with spies, and the hunt to ferret out the moles left little room for overthrowing governments.

As Effinger's paranoia grew, those he trusted became increasingly moronic, degenerate, and psychopathic. One of Effinger's inner circle was Detroit's Dayton Dean, who on May 12, 1936, in night-rider fashion, kidnapped a Catholic coworker because he was married to a Protestant woman. The legionnaires took the man to a deserted spot, shot him eight times in the head, and left him in a ditch. Because the victim was a white man, police had to do something and quickly arrested Dean. The instigator turned stool pigeon, and the story came out. Dean's testimony against his fellow legionnaires got the attention of Harry Warner, and the Legion became the subject of a Warner Bros. movie, producer Hal Wallis in charge of the project.

Wallis initially wanted to cast Edward G. Robinson in the lead, but Robinson "didn't look American enough," so the newly hot Humphrey Bogart was cast instead. There were security concerns during production and sets were given extra security, but there were no attempts to disrupt the making of the movie.

The only legal trouble the film encountered came after its release, when the KKK sued because Warner Bros. had stolen the design of their hooded uniforms. A California judge threw out the suit.

Bogart plays an affable factory worker whose anticipated promotion goes instead to an immigrant, a foreigner. He turns on the radio and someone imitating Father Coughlin comes on, kindling our hero's frustration into hate and xenophobia.

A coworker recruits Bogart into the Black Legion. To get around the PCA, the film had to be vague about the hate's target. The enemy, according to the script, is defined as those who "cling to foreign doctrines, foreign faiths, and un-American morals."

Bogart is initiated in the woods by men in black robes who hold a loaded gun to his head. Once in, Bogart must prove he's capable of violence—*make his bones*, as the Mafia says—so when a coworker refuses to join the legion, Bogart has him punished. Legionnaires drag him into a secluded spot and whip him. Bogart then shoots the man in the back and kills him.

The movie ends with the murder trial. The judge gets the last word: "Your idea of patriotism and Americanism is hideous to all decent citizens. We cannot permit racial or religious hatreds to be stirred up so that innocent citizens become the victims of accusations brought in secrecy."

The movie was well-reviewed, called "courageous" and a sign that Hollywood was "growing up."

Looney Tunes and Merry Melodies (1937–41), Warner Bros. cartoon series. 6 minutes.

These increasingly featured the WB stars (Bugs Bunny, Daffy Duck, Porky Pig, Elmer Fudd, all voiced by Mel Blanc) enlisting or being drafted, helping to ready America for the upcoming battle. Probably the most famous was the 1939 *Old Glory*, in which Porky Pig doesn't want to memorize the Pledge of Allegiance until kindly old Uncle Sam visits him in a dream to give him a lesson in patriotism.

Hitler: Beast of Berlin (1939), Producers Releasing Corporation (PRC). Director: Sherman Scott (pseudonym for Sam Newfield). Writer: Fred Myton. Cast: Roland Drew, Steffi Duna, Greta Granstedt, and Alan Ladd. 87 minutes.

Poverty Row feature based on the novel *Goose Step* by Shepard Traube. A couple producing anti-Nazi propaganda in Berlin are caught. The man is sent to a concentration camp. Will he be able to escape and flee to Switzerland? Contains newsreel footage of Hitler. Criticized for merely "scratching at the surface" of Hitler's evil.

Confessions of a Nazi Spy (1939) (see Chapter 21).

Warner Bros. uses the Mighty Voice.

The Nine Million (1939), Warner Bros. Producer: Sam Sax. Director: Roy Mack. Starring Burnet Hershey. 10 minutes.

Made in conjunction with United Jewish Appeal, it combines newsreel footage with studio-shot scenes. It was a call-to-action film regarding the refugee crisis caused by European Jews fleeing Hitler. The film urges the government to raise immigration quotas and the public to offer haven for "refugees fleeing fascism."

Crisis (1939), released by foreign-film importers Arthur Mayer and Joseph Burstyn, produced by Herbert Kline. Written by Hans

Berger and Alexander Hammid. Starring Leif Erickson (narrator), Eduard Benes, and Konrad Henlein. 95 minutes.

Using archival footage, much of it previously seen on *The March of Time*, the film pulled no punches. It opens with a shot of the book *Mein Kampf*, followed by an animated map in which Germany morphs into a wolf's head that hungrily takes bites out of its neighbors. The film's narrator describes Hitler's ambitions and methods, and concludes, "The human race itself is impoverished and humiliated by these events."

FDR saw the movie and urged all theater operators to book it. "You must show this film everywhere in the country to help counter the 'America Firsters' propaganda calling me a war monger," the president said.

You Nazty Spy! (1940), Columbia. Director: Jules White. Writers: Felix Adler and Clyde Bruckman. Cast: Moe Howard, Jerome "Curly" Howard, and Larry Fine. 18 minutes.

The Three Stooges deliver the first anti-Nazi film to be made by a major studio other than WB. Despite it being a silly Stooges short, with the normal reliance on slapstick, Moe Howard's Hitler impression remains a Hollywood vs. Nazis highlight.

The short opens with a gag that doubles as a legal disclaimer: "Any resemblance between the characters in this picture and any persons living or dead is a miracle."

Moe actually plays a paperhanger who inadvertently stages a coup and becomes dictator of Moronica. His transformation into Hitler becomes complete when he gets a piece of black electric tape stuck to his upper lip.

With Curly Howard playing Gallstone, a Mussolini type fellow, and Larry Fine as Pebble, a Goebbels-like propaganda king, they eye-poke and slap each other in the usual Stooge order, Curly and Larry taunting Moe because he promised to invade "Great Mitten" but hasn't gotten around to it.

The two comic impressions of Hitler in Hollywood movies

were Moe Howard's and Charlie Chaplin's, which we'll get to. Only Howard captured the intense anger that was key to Hitler's charisma.

Foreign Correspondent (1940), United Artists. 120 minutes.

Another anti-Nazi thriller produced by Walter Wanger. To direct, Wanger hired the future king of suspense Alfred Hitchcock, who wasn't yet the superstar he'd become but was seen by both producers and audiences as a top edge-of-your-seat auteur.

It was based on a book called *Personal History* by real-life foreign correspondent Vincent Sheehan. The book included sections on the Russian Revolution, the Spanish Civil War, and on the rise of Nazism in Europe. Wanger had already brought in Hitchcock and writers Charles Bennett and Joan Harrison, who wrote a script relevant to 1940 audiences. The final script was credited to Bennett and Harrison, but included dialogue added by some notable Hollywood figures including Budd Schulberg (*On the Waterfront*, *The Harder They Fall*), and wisecracking sophisticate Robert Benchley, who lent roundtable wit to humorous shorts for MGM.

Released by United Artists, it was by far the best received of the pre–Pearl Harbor anti-Nazi pictures. Nominated for six Academy Awards, including Best Picture.

Starring Joel McRae and Laraine Day, it tells the story of an American reporter who stumbles upon a sect of Nazi agents in England. The film contains a difficult-to-watch torture scene in which the Nazi villains are shown to be animalistic sadists. The film concludes with an obvious call-to-action to stop the spreading menace.

Among the inspirational quotes to come out of that script were: "You don't keep out of war just by being peaceful while other people are slowly digging away at the ground under your feet. That's not how you keep out of a war. That's how you lose a war." And: "Hello, America. Hang onto your lights. They're the only lights left in the world."

The Great Dictator (1940), United Artists. 125 minutes.

Producer, director, and star Charlie Chaplin mocks Hitler. The BBC called it "a spookily accurate insight into Hitler's psychology." Chaplin, who'd stubbornly continued to make silent pictures well into the talkies era, makes his first real sound picture here, portraying the title character, called Adenoid Hynkel, leader of Tomania. The most famous scene depicts the world as a large balloon, one that bounces up and down as the exceedingly graceful Chaplin plays with it as a toy. Chaplin plays a dual part, also portraying a poor amnesiac Jewish barber who has just been released from a hospital due to a wound suffered in the First World War. The picture is a vivid indictment of Nazi evil, despite its technical status as a comedy. (The scene with the balloon frustrated some, because it gave the Hitler character a gracefulness and gentleness that the actual dirtbag lacked.)

Hidden Enemy (1940), Monogram Pictures. Director: Howard Bretherton. Writers: Charles Williams and Marion Orth. 63 minutes.

A newspaper reporter battles German spies in the U.S. seeking industrial secrets. The MacGuffin is the formula for a new metal "lighter than aluminum and stronger than steel." Stars Warren Hull, best known as the *Werewolf of London* (1935). Available on YouTube.

Escape (1940), MGM. Director: Mervyn LeRoy. Writers: Arch Oboler and Marguerite Roberts. Stars: Robert Taylor and Norma Shearer. 98 minutes.

Film tells of a young man searching for his mother, who's been thrown into a concentration camp by the Nazis. The studio had difficulty finding Jewish cast and crew as they were fearful of Nazi reprisals.

During production, things in Europe went from bad to worse. Germany invaded Scandinavia, and Belgium surrendered.

The Mortal Storm (1940), MGM. 100 minutes.

In June 1940, MGM released *The Mortal Storm*, which depicted Nazi Germany as a gangster state, seen through the eyes of one German family. It was based on the novel of the same name, published in 1937, written by British author Phyllis Bottome, who had lived in Germany during the first years of Hitler's reign and had seen the dramatic change that came over the country. To direct the picture, Louis B. Mayer hired Frank Borzage, known for his dozens of filmed romances and potboilers dating back to the silent-movie era.

Production encountered unexpected difficulties. The art director called for one hundred Nazi flags, but there wasn't a flag maker in southern California willing to fill the order, so the seamstresses in the MGM prop department went to work and made them.

The script did pull a few punches. The word Jew or Jewish is absent. The poor folks being persecuted by the SS were referred to as "non-Aryans." The only hint at what it's all about comes after one of our protagonists is rounded up and sent to a concentration camp, there is a large J drawn on his prison uniform.

When *The Mortal Storm* came out, the MGM publicity department tub-thumped the film as a romance. Posters showed stars James Stewart and Margaret Sullavan in full embrace. No swastikas, no Nazis anywhere to be seen.

This pattern of eliminating the anti-Nazi bent of future MGM pictures continued. A comedy script about Nazis called *Heil, Jennie* was released just as *Jennie*. A film called *I Married a Nazi* had a last-minute title change to *The Man I Married* (see below).

At Twentieth Century-Fox, as war approached, Darryl F. Zanuck wanted to make a picture about religious intolerance called *Brigham Young*. Fox boss Joe Schenck didn't like the idea, saying, "The European war is going from bad to worse. By the time your picture is done, the intolerance of Brigham Young's day will seem pleasant compared to Nazi brutality."

Zanuck talked Schenck out of his objection and the picture was made, but Joe had been right. It wasn't the big hit that Zanuck thought it would be.

The Man I Married (1940), Twentieth Century-Fox. Producer: Darryl F. Zanuck. Director: Irving Pichel. Writer: Oliver H. P. Garrett, based on a short story by Oscar Schisgall. Cast: Joan Bennett, Francis Lederer, Lloyd Nolan, and Anna Sten. 77 minutes.

Originally entitled *I Married a Nazi.*

I'll Never Heil Again (1941), Columbia Pictures. Director: Jules White. Writers: Felix Adler and Clyde Bruckman. Cast: Moe Howard, Jerome "Curly" Howard, and Larry Fine. 18 minutes.

The release date, appropriately enough, was July 4, 1941. Tag line: "Hilarious howls with Hollywood's daffy dictators!"

The Three Stooges' first send-up of the Führer and his boys went over so well, they came back for an encore a year later. The title is a takeoff on an early Frank Sinatra tearjerker, "I'll Never Smile Again," which had the honor of being *Billboard* magazine's first number-one hit, where it remained for twelve weeks, most of the summer of 1940.

At one point in the short, Moe has his mustache ripped off.

"Give me back my personality," he says.

Moe caused a furor, no pun intended, when after a late day of shooting, still wearing his personality, he had to rush to his daughter's birthday party, causing concerned Angelinos to call the LAPD reporting that Hitler was running red lights.

In the distance, across this company town, Hollywood U.S.A., still anti-Nazi and free, a squawky band played the Three Stooges theme, the verse to "Listen to the Mockingbird."

SOURCES

Books

Arad, Gulie Ne'eman. *America, Its Jews, and the Rise of Nazism.* Bloomington: Indiana University Press, 2000.

Beekman, Scott. *William Dudley Pelley.* Syracuse, NY: Syracuse University Press, 2005.

Bernstein, Arnie. *Swastika Nation.* New York: St. Martin's Press, 2013.

Bernstein, Matthew. *Controlling Hollywood.* New Brunswick, NJ: Rutgers University Press, 1999.

Birdwell, Michael E. *Celluloid Soldiers.* New York: NYU Press, 1999.

Brinkley, Alan. *Voices of Protest.* New York: Knopf, 1982.

Buntin, John. *L.A. Noir.* New York: Broadway Books, 2009.

Carr, Steven Alan. *Hollywood and Anti-Semitism.* New York: Cambridge University Press, 2001.

Cohen, Mickey, and John Peer Nugent. *In My Own Words.* Englewood Cliffs, NJ: Prentice-Hall, 1975.

Diamond, Sander. *The Nazi Movement in the United States, 1924–1941.* Ithaca, NY: Cornell University Press, 1974.

Dinnerstein, Leonard. *Antisemitism in America.* New York: Oxford University Press, 1994.

Doherty, Thomas. *Hollywood and Hitler, 1933–1939.* New York: Columbia University Press, 2013.

Duncan, Paul, ed. *Alfred Hitchcock: The Complete Films*. Los Angeles: Taschen, 2019.

Fleming, E. J. *The Fixers*. Jefferson, NC: McFarland & Company, 2005.

Frye, Alton. *Nazi Germany and the American Hemisphere*. New Haven, CT: Yale University Press, 1967.

Gabler, Neal. *An Empire of Their Own*. New York: Crown, 1986.

Hart, Bradley W. *Hitler's American Friends: The Third Reich's Supporters in the United States*. New York: St. Martin's Press, 2018.

Higham, Charles. *American Swastika*. Garden City, NY: Doubleday, 1985.

Hoke, Travis. *Shirts!* New York: American Civil Liberties Union Press, 1934.

Kahn, Ava. *Jews of the Pacific Coast*. Seattle: University of Washington Press, 2010.

Mann, William J. *Tinseltown*. New York: Harper, 2014.

Ross, Steven J. *Hitler in Los Angeles*. New York: Bloomsbury, 2019.

Spivak, John. *Secret Armies*. New York: Modern Age, 1939.

Vorspan, Max, and Lloyd P. Gartner. *History of the Jews of Los Angeles*. Philadelphia: Jewish Publication Society of America, 1970.

Whitman, James Q. *Hitler's American Model*. Princeton, NJ: Princeton University Press, 2018.

Periodicals

The American Hebrew & Jewish Messenger

The American Israelite

The American Magazine
Architectural Digest
B'nai B'rith Messenger
California Jewish Voice
California Weckruf
Chicago Tribune
Eastside Journal
Film Weekly
Hollywood Citizen-News
Hollywood Now
The Hollywood Reporter
Hollywood Spectator
The Jewish Exponent
Jewish Review
Ken
Life
The Literary Digest
The Long Beach Morning Sun
Los Angeles Evening Citizen News
Los Angeles Evening Herald Express
Los Angeles Examiner
Los Angeles Times
Military Technical Journal
Mosaic Magazine
Motion Picture Daily
Nevada State Journal
The New York Times

The New Yorker

The Pasadena Post

The Pomona Progress Bulletin

The San Diego Union-Tribune

Santa Cruz Sentinel

The Saturday Evening Post

Sunday Worker

Tablet

World Service

World War II

Websites

Dav.org

law.uchicago.edu

jta.org

mosaicmagazine.com

Myjewishlearning.com

Pbssocal.org

Smithsonianmag.com

Timesofisrael.com

Usc.edu

ACKNOWLEDGMENTS

The author would like to thank the following persons and organizations without whose help the writing of this book would have been impossible: editor James Abbate; photographer Matthew Benson; the Reference Services staff at the Center for Jewish History; Rebecca Cremonese, Mallory Furnier, Special Collections & Archives Librarian and David N. Sigler, Reading Room Supervisor at University Library, California State University, Northridge; Sandra Garcia-Myers, PhD, USC Cinematic Arts Library and Archives; my agent extraordinaire, Doug Grad; Lisa Grasso-Benson; Shira Hudson at the United Jewish Appeal; Sue Luftschein, Head, Special Collections, Doheny Library, University of Southern California; Susan Elia MacNeal; editor with the deft touch, Arthur Maisel; Melanie Myers, Deputy Director, and Megan Scauri, Senior Librarian for Special Collections and Digital Projects at the American Jewish Historical Society; Rivka Schiller, Reference Librarian, The David M. Rubenstein National Institute for Holocaust Documentation, United States, Holocaust Memorial Museum; Craig Singer; Eve Smith; Deb Sperling.

INDEX